# Schelling's Political Thought

ALSO AVAILABLE FROM BLOOMSBURY

*The Schelling Reader*, ed. Daniel Whistler and Benjamin Berger
The Absolute and the Event: Schelling after Heidegger, *Emilio Carlo Corriero*
Kielmeyer and the Organic World: Texts and Interpretations, *ed. Lydia Azadpour and Daniel Whistler*

# Schelling's Political Thought

*Nature, Freedom, and Recognition*

*Velimir Stojkovski*

BLOOMSBURY ACADEMIC
LONDON • NEW YORK • OXFORD • NEW DELHI • SYDNEY

BLOOMSBURY ACADEMIC
Bloomsbury Publishing Plc
50 Bedford Square, London, WC1B 3DP, UK
1385 Broadway, New York, NY 10018, USA
29 Earlsfort Terrace, Dublin 2, Ireland

BLOOMSBURY, BLOOMSBURY ACADEMIC and the Diana logo are trademarks of
Bloomsbury Publishing Plc

First published in Great Britain 2023
This paperback published 2024

Copyright © Velimir Stojkovski, 2023

Velimir Stojkovski has asserted his right under the Copyright, Designs and Patents Act,
1988, to be identified as Author of this work.

For legal purposes the Acknowledgements on p. viii constitute an extension of this
copyright page.

Series design by Charlotte Daniels
Cover image: Trees without leaves (© Vicente Méndez / Getty Images)

All rights reserved. No part of this publication may be reproduced or
transmitted in any form or by any means, electronic or mechanical,
including photocopying, recording, or any information storage or retrieval
system, without prior permission in writing from the publishers.

Bloomsbury Publishing Plc does not have any control over, or responsibility for, any third-party
websites referred to or in this book. All internet addresses given in this book were
correct at the time of going to press. The author and publisher regret any inconvenience
caused if addresses have changed or sites have ceased to exist, but can accept no
responsibility for any such changes.

A catalogue record for this book is available from the British Library.

Library of Congress Cataloging-in-Publication Data

Names: Stojkovski, Velimir, author.
Title: Schelling's political thought : nature, freedom, and recognition / Velimir Stojkovski.
Description: London; New York : Bloomsbury Academic, 2023. |
Includes bibliographical references and index.
Identifiers: LCCN 2022039901 (print) | LCCN 2022039902 (ebook) |
ISBN 9781350177857 (hardback) | ISBN 9781350188501 (paperback) |
ISBN 9781350177864 (adobe pdf) | ISBN 9781350177871 (epub)
Subjects: LCSH: Schelling, Friedrich Wilhelm Joseph von,
1775-1854–Political and social views. | Political science–Philosophy. |
Philosophy of nature. | Idealism, German. | Liberty–Philosophy.
Classification: LCC JC233.S29 S76 2023 (print) |
LCC JC233.S29 (ebook) | DDC 320.01–dc23/eng/20221025
LC record available at https://lccn.loc.gov/2022039901
LC ebook record available at https://lccn.loc.gov/2022039902

ISBN: HB: 978-1-3501-7785-7
PB: 978-1-3501-8850-1
ePDF: 978-1-3501-7786-4
eBook: 978-1-3501-7787-1

Typeset by Deanta Global Publishing Services, Chennai, India

To find out more about our authors and books visit www.bloomsbury.com and
sign up for our newsletters.

*For Živka—*

*a philosophy of life for one who loved life*

# Contents

*Acknowledgments* viii

Introduction 1

1   A Youthful Foray into Political Thought: Schelling's *New Deduction of Natural Right* 25
2   The Unconscious Roots of Consciousness: Recognition in the *System of Transcendental Idealism* 59
3   *Naturphilosophie* as Political Theory 85
4   The Politics of the Neoplatonic Ground of Freedom in Schelling's: *Philosophical Investigations into the Essence of Human Freedom* 141

Conclusion: A Schellingian Political Philosophy: Merging the Negative with the Positive 181

*Notes* 191
*Bibliography* 220
*Index* 227

# *Acknowledgments*

I would like to thank all of my wonderful colleagues and students at the University of Michigan—Dearborn. My approach to philosophy has always been guided by the principle of ongoing dialectical praxis, and without you this would be impossible. I am especially grateful to Imran Aijaz and Maureen Linker for their friendship and support. I owe a great debt of gratitude to my friend Bob Fraser. He read the complete manuscript at a couple of stages and caught countless discrepancies that my eyes skirted over again and again. I would also like to thank my partner, Christy, for more reasons than could possibly be articulated in an acknowledgment page. A big thanks to Liza Thompson and Lucy Russell at Bloomsbury for their guidance through the entire process, as well as the anonymous reviewers for their invaluable and supportive comments. Last, but certainly not least of all, a giant thank you to my family and friends.

# *Introduction*

"Schelling is not a political thinker,"[1] Habermas boldly proclaims, thus seemingly putting to rest the question of what a Schellingian political theory would look like before it was even asked. His reasoning for why this is the case is understandable, and I share some of his concerns: Schelling only ever sketched out his political views, and these sketches often clash with one another. A brief foray in the *System of Transcendental Idealism*, a scathing critique of the state in the 1810 *Stuttgart Seminars*, tantalizing hints about our responsibilities to Nature scattered throughout his vast writings on *Naturphilosophie*, and a seemingly conservative, statist turn during the positive philosophy period. Unlike his fellow Idealists Fichte and Hegel, he has no long-form manuscript such as *Foundations of Natural Right* or *Philosophy of Right*. The closest we have to such a work is the *New Deduction of Natural Right*, a terse, nearly Spinozistic style text published in 1796. What one sees while excavating his vast, labyrinthine authorship are wide-ranging concerns with issues of metaphysics/ontology, Nature, transcendental and absolute idealism, art, religion, and as is the case in the last years of his productive life, a deep-seated concern with what can retroactively be described as existential issues. Despite all of this, in this this particular instance Habermas is profoundly wrong. Much has changed since he penned those words in 1971. New approaches to Critical Theory are in order, and Schelling emerges as an untimely thinker to guide us through them.

Schelling's oldest concerns about our theoretical and practical neglect of Nature are mind-bogglingly prescient. We are living through the consequences of this neglect, witnessing it on a nearly daily basis. His view of freedom as *dissent*,[2] as found in the *New Deduction of Natural Right*, can help us understand and navigate through current social movements—movements for a greater and greater inclusivity of historically neglected peoples. These movements also form strong counter-movements, as the dialectical pendulum ever swings in the opposite direction. This too must eventually be worked through. The moments of Hegelian (and Marxist) sublation don't seem so forthcoming, however, even at dusk. We've collectively lost the faith the world is progressing in a meaningful direction, despite our pretenses to the contrary, and we must come to terms with a dialectic that oscillates, ebbs, and flows in certain directions, but does not necessarily absorb the earlier positions into a higher order form. Furthermore, Schelling's theory of recognition, a centerpiece of German Idealist thought from Fichte to Schelling to Hegel, is shown by Schelling in *System of Transcendental Idealism* to be more murky and messy than suggested by either Fichte or Hegel. Schelling's notion of self-consciousness develops in a recognitive framework in a manner similar to both Fichte and Hegel, but his notion of consciousness is not at all a brute starting position as it is in his early Fichtean days. Rather, as Theresa Fenichel,[3] Matt ffychte,[4] and S.J. McGrath[5] have each demonstrated in their respective studies, consciousness for Schelling is *always and necessarily* grounded in the unconscious. Thus recognition becomes more difficult, murkier, and more prone to misrecognition. One must account for that which can be acknowledged and recognized in the Other while at the same time accounting for the hidden predispositions in the self that make recognizing the Other all the more difficult (and Fichte and Hegel are well aware of the potential pitfalls of recognition, as is Axel Honneth from a contemporary angle). Last of all, evil has been shown by Schelling to be a fundamental concept of lived human reality, a central feature of freedom itself, and freedom is of course the universal presupposition of ethical and political life. Thus, one must contend with the lived reality of evil, as articulated by Schelling in the *Philosophical Investigations into the Essence of Human Freedom*.

Hence the need for a book such as this one. It is not simply the case that we need to look at Schelling's disparate and occasional forays into political philosophy proper in order to fill a gap in our historical knowledge, although that is certainly one of the outcomes, but rather to think along with Schelling[6] about how to theoretically and practically address the most pressing political concerns of our time—concerns that are divided here along the universals of Nature and our responsibility to it (which is easily and by a long shot the single most pressing issue of our time), recognition, and freedom. As such, the study is meant to be a piece of Schellingian-inspired political philosophy and Critical Theory, an effort to systematize a thinker who was the first of the major Idealists to break with the notion of system (and with Idealism proper, for that matter). Yet I have stayed as faithful to Schelling's own arguments as hermeneutically possible throughout the study. I have simply followed him along to the natural conclusions of his arguments rather than anachronistically working backward from our time back into the 19th century. The very structure of the book is meant to mirror Schelling's own development from the earliest days of his authorship to what I take to be his undisputed masterpiece, the *Freedom Essay*. The central grounding[7] metaphor developed there is what grounds this text as well, thus systematizing a wide-ranging set of concerns scattered throughout multiple texts across multiple shifts in position. Taking the simple, natural imagery of a tree, one can think of the first two chapters as the various branches of the sociopolitical. They twist and turn along the lines of dissent, recognition, freedom as expressed in the practical realm rather than at the level of fundamental ontology (and beyond), and the very fact of our historicity introduces contingency that makes it impossible what shape they will ultimately take. Nonetheless they must ultimately take a shape. The third chapter forms the heavy trunk of this tree. It concerns our responsibility to Nature, which I argue is the condition for the possibility of the social and recognitive in the first place. Schelling is right in insisting repeatedly throughout the vast corpus of the *Naturphilosophie* that Nature has been forgotten by humans, and there is a price to be paid for this forgetting. It's time that we remember again or further suffer the consequences of the initial forgetting—consequences that get more and more dire with each passing year. Finally, the end of the book represents the dark, buried roots of the tree—the dark ground of being beyond being—where we find what freedom truly "is" and what its reverberations are from root to branch.

In following this metaphor through I simultaneously follow Schelling's own intellectual development from the 1796 *New Deduction of Natural Right* to the *Freedom Essay* of 1809. Each twist in the development, each change of position and restart, is taken by Schelling because he is not happy with how far down he has dug, how well he has grounded the previous position. He ever-increasingly wants to peer deeper down the proverbial rabbit hole, eventually taking it past the point of where human categories break down in the dark ground of being. First there is a discontentment with the Kantian and Fichtean transcendental framework, where the "I" is abandoned as a possible starting point due to its exclusion of Nature, a vast self-organizing realm reduced to mere "not-I" rightfully did not sit well with Schelling. After all, the only logical question after developing the notion of a transcendental I or ego is what makes this possible in the first place. Right as he is developing his *Naturphilosophie* with simultaneous inquiry into the cutting-edge scientific experimentation of the time period along with the philosophical extrapolations from these findings, he is looking for a way to ground Nature itself into a more fundamental philosophical principle. Hence the transition to the Identity Philosophy, where self and Other, thinking and being, subject and object collapse into the identity of identity and difference. This too he is not happy with. After retroactively inserting insights from the Identity period into his *Ideas for a Philosophy of Nature*, he is unhappy with its conclusions, leading him to articulate the notion of the dark ground of being (the *Ungrund* or *Urgrund* depending on the point he is trying to make) in the 1809 *Freedom Essay*.

## Schelling's Authorship: A Brief Sketch

In order to situate the reader who is unfamiliar with Schelling, it is necessary to draw a brief sketch of the various phases of his authorship that are mentioned in the section directly above. A full introduction in a book such as this one, whose aim is to study a hereto neglected element of the vast authorship, is both well beyond the scope of the book and, more importantly, decidedly outside the central aim of the overarching argument. There are several excellent texts the reader could refer back to in English, German, and French. In English the reader can refer to Dale E. Snow's *Schelling and the End of Idealism*,[8] a book that both situates Schelling in his historical period and surveys his work from its inception and into his middle period in the *Ages of the World*. Snow demonstrates how Schelling is at the forefront of the developments of German Idealism from its transcendental roots into the notion of Absolute Idealism that Schelling himself coins early in his authorship, all the way through his break with the overarching approach as he contemplates the limits of system building and the notion of temporality. Andrew Bowie's *Schelling and Modern European Philosophy: An Introduction*[9] is both a systematic overview of the various periods as well a direct engagement with a series of analytic and continental thinkers whose thought parallels Schelling's own.[10] Both Bowie and Snow take Schelling seriously as a major thinker in his own right rather than a stepping stone to Hegel, which is often where he was placed by commentators unreflectively accepting the Hegelian story of a direct progress to the dialectic. Both are also honestly critical in places where they find philosophical misgivings with his approach, which I take to be the true hallmark of a philosopher being taken seriously rather than being treated as a mere historical curiosity. Frederick Beiser's work is indispensable for the English-speaking reader looking to gain a foothold in 19th-century German philosophy.[11] While he has no standalone volume on Schelling, his work *German Idealism: The Struggle against Subjectivism 1781-1801*[12] devotes a substantial amount of time to Schelling's early work. The German reader naturally has more access to material since the scholarship on Schelling was largely confined to Germany for the last hundred and fifty years, and even there he was relatively neglected in favor of Kant, Fichte, and Hegel. Manfred Frank's work in many ways kept the spark of Schelling scholarship alive, especially since Frank has always taken Schelling seriously. His *Eine Einführung in Schellings Philosophie*[13] is an excellent overview. Finally, Xavier Tilliette's two-volume study of Schelling—*Schelling une Philosiphie en Devinir*[14]—is quite possibly the most substantive single engagement with the totality of Schelling's work in any language. Tielliete begins with the earliest publications and excavates everything until Schelling's death.[15] Thus, in lieu of a long introduction we instead begin here with a sketch of the thinkers that have most influenced Schelling, and subsequently turn to a general overview of the texts that are the foundation for the argument being made throughout this study.

# Schelling's Authorship: Background

## Kant

As Bruce Matthews[16] and Bernard Freydberg[17] decisively demonstrate, Schelling's earliest work (which began when Schelling was a mere teenager!) cannot be untangled from his interest in ancient Greek philosophy, and especially the work of Plato, and Kant. Kant is easily the most towering influence on Schelling, and he draws on the three *Critiques* extensively at nearly every juncture of his corpus even as he often breaks with them substantially. From the *Critique of Pure Reason* Schelling absorbs a general framework of argumentation that sets a limit on metaphysical speculation which does not take empirical findings into account. Even when he and Fichte break off their collaborative relationship[18] over Schelling's inclusion of the Real, of Nature, into a transcendental framework one can see an implicit acceptance of the Kantian position that concepts without intuitions are in fact blind. While Kant himself contends that he is not concerned with system building but rather with the *principles* which would make such a system possible,[19] Schelling *is* concerned with system building (at least in the early authorship). This system, however, is not the *a priori* conceptual system of the pre-critical philosophers that Kant himself rejects (Leibniz,[20] Wolff, Baumgarten) but rather one that takes Kant seriously at his word and argument that any viable system, which was a task that Kant himself never properly undertakes after the three *Critiques*, must in fact be informed by empirical concerns. As such, the *Naturphilosophie* represents the first attempt to build a system that will be informed completely by the findings of the empirical sciences while at the same time delving into a speculative direction, and the *System of Transcendental Idealism* further solidifies this general approach by adopting the standpoint of the transcendental framework in the first portion of the text, a philosophy of Nature in the second, and an attempt to theorize the curveball that history hurls into any neat notion of system building by messy contingency. Furthermore, we can see Kant inching in a similar direction with his critical edifice in place in his *Metaphysical Foundations of Natural Science*,[21] without taking the decisive step toward full-blown system building.

The *Critique of Practical Reason* likewise looms large, and is especially indispensable for understanding the *New Deduction of Natural Right* that we will be working through in the first chapter. There Kant brings back that which he had banished from theory in the *Critique of Pure Reason*—namely God, freedom, and the immortality of the soul. For our purposes, however, we can simply focus on *freedom* given its disproportionate influence on any and all normative philosophical frameworks. In a letter written to Hegel, Schelling unequivocally states that "freedom is the alpha and omega of all of philosophy." This dictum follows Schelling from the earliest days of his authorship until the very end. For Kant, freedom is simply the precondition for all moral, legal, and political reasoning. Given that we have no direct, empirical experience of freedom itself,[22] we cannot accept any theoretical arguments for its existence. As the antinomies of the first *Critique* show, there are equally good arguments for and against the existence of freedom, and that particular debate has gone virtually nowhere from the standpoint of theory since its original inception (which is still true, despite the fact that newer theories have a shiny contemporary coat of neuroscience paint over them, they function with the exact same logic of the earliest theories). As we will see in Chapter 1 and again in the final chapter (befitting of Schelling's "alpha and omega" claim), for Schelling freedom is first the "unconditioned," that which cannot be subsumed under the rubric of empirical necessity, and in the end it remains a much more developed unconditioned, one that takes us into the very limits of human rationality into the dark ground of Being where freedom finds its seat. Unlike Kant, however, Schelling is never satisfied with making freedom as the mere condition for the possibility of ethical and political life. As it is the case with Hegel, for him this would be a merely "formal" concept of human freedom and freedom in general; a concept that cannot fully capture the lived experience of freedom and its penchant for good *and* evil. Thus, this insight, along with many of the insights that often have their grounding in Kant, moves past the confines that are imposed by Kantian critical philosophy as they are reworked again and again, from the bottom-up, by Schelling.

This brings us to the *Critique of Judgement*, the last of the critical edifice developed by Kant and the book that is perhaps the most influential to Schelling's overall project. It is doubly influential on Schelling insofar as it deals with teleological judgments that are not to be directly found in Nature itself and yet, as Kant argues, are nonetheless found in Nature by the transcendental subject that inescapably places them there, and it is also influential in its excavation of artistic judgment, a topic near and dear to Schelling and his fellow Romantics. In many ways, however, the influence of the third *Critique* on German Idealism lies not in what Kant demonstrates in its pages, but in what he *suggests* is possible to ultimately demonstrate by using the faculty of judgment as the mediating link between reason and the understanding. While Kant's work on the nature of aesthetic judgment is of great importance for understanding both Schelling's and the Romantic Movement's engagement with artistic creation, it is his suggestive comments concerning the potential unification of the supersensible that underpins Nature and the supersensible that underpins freedom[23] and his hints at a system of reason that set the tone for the future trajectory of Schelling's research (as well as Hegel's, but that is a matter for a different study.) For instance, Kant states that "judgement must assume, as an a priori principle for its own use, that what to human insight is contingent in the particular (empirical) natural laws does nevertheless contain a law-governed unity, unfathomable but still conceivable by us, in the combination of what is diverse in them to [form] an experience that is intrinsically possible."[24] In many ways it is this "unfathomable" unity which Schelling seeks to fathom in his *Naturphilosophie*, *System of Transcendental Idealism*, *New Deduction on Natural Right*, and the *Freedom Essay*, thus giving us a roadmap to unifying his quite unsystematic reflections on political philosophy into the coherent whole outlined above.

## Fichte

The Fichtean influence on Schelling has the peculiar feature of being simultaneously decisive and yet transient. Yes, it is inarguable that Schelling had a "Fichtean" phase very early in his work, a phase where he too follows Fichte down the path of a transcendental idealism grounded *purely* in the working of the ego. It is also inarguable that he quite rapidly moves past this phase of his research as the transition between *Of the I as Principle of Philosophy* and *Ideas for a Philosophy of Nature* is a mere two years apart (1795–1797, respectively, thus heavily hinting at the possibility that Schelling was moving away from Fichte even as he was defending his basic framework, especially since Spinoza is already being invoked in 1795). I personally take the Fichtean position to be infinitely more fascinating when studied in its own right rather than as a path to Schelling (or Hegel), given that Fichte is the most adept of all the German Idealists at articulating the details that go into building a robust theory of *subjectivity* qua subjectivity. In both tone and content Fichte can be thought of as a very early phenomenologist. Furthermore, the reception of Fichte in Germany at large as well as among the individual post-Kantian Idealists is, unfortunately, most heavily indebted to his murkiest text: the 1794 *Wissenschaftslehre* (translated into English as *The Science of Knowledge*[25]). Compiled rather hastily over a brief period of time, often writing the text as a way of teaching the material to his students, Fichte spends his remaining years intensely revising and, more often than not, completely restarting the project from scratch. A rough breakdown of the work has these general parameters.

The 1794 *Wissenschaftslehre* begins with Fichte arguing that a series of logical steps, assumed as true at the beginning of philosophizing but only proven to be true upon the completion of the *Wissenschaftslehre* from the standpoint of transcendental subjectivity, can show how we can ground philosophy in nothing other than the activity of the transcendental ego.[26] He tells us that "the presupposition A is A (or A=A, since that is the meaning of the logical copula) is accepted by everyone and that without a moment's thought: it is admitted to be perfectly certain and established."[27] This logical truth is then applied to transcendental subjectivity. The I *posits* itself freely, resulting in the notion that "I=I." Connecting the notion of I=I back to the tautology A=A, Fichte tells us that "I, who posit A in the predicate position, necessarily know, *because the same was posited in the subject position*, about my positing of the subject, and hence know myself, again contemplate myself, on the same with myself."[28] What Fichte means here is that through its own activity, what he calls "positing," the subject is immediately self-aware. As is the case for all philosophers who write in the German Idealist and phenomenological tradition, for Fichte consciousness is necessarily intentional. When the I or ego begins philosophizing it realizes that it is immediately conscious of its own self, because consciousness is necessarily consciousness *of* something. We know that the self exists, Fichte argues, because "it has posited itself."[29] This is merely the beginning, however. Through a series of dialectical movements (which Fichte calls thesis, antithesis, and synthesis, a formulation that is often mistakenly attributed to Hegel), Fichte looks to ground all of philosophy and all human knowledge in the positing activity of the I.

The next step in the dialectic from A=A (I=I), which is the considered to be the thesis, is to posit the antithesis. The antithesis of pure identity is difference. Thus, the next step is to argue that logic necessitates that if these is an A there must be a not-A. Transferring this logical move to the activity of the I, Fichte argues that if there is an I, there must be a not-I. To explain it in a more phenomenological fashion, subjectivity also requires objectivity—it needs something to be conscious of. (We could also say that subject and object co-constitute each other, even though Fichte would not use such language.) However, this is not quite the case at the outset for Fichte. He states that at first "I know of ~A *that* it is opposed to some A. But what that thing may or may not be, of which I know this, can be known by me only on the assumption that I am acquainted with A."[30] So, at first the knowledge of the necessity of an object in order for there to be a subject is not an acquaintance with actual objects in the world. Rather it is a *formal* necessity required by an elaboration of transcendental idealist principles. As such, all philosophy, and even objectivity, is initially grounded in the activity of the Ego as I: "Both self and not self are like products of original acts of the self, and consciousness itself is similarly a product of the self's first-original act, its own positing of itself."[31] That is, the foundational principle *must* be the transcendental subject, which leads Schelling and Hegel to later criticize Fichte, perhaps unfairly, that he ultimately falls into mere subjective idealism and solipsism (see for example Schelling's *System of Transcendental Idealism* and Hegel's *The Difference Between Fichte's and Schelling's System of Philosophy*[32]).

After establishing the principles I=I and I=~not-I, the thesis and the antithesis, Fichte moves on to speak of the synthesis between self and not self, telling us that "in the first synthetic act, the fundamental synthesis (of self and not self) we have… established a context for all possible future syntheses."[33] The synthesis shows that there is a higher unity between the self and the not self. The self knows that consciousness exists insofar as it posits itself, but it also knows that it is determined, or shaped by objects. I can only know that I am a subject if there is an object that opposes me. If the not-I is to actually and actively determine or shape the I, then it cannot simply be a mere negation, because, Fichte argues, a mere negation does not have any reality. In order to determine the I, then, the not-I must have some sort of concrete reality.[34] It is at this point that the argument becomes opaque in its original formulation, and it is ultimately over the status of the "not-I" that Fichte and Schelling break both philosophically and publically, with Schelling accusing Fichte of reducing the entirety of Nature to a mere postulate of the ego and Fichte accusing Schelling of reverting back to a dogmatic, pre-critical position by introducing Nature back into transcendental idealism.[35]

## Spinoza

The irony of the above accusations is that they both have substantive merit. Fichte simply does not care about Nature as such and does in fact reduce it to a not-I, but he does so in order to ground his *epistemological* project into a single principle. As an epistemologist and transcendental idealist first, especially one who makes practical philosophy as first philosophy, Fichte simply leaves Nature to the natural scientist. Likewise, the accusation that Schelling is introducing "dogmatist" or pre-critical ideas into his system is factually true. It is Schelling's reading of Spinoza, along with his fascination of the newly emerging discoveries in chemistry and biology, which lead Schelling to break with transcendental idealism proper. It is to Spinoza that we now briefly turn to. The rediscovery of Spinoza in Germany after nearly a century of neglect happens virtually due to an accident that spirals into a full-blown drama that is the Pantheism Controversy.[36] Lessing, Germany's pre-eminent enlightenment thinker, confesses to his friend Jacobi that he is a Spinozist. Given the cultural ascendency of the work of Leibniz through Christian Wolff and Alexander Baumgarten in the German intellectual tradition—work that is meant to give a purely rational justification to traditional Christian orthodoxy concerning God, freedom, and immortality of the soul—this confession was seen as tantamount to an admission of atheism. While the controversy is absolutely fascinating both philosophically and culturally, what is of interest here is the renewed spotlight it shines on Spinoza. Rather than being a philosopher who was essentially headed for the dustbin of history, Spinoza overshadows[37] all the other pre-Kantian modern thinkers. One simply can't understand the development of Schelling and Hegel without a recourse to Spinoza.

What those two take from Spinoza follows both of them for much of their life, and, along with Kant, it sets the tone and general structure for Absolute Idealism. In the *Ethics*[38] Spinoza infamously argues for a monistic vision of reality. Guided by a merciless use of the Principle of Sufficient Reason,[39] Spinoza argues that the only way to get rid of the various problems that plague dualism of all kinds is to conceptualize reality as a single, infinite substance (God) that has an infinite amount of attributes or essences. The two attributes that are accessible to the human reason are mind and body, both of which are unified at the level of fundamental ontology, thus sidestepping the pesky problem of interaction that Cartesian thought had no good answer for. This infinite substance with infinite attributes, the grand totality of all reality, can be likewise modified in an infinite amount of ways, giving rise to the great variety of life that we observe all around us. Thus with one neat argument, which is developed in geometrical order with nearly geometrical precision in the *Ethics*, Spinoza hands the post-Kantian idealists the basic blueprint for the Absolute. As Spinoza puts it in Proposition 7, Part II of the *Ethics*, "*the order of connection of ideas is the same as the order and connection of things.*"[40] That is, at the most basic level of metaphysics/ontology, the Ideal and the Real are inextricably intertwined. The banishing of the Real to the *noumenal* realms is rejected by Schelling (as well as Hegel), and a new form of speculative thought it inaugurated.

This new form of speculative thought incorporates the overarching framework provided by Spinoza, but fundamentally alters it in ways that make it substantially different in tone and content to what Spinoza had in mind. Freedom is introduced into the system, thus undermining Spinoza's rigid necessatarianism; the *subject* of Kant and Fichte is likewise added, thus ensuring that philosophy can only understand the Whole or the Absolute if and only if it also understands the ways in which the subject is constituted, while at the same time making subjectivity a basic constitutive part of Nature; and, finally, Nature is conceptualized in *organic* rather than mechanistic terms, which brings to the forefront what Jason Wirth dubs "the conspiracy of life."[41] Rather than thinking of Nature as a single, nearly static substance where everything follows with mechanistic necessity, Schelling instead conceptualizes it as inherently *alive* and *organic*. This is not to say that he replaces it with a naively romantic conception of Nature as a kind of giant super-organism, but rather that it has principles in it which make it *inherently self-organizing*. Ultimately, it is the biological notion of self-organization, with its messy often non-linear causality, that takes explanatory precedence in his thinking.

## Böhme

The German mystic Jakob Böhme looms large over all Absolute Idealism. His influence on Schelling[42] and Hegel is decisive and profound, yet he remains a difficult and enigmatic figure to write on given his deeply original mystical insights (often quite different from the more purely Neo platonic mystics such as Meister Eckhart or Pseudo-Dionysius), his penchant for alchemical language to convey his insights (which is quite far removed from the contemporary worldview), and his relative lack of care for systematic, philosophically rigorous arguments. Although the last is somewhat unfair to Böhme as his concerns are not philosophical in our sense, but rather theosophical and, furthermore, borne from *experiential* insight rather than logical/conceptual speculation (although that certainly plays a role). What is of particular interest to us here is Böhme's notion of the "*centrum*," the hidden, unconscious core of subjectivity and drive,[43] his conception of evil as a positive reality rather than a mere privation, his general picture of dueling polarities[44] that will be of import to the *Naturphilosophie*, his distinction between the ground (or rather non-ground) of being and being itself, and his insistence on the primacy of the will over reason.[45] All of these are fundamentally reworked by Schelling with philosophical rigor, and when combined with the thinkers above, serve as the bedrock upon which he builds his highly original, untimely philosophical output.

The notion of the *centrum* is both highly fruitful theoretically and metaphorically, and yet difficult to pin down due to its very nature in Böhme's conception of reality. The notion of the *centrum* also simultaneously describes his explanation for the origin of evil as well as the hidden, dark core of personality that is inaccessible to rational thinking. In the *Way to Christ*,

Böhme captures the idea through a discussion now quite alien to the halls of philosophy: the nature of the devil. He writes:

> The devil stayed in his place of ruling, but not in the one in which God created him; rather [he stayed] in the one into which he himself went, not in the work of creation, but into the groaning birth of eternity in the *centrum* of nature…in a kingdom of darkness, in the abyss… In all things there is good that keeps and locks evil in itself. Thus he [the devil] can only go to and rule the evil when it raises and leads its desire into wickedness. This an inanimate creature cannot do, but man can do easily through the inanimate creature when he leads the *centrum* of his will, with his desire, out of the eternal *centrum* into them.[46]

What is of interest to us here is not the devil as such, but how Böhme's conception of the *centrum* plays out in the reality of Nature, the origin of evil, and the notion of unconscious drives emerging from the human will. First of all, we see a component of reality that cannot be captured in reality itself, but rather in that which makes reality possible and is thus incapable of ever being neatly categorized. The above description in the *Way to Christ*, a book written in the very final portion of Böhme's life, contends that what makes the devil the Devil is the fact that he attempts to usurp the very forces of creation that are guided by God in his *willful desire* to create. (Böhme's God is not the God of the rationalists or even quite the God of classical theology.) These forces lie in the hidden core, the dark ground or being that is not Being *qua* Being, and are accessible to God, the devil, and humans. Humans, unlike the devil, perpetrate evil not when they retreat purely into the *centrum*, but when they transfer their willing away from the eternal willing and into creation itself. God's will in the *centrum* is the desire for creation, and the transference of this will in humans is away from the eternal creation and toward blind consumption, one that is in principle non-rational.

The notion of the non-ground and the primacy of the will over reason is one of Böhme's core insights—the second one upends the Western philosophical tradition's insistence that humans share with God the notion of *intellect* first and foremost. It is in the intellectual sense that we are most like the divine. For Böhme neither we nor God are first and foremost intellect. What we share is *will*, a blind drive or urge, which thus paves the way for Schelling's and

Schopenhauer's arguments for the primacy of the will and for the subsequent psychoanalytic tradition that jumps off from their insights. In the *Mysterium Pansophicum*,[47] Böhme begins with a notion that is central, indeed indispensable, for understanding Schelling from 1809 forward: the non-ground. He tells us that "the non-ground is an eternal nothing but forms an eternal beginning as a craving. For the nothing is a craving for something."[48] This notion of a "non-ground" a groundless ground or *Ungrund*, is a grounding principle that is itself "outside" any and all rational categories for it is a *nothing*, literally no-one-thing or even thing, and, as such, inaugurates a distinction between Being and its unknowable ground that cannot be Being. This principle follows us from Schelling to Hegel (where it is transformed as the opening move of the dialectic in the *Science of Logic* between the copula of being and nothing, thus eliminating all the mysticism inherent in it) to Heidegger. The nothing is a craving, "the same craving is also a nothing as only a mere will."[49] Furthermore, this will, when accounted for from the standpoint of the divine, guides or "rules over"[50] the craving, "and we thus recognize the eternal will-spirit as God and the stirring life of the craving as nature. For there is nothing prior, and both are without beginning; and each is the cause of the other and as an eternal bond."[51] The will/God and the craving/Nature are succinctly conceptualized here as two poles of the same process, both co-eternal and seemingly needing one another for their existence—Nature needs the will to guide the blind craving, and the will needs Nature to have something to will, thus rendering each as co-constitutive of the other and yet emerging from a similar, nonrational source. It is upon this framework that Schelling builds his argument concerning human freedom, fundamentally and philosophically reconstructing Böhme. This, along with Spinoza, Kant, and Fichte, form a backdrop for what is easily one of the most creative and profound philosophical outputs of the 19th century (or any century for that matter).

## Schelling's Authorship: The Key Works for our Study (1796–1810)

As has been established above, the aim of this study is to excavate the various texts where Schelling deals *explicitly* with political philosophy, and this reconstruct from the primary textual data an overarching Schellingian political theory, a theory that will be able to deal with what I take to be the most pressing and pertinent political problems of the 21st century—our responsibility to the Natural world, issues surrounding recognition over various marginalized peoples, the freedom to dissent and enact political change, and the difficulty of enacting said change due to our capacity for good *and* evil. With the exception of the 1796 *New Deduction of Natural Right*, much of these dealings are buried in texts that have aims that are other than political. The *Naturphilosophie* texts that we examine here[52] have tantalizing hints about normativity, Schelling's notion of recognition is found in a text that is not first and foremost political (*The System of Transcendental Idealism*), and the *Philosophical Investigations into the Essence of Human Freedom* is work of metaphysics/ontology that takes us to the utmost limits of those key inquiries. As such, the organization I have adopted is largely developmental, and it takes Schelling's own search for a grounding principle as the chief inspiration for argumentative arc developed throughout.

We thus begin with the earliest text, *New Deduction of Natural Right*.[53] Composed sometime during the period 1795–1796, and published in 1796, the *New Deduction* is a terse aphoristic text, somewhat resembling Spinoza's axiomatic efforts but without the explicitly Euclidian structure. In it Schelling is concerned with articulating the ground for practical philosophy, for the manifestation of the unconditioned *noumenal* nature of freedom into the phenomenal realm.[54] The process by which this occurs is the unfolding of individual free action into a Natural world filled with objects and subjects, respectively, who bump against my own activity.[55] In bumping into the world I directly observe freedom itself, and see both its efficacy as well as its limitation. Its efficacy can be observed on the literal mark one leaves on the world itself, and its limitation is twofold: First and foremost for Schelling, there is the awesome power of Nature itself which overwhelms the individual subject with its awesome power, leading said subject essentially speechless. All they can do is "bow" to Nature.[56] Secondly, in a move that echoes all the great modern political thinkers (Hobbes, Locke, Rousseau, and Kant) we bump into other manifestation of individual will—other humans—and we see the need to limit our absolute freedom in the practical realm in order to coexist.[57]

Here Schelling invokes and reworks Rousseau's central insight concerning the interaction between the general will and the individual will. In the *Social Contract*,[58] Rousseau argues that the fundamental basis for the body politic, that which makes government possible and gives authority to the said government to legislate and execute laws, is the *general will* as made manifest by a social contract. For Rousseau this general will is that which is concerned with the universal good of the state as a whole,[59] and its generality is to be found in the fact that it obligates each individual with equal weight. "It must issue from all in order to apply to all."[60] Famously for Rousseau, the initial chains by which we are all bound after our move away from the idyllic state of nature is acceptable if and only if they are self-imposed. Like the Kantian extrapolation in the realm of morality, one is free as long as one imposes rules on oneself, thus fostering an account that later thinkers such as Isaiah Berlin will dub "positive" right.[61] The difference in the Rousseauian formulation is that it isn't mere individualistic self-legislation which obligates, but rather the legislation of the general will which is the condition for the possibility of sovereignty. Schelling retains the language of the general will, but *explicitly* favors (at least in this particular text) a heavily individualistic read of it that is somewhat at odds with Rousseau of the *Social Contract* but not Rousseau as such since he notoriously wavers between a collectivist and individualist perspective in his authorship.[62] For Schelling, "*the content of the general will is determined by the form of the individual will*, not vice versa."[63]

Perhaps over the worry of the Reign of Terror that had just concluded shortly before the composition of the *New Deduction*, a worry that cools the young German Idealists to the French Revolution that they all had seen as an amazing manifestation of human freedom, leads Schelling in this more individualistic account. Nevertheless, he is quite clear and adamant that it is *individual* freedom that he is concerned with here, and this concern never truly leaves his writings even after he moves in a much less individualistic direction during his *Naturphilosophie* and *System of Transcendental Idealism Period*. It is also this worry over individual freedom that will have him articulate one of the earliest and most powerful defenses on the need of *dissent*[64] in order to truly articulate and ground freedom in the realm of the practical. This notion puts him along an argumentative trajectory that is also found in Hegelian recognition, both in the early unpublished manuscripts as well as throughout Hegel's corpus, as well as contemporary accounts of recognition as found in the work of Axel Honneth and his sister (or perhaps even synonymous) notion of *struggle*. Thus, the first chapter of our study will excavate and give a running commentary to the *New Deduction of Natural Right*, and then situate this commentary through the lens of historical and contemporary concerns surrounding dissent by briefly examining the Haitian Revolution and contemporary struggles for recognition through dissent. As such, we will tie this early *completely* political piece of philosophy with the notion of recognition that is found in the *System of Transcendental Idealism*.

The *System of Transcendental Idealism* is in many ways the book by which Schelling's reputation was solidified, both in his time and in his later reception, and yet it remains a somewhat strange work. As the title clearly indicates this is Schelling's first and truly only book to attempt a systematic reconciliation between the various sub-branches of philosophy, but in execution its systematicity is somewhat fragmented, which might be one of the reasons why he eventually gives up on the dream of system building. The first half of the book works along Kantian/Fichtean lines even as it ultimately breaks with both and should be familiar to readers of transcendental idealism in general. It is a systematic effort to deduce the conditions for the possibility of knowledge, to reconcile the subject and the object. The way that Schelling goes about the project is immediately different from Kant and Fichte however, for the first places the purely objective in the realm of the *noumenal*, leaving the study of the phenomenal to the working scientist, while the second essentially reduces the objective to mere "not-I." Schelling is not content with either move, as is evidenced in his very framing of the argument for transcendental philosophy and its need to include Nature *qua* Nature as the objective counterpoint to the subjective transcendental conditions for the possibility of knowledge. In a succinct summary of the structure of the entire project, Schelling writes:

> The intrinsic notion of everything merely *objective* in our knowledge, we may speak of as *nature*. The notion of everything *subjective* is called, on the contrary, the *self*, or the *intelligence*. The two concepts are mutually

opposed. The intelligence is initially conceived of as the purely presentative, nature purely as what can be presented; the one as the conscious, the other as the nonconscious. But now in every *knowing* a reciprocal concurrence of the two (the conscious and the intrinsically nonconscious) is necessary; the problem is to explain their concurrence.[65]

Taking seriously the notion that transcendental idealism is an epistemological project, Schelling begins by framing the discussion in terms of what can be known and yet he immediately breaks with the representational knowledge of Kant and the moderns and insists up front the moment of knowledge is one where subject and object concur—they coincide with one another such that the pure distinction between the two must be collapsed. As he puts it, he wants to know how this can be possible in the first place.

The answer to that question is developed throughout the whole book, and yet it seems that Schelling himself is not content with his own conclusions for he moves almost *immediately* past his own findings and within a year is working on his Identity Philosophy. The general argument of the book however is to found in the meeting point between transcendental philosophy and *Naturphilosophie*, the second of which he had already been developing for many years and, as Grant convincingly shows, continues to develop throughout his entire career.[66] At the meeting point, epistemology and ontology coincide and subject and object are shown to be two poles of the same underlying substrate that we may dub the Absolute. Thus, here transcendental inquiry is *fundamentally transformed* from its initial formulation for it is developed from subject to object (Nature) in the first half and from object (Nature) to subject in the second half of the work, which entails that the transcendental categories are possible in the subject only if they have a prior origin point in Nature. It is over this that Schelling and Fichte break their collaborative relationship and friendship. By naturalizing the transcendental Schelling substantially breaks with the critical epistemological project of Kant and Fichte and inaugurates Absolute Idealism. Yet this framework is shortly lived since Schelling introduces *history* at the end of the text, and history muddies the neatness of any and all purely philosophical accounts for it introduces *contingency* at the very heart of our inquiry.

What is important for our political project here, however, is not the work as a whole but rather two key interrelated points that emerge out of it: the Schellingian formulation of recognition and its grounding in the *unconscious*. Like Fichte and Hegel, Schelling develops a theory of recognition[67] in order to explain the condition for the possibility of self-consciousness. Unlike Hegel, who speaks of recognition throughout his corpus,[68] and unlike Fichte who develops his *entire* political philosophy from recognition,[69] Schelling's notion emerges out of the attempt to bridge transcendental and naturalistic inquiry and is relegated to one portion of the *System of Transcendental Idealism*. There he argues that the only way that I can get a hold of myself as a self, as an independently existing and *free* 'I,' is in and through the recognition of other selves that are independent of me.[70] As he explicitly puts it: "no rational being can substantiate itself as such, save by recognition of others as such."[71] For Schelling, recognition is inherently tied up with *freedom*, such that what is being recognized is not only my subjectivity and self-consciousness, but also (and primarily) my free efficacy in the world. It is thus the case that what has been established on transcendental idealist grounds throughout much of the book is shown to be ultimately a function of the social/practical sphere in philosophy. That is, while freedom is the alpha and omega of philosophy, the purely formal or theoretical notion of freedom is inherently meaningless if not filtered through free action, and free action is only meaningful when done in *praxis*. This praxis is understood by Schelling to be a lifelong project of education.[72] It is the Other, those who predate me and form the social structure into which I am thrown at birth, who call upon me to understand my freedom through an ongoing process of education, understood broadly as lifelong learning rather than merely formal schooling. Only in this manner can I truly understand my moral obligations that result from being a free being.

What is exceptionally unique in Schelling's contribution to the recognitive framework is not the above insight. Indeed, in many the above simply echoes Fichte's notion of "summons" in the *Foundations of Natural Right* and Hegel's notion *Bildung* as found all throughout the *Philosophy of Right*. Unlike Fichte, who begins and ends his theorizing with the activity of the transcendental ego in its practical manifestations, and unlike Hegel who is a philosopher of the social[73] *par excellence*, Schelling's entire philosophical career can be interpreted through his ever-expanding search for a deeper and deeper *grounding* principle, and this grounding principle is first found in Nature and explicitly articulated as *unconscious*. "The world brought about through unconscious production"[74] is Nature itself. Rather than finding the conditions for the possibility of consciousness in the realm of the transcendental, as Kant does, Schelling finds them in Nature itself, and Nature itself has productive forces that are not in and of themselves conscious. Yet they serve as the condition for the possibility of consciousness. As McGrath points out, "the unconscious is the other pole of consciousness, the limit of the ego, and the abyss of unfathomable freedom at the ground of culture and nature."[75] As such, it turns out that the Kantian condition for the possibility of experience is itself further conditioned, and it is done in a way that the limitations of transcendental idealism are overstepped in a work that is ostensibly about transcendental idealism. This radical move entails that the recognitive process itself is underpinned by unconscious factors, which in turn means that there are elements of the subject that are inaccessible to self and to other in the process of recognition. The unconscious, then, will forever permeate the ongoing process of recognition unfolding in the political realm, and thus demonstrate why it is so difficult to shake entrenched negative attitudes of the Other at both the individual and structural levels.

Given the hermeneutic metaphor employed throughout the book of a branching tree in need of grounding, a metaphor that is not so much a metaphor but a mirror of Schelling's own ontological development, we move from the *System of Transcendental Idealism* to the *Naturphilosophie*. Here and only here do I break slightly with the purely historical development and work back from the *System* published in 1800 to the *Ideas for a Philosophy of Nature* (1797/1803)[76] and the *First Outline of a System of the Philosophy of Nature* (1799). While these works are not in and of themselves primarily political, they paint a picture of Nature that has a staggering implication for our collective political responsibility to Nature. Before the advent of environmental ethics and environmental philosophy, Schelling stands virtually in a category of one when it comes to overarching concerns about our responsibility to Nature (at least in the West[77]). Weaving through and connecting the ideas of (a) transcendental categories embedded in Nature itself; (b) the naturalization of the transcendental and the transcendentalizing of naturalism in the development of Absolute Idealism; and (c) the distinction between Nature as productivity and Nature as product, I argue throughout this chapter that the heart and soul of Schelling's ontology and the subsequent implications of our political responsibility to the natural world is to be found first and foremost in his *Naturphilosophie*. It is here that we move away from the mechanistic picture of reality that plagues modernity and is crucially responsible for our view of the world as mere object, a resource for our use rather than what it actually is—the source of life itself and its continued existence. What we find instead in the worldview of the *Naturphilosophie* is a speculative[78] view of Nature informed by the then-emerging sciences of biology and chemistry, and this speculation is only more forcefully substantiated by current findings in evolutionary biology, chemistry, and cosmology. For Schelling, Nature itself is to be understood first and foremost in line of its *productive* forces rather than individual product, making the heart of being a *process* through and through. This process is structured by dueling polarities that never exhaust themselves in any finite product, and this process takes us well away from the substance metaphysics of the pre-Kantian moderns (although some elements of this worldview are retained through Schelling's engagement with Spinoza and Leibniz). This process also entails that we are in a continuum with the rest of Nature itself, one of its infinite products rather than a separable entity. As such, our political and normative collective responsibility to Nature is primordial and profound. Without it we cannot *be*, and this entails a wholesale reversal and restructuring of the modern political picture that one inherits from Hobbes and Locke which begins with atomic agents struggling against Nature. This picture is one of the root causes of our treatment of Nature and each other as antagonistic forces to be tolerated or overcome, and reorients the body politic toward a new ground—a ground that was in fact always-already there but has been forgotten and continues to be neglected, pushed back into the unconscious despite the fact that as I write these words *one in three* human beings on the planet have directly felt our shared neglect of our responsibility to Nature itself.

Finally, we examine the *Philosophical Investigations into the Essence of Human Freedom*, which very well could be Schelling's magnum opus despite its brevity. The book is in many ways a philosophical masterpiece, syncretizing

Spinozistic monism; *Naturphilosophie*; Neoplatonism (from which it gets its core logical structure); Böhmian mysticism; and realism/idealism. In it Schelling is concerned with both the possibility and the reality of human freedom, its origin point and its concrete reverberations into lived reality as the freedom for good *and* evil. It falls in line with many attempts of the theodicy project that one sees throughout the development of monotheistic philosophy of religion in the middle ages and, especially, into modernity with works such as Leibniz's *Theodicy*. Unlike any of these other works of theodicy, which almost invariably defend a notion of evil as privation that has its roots in the Augustinian Christening of Neoplatonism, Schelling wants to give a more positive weight to the possibility of evil all the while keeping his (mostly) pantheistic God free of the blame. Put succinctly, he argues that the possibility and lived reality of evil has its roots in the same ground from which God and the rest of reality (Nature) emerge. This is the dark ground of Being that is not Being itself, but rather its conditioning principle, the root of our metaphorical tree where reason reaches its utmost limit, Schelling's "indivisible remainder."[79]

The above is admittedly a brief window into a book with enough layer and depth that it warrants years of careful study. The final chapter of this book will look to unpack the work with an eye toward our primary objective here—how is it that the notion of freedom as freedom for good and evil, admittedly a metaphysical question, have direct and reverberating impact through the body politic? First and foremost, politics and all normative inquiry inherently presupposes and *must* deal with freedom. Kant was absolutely correct in positing that ethics and politics are impossible without freedom. In tackling a robust inquiry into freedom that does not begin and end with the liberal obsession with negative freedom one finds in thinkers such as Mill and Berlin, and instead looks at the lived reality of freedom with its inherent tendency to polarize toward the extremes to good and evil Schelling is showing us the fragility of all our political organization. Utopia is to be abandoned; it is not of much use even as a regulative ideal. Humans are invariably the villain at the end of all our stories, and societies must be built resiliently to account for the fact that when we retreat deep into the self, as Schelling will argue throughout the *Freedom Essay*, we perpetuate literal evil. This evil is always multifaceted, appearing as oppression, environmental degradation, racism, and sexism, to name but a few overarching issues. It happens on the individual and structural level, and must be guarded against. Our guardrails are our capacity for much good along with evil, as well our capacity for recognition, dissent, and our responsibility to Nature found in the previous chapters. To attempt to tackle as many possible solutions to the world's myriad problems we must take all of these into account (as well as findings from hundreds of diverse empirical fields, which is something that no philosophical account can accomplish in and of itself), understanding each solution to be an ongoing tentative process, with no guarantee of final success. Secondly, and perhaps just as importantly, we must rethink the relationship between freedom and necessity, our positive and negative political responsibilities to one another. Rather than conceptualizing these issues as diametrical opposites I contend that we must think of them as dialectical copulas, each needing the other in order to make sense of both, and each ultimately grounded in the very ontological structure of reality. Thus, the least of the explicitly political German Idealists is shown to be political through and through, an unlikely guide to yet another tumultuous century. In every sense that counts, Schelling shows himself to be *untimely* through and through.

# 1

# *A Youthful Foray into Political Thought*

# *Schelling's* New Deduction of Natural Right

## Introduction

Written in 1796 during his time as a tutor in Jena, the *New Deduction of Natural Right* is one of the few rare instances of Schelling explicitly articulating and writing on political *philosophy* as such.[1] Presented in the Spinozistic manner of a *deduction*, each piece of an essay flows in a series of terse aphorisms meant to build upon each other. The topic should be of no surprise to anyone with even a passing familiarity of Schelling's thought as it is directly concerned with the "alpha and omega of all philosophy"[2]—freedom. Schelling's entire corpus is animated by the notion and lived reality of freedom itself, making Schelling a philosopher of freedom *par excellence*, and a key precursor for existential tradition, which owes a greater debt to his thought than has been traditionally conceived. The freedom articulated here, however, clearly owes its greatest debt to Kant and Rousseau, as evidenced by an overwhelming attention that he pays to the interplay between the individual and the general will.

The aim of this chapter is thus threefold. First, I will provide an argumentative overview of this relatively short but dense essay, demonstrating throughout how the deduction deals with the articulation of freedom, rights, and morality. Secondly, I will explicitly focus on what is a significant insight of the text itself, one that will be echoed again and again throughout the subsequent two centuries: the notion of *dissent*[3] as a key moment of the concrete emergence of freedom in political life. Dissent, I argue here, is one of the key pieces, and perhaps even *the* key piece, of contemporary struggles for recognition by marginalized communities. It plays a prominent role in the work of contemporary critical theorist Axel Honneth in the form of "struggle," as well as in the Hegelian articulation of recognition that runs throughout his corpus, but with the exception of Emiliano Acosta's essay, it has been woefully undertheorized in the literature on Schelling. Furthermore, this account of dissent offers a key piece of the larger puzzle of making Schelling deeply relevant to contemporary political concerns and of synthesizing his disparate contributions to matters political into a coherent whole. As such, the notion of dissent will be examined not simply through the abstract lens of philosophy, but also through some concrete political struggles: those of the Haitian Revolution and the women's suffrage movement. Last of all, we will examine how the interplay between the general and particular will has direct bearing on the inner workings of the body politic. I take this to be especially pertinent in the context of the current political landscape of the United States, where we are experiencing what can succinctly be described as the fracture of the general will into two dueling factions, which, despite their underlying adherence to a neoliberal capitalist framework, have ground the political machinery to virtual standstill when it comes to anything other than the indefinite perpetuation of the said framework.

## *New Deduction of Natural Right* Part I: Freedom and Dissent

*New Deduction of Natural Right* begins with a question that has its origins (as does much of Schelling's thought) in Kant—how to articulate *freedom* theoretically into a world where it will fall under the strict iron necessity of physical law that determines and structures all other phenomena, thus undercutting its very status as freedom at the outset. In the Schellingian parlance, the question is one of bringing the "unconditioned" into reality.[4] To bring the said unconditioned (i.e., freedom) theoretically is to break its status as unconditioned, given that phenomena are always-already conditioned, so, invoking Kant again, one does not in fact bring the unconditioned into reality theoretically—like in Fichte's *Wissenschaftslehre*, it must be done *practically*. While this move has its roots in both Kant and Fichte, Schelling is never content to relay exclusively on the insights of his predecessors, and he immediately proceeds to give the notion a new twist which demonstrates how he will break with *both* the Kantian and Fichtean paradigms. Schelling states: "Be! In the highest sense of the word; cease to be *yourself* as a phenomenon: endeavor to be a noumenon as such! This is the highest call of all practical philosophy."[5] The ontological implications of this statement offer a fascinating rethinking and restructuring of the noumenal/phenomenal relationship. While Fichte will famously drop the noumenal as an unwarranted posit, ushering in *practical* philosophy as the grounding for theoretical insights, Schelling is suggesting in this above statement, still not elevated to the level of a proper argument as such, that *being* itself traverses the chasm between noumena and phenomena at the level of political praxis. This represents an early germ of the now infamous distinction, one that ends up having a decisive influence on Continental thought through Heidegger, of being and the ground of being that is to be found in the *Philosophical Investigations into the Essence of Human Freedom* (which will be examined in detail in the final chapter of this work). As we shall see, there Schelling argues that freedom is grounded not in in the realm of being but that which grounds all being, both in Nature itself and in God.

The commandment to *be* free, arising out of the noumenal is "unconditioned" because it demands that freedom itself is not constrained by any external forces, be they conceptualized in the deterministic manner of a Spinozistic system of in the organic, non-linear fashion of the *Naturphilosophie* that is in its beginning stages at the time of the publication of the *New Deduction*. As Schelling puts it to be free is "unconditioned, because it demands something unconditioned. Therefore the demanded endeavor itself must be *unconditional,* that is, it must depend only on itself and cannot be determined by foreign law."[6] By beginning with a call of myself to myself to *be* free, I do not and conceptually cannot depend upon previous determinations, be they normative, legal, or natural, for the articulation of my freedom would then collapse into some series of conditions, thus immediately nullifying itself and collapsing into unfreedom rather than freedom. As such, Schelling contends here that freedom can be freedom if and only if it emerges as a primary principle out of the noumenal or unconditioned, but it can only manifest itself with anything resembling causal efficacy when it shows itself in Nature as life, leading him to write: "the name of this causality is *life.* Life is the autonomy in the phenomenon; it is the (Schema) of freedom, insofar as it reveals itself in nature."[7]

What occurs next in the deduction of freedom is a set of moves that ought to be intimately familiar to even the casual reader of modern political thought (Hobbes, Locke, Rousseau); Fichte's transcendental deduction of the natural world from the free activity of the transcendental "I" positing itself and its opposite (the not=I); and of Hegel's derivation of self-consciousness in the Master/Slave dialectic, where the self fails to determine itself in the moment of consumption or destruction of the natural objects it encounters. Schelling states: "as far as my *physical* power reaches I give my form to everything in existence, I force my purpose upon it, I use it as a means of my boundless will."[8] In the classic liberal thought of one such as Locke (or Hobbes, for that matter) the initial formulation of rights surrounds one's mingling of their labor with the "raw material" of the world around them, thus transforming that which no one owns into something of one's own—property emerges. In the Fichtean transcendental account, the "I" or transcendental ego only comes to self-realization in and through an encounter with the Other, but this encounter does not happen in a *purely* transcendental fashion given that the sheer materiality of the world asserts itself against the "I" and given the Fichtean reversal by which *practical* philosophy, rather than theoretical, becomes first philosophy. As such, Fichte identifies the body and embodiment itself as the locus around which efficacy is exerted in the world, thus echoing what Schelling writes above concerning our physical power[9]:

To say that a rational being as an individual has been affected is to say that an activity that belongs to it as an individual has been canceled. Now the complete sphere of the rational being's activity, as an individual, is its body; thus the efficacy in this body, the capacity in it to be a cause merely by means of the will, would have to be restricted, or—more concisely—an influence would have to have been exercised upon the person's body.[10]

As such, for *both* Schelling and Fichte, the will is mediated by the physicality of the human body. The "boundless will" described by Schelling, imparting form on the objects it surrounds, can only work in and through the medium of *physicality or embodiment* for him as well as for Fichte.

The next move that Schelling makes, however, is quite uniquely his. My sheer physical impositions upon nature are struck back in light of Nature's overwhelming power: "where my *physical* power finds resistance, there is *nature*. I acknowledge the superiority of nature over my physical strength; as a being of sense I bow to it; I *cannot* do more."[11] This terse step in the deduction has moral, political, and pragmatic implications in how Nature itself is viewed, ones that simply cannot be found in the vast majority of modern thinkers writing on political theory.[12] The modern project of a boundless will probing nature and taming it for its own purposes through the technological advances of the then-emerging natural sciences is called into question by Schelling in one short sentence. In my encounter with Nature, I am not the Hegelian unself-aware destroyer failing to find recognition, or Francis Bacon's subject that will probe the depths of Nature in order to tame and shape it purely in the human image,[13] or even the Lockean laborer who finds his natural right in and through making Nature one's own through said labor. The Schellingian free, unconditioned subject encounters nature and "*bows*" to it in light of its overwhelming power. We can safely assert that this conception of Nature, the awe that one has when faced with it, is carried by Schelling throughout his corpus, in everything from the early work, as we already see here, until his final speculation concerning positive philosophy.[14]

At this point in his argument, Schelling sets aside the consideration of Nature itself; that consideration will re-emerge and permeate nearly the entirety of the Schellingian corpus.[15] The next step happens in light of the inevitable encounter of human to human, one that obviously extrapolates from the actual empirical encounter, which is always-already a done deal given our basic biological constitution, and presents instead an idealized extrapolation by which the self comes to concrete self-understanding. In the inevitable encounter of human and human, "where my *moral* power finds resistance, there can no longer be *nature*. I shudder and stop. I hear the warning: Here is *humanity! I may* not do more."[16] As was the case in Fichte's deduction of recognition, and as it will be the case in Hegel's Master/Slave dialectic both in the early unpublished manuscripts as well as in the *Phenomenology of Spirit* and the *Encyclopedia Philosophy of Mind*, freedom, subjectivity, and humanity become inextricably combined in our primordial encounter with the other, an encounter that is *ontological* in nature, for there never was a well-defined or delineated historical moment in which humans are not among others. However, while we are always-already embedded in a social nexus, or, to borrow from Heidegger, thrown in a world not of our own making, there is in fact a *historical* moment in which freedom and rights become salient features of human political life (and struggle). For the young German Idealists, rabidly following any and all events unfolding during the tumultuous French Revolution, that *moment* is quite literally unfolding before their very eyes.

This encounter with the other leads to what is perhaps the key development of the mechanism by which freedom and, subsequently, rights, are established in Schelling's early political treatise. As indicated above, I follow Emiliano Acosta in labeling this moment as one of a *necessary* "dissent." Schelling states:

> When I feel that my freedom is limited, I recognize that I am not alone in the moral world, and the manifold experiences of limited freedom teach me that I am in the realm of moral beings, all of whom have the same unlimited freedom… Only when I address the *will* of another and when he rejects my demands with his categorical '*I will not!*' or else when he is willing to give up his freedom for the price of mine, do I recognize that behind his face there dwells humanity.[17]

This notion of *dissent*[18] is absolutely indispensable both for articulating the historical roots of recognition as well as rights discourse as re-envisioned through the lens of German Idealism.

As we see in the above quote, Schelling is arguing (quite correctly) that the key moment of freedom and its concrete emergence into sociopolitical institutions is decisively contingent upon the human ability to assert one's agency. This assertion happens when the self stands up for oneself in light of direct adversity and pushback from others. If one thinks here of the larger historical picture in which philosophical ideas are concretely played out, the history of humanity is in many ways the history of ever-emergent struggles for the articulation of individual and group agency.[19] (I find it that the individual and the group cannot ever be decoupled from one another except by means of abstraction. That is, they are so completely entangled that any notion that attempts to theorize from the primacy of either the individual or the group is doing so at the expense of reality.) That is, if one does not assert oneself decisively with the "categorical '*I will not!*'" articulated by Schelling above, there is little to no chance of being recognized as a fully autonomous agent. This *I will not!* is of course absolutely no guarantee that the Other will in fact recognize one's demands or freedoms, but it is the indispensable starting point for change that is very often quite slow and painful (sometimes violently painful) in world events. The reversal of values that happens at the onset of modernity is one key example of how this process takes place. It is by now conventional wisdom that for the vast majority of human history top-heavy hierarchical organizations are the default norm. These organizations see the right of aristocracy to rule to be embedded in the very ontological structure of reality, with kings and nobles being given the said right either by God himself, as was the case all throughout Europe in conceptions of the Great Chain of Being, or the Mandate of Heaven, as would have been the case in China and much of Southeast Asia. Modernity changes this picture by flipping the script to an idea that is already implicit in the older norm—that one rules or has the mandate if and only if there is broad (or good enough) support from the public. Modernity takes this quite a bit further and reverses the traditional order completely in articulating that it is really *individuals* who are the ultimate unit of society, and they bear intrinsic rights that cannot be trampled on by the ones in charge. This of course leads to a series of revolutionary changes in the very basic ways in which government is construed in the first place, but the resistance to aristocratic norms of rule constitutes a key starting point for what later become ever more nuanced struggles and dissents: the wars for the elimination of slavery, especially including the Haitian revolution; the women's suffrage movement, which was largely nonviolent but yet full of examples of dissent; the various worker rights movements that often ended in bloodshed in the late 19th and early 20th centuries, and are ongoing well into today; the right of homosexual couples to marry and live in the open; the right of trans people to simply be acknowledged as even being a possibility outside of the male and female binary; and the list could go on and on.

Connecting this notion of *dissent* explicitly with freedom, rights, and recognition (a process that will begin in this chapter and follow us throughout the length of this book) has multiple advantages for understanding and diagnosing what are a series of ever-pressing contemporary moral concerns. If we think here of the suffrage movement and the fight over Jim Crow in the 20th century, we have two crystal clear instances of how political life is entirely enmeshed with dissent. The civil rights movement is an especially vivid and relatively current instance where dissent, the "*I Will Not!*" is on public display in nearly every encounter. Images of human beings beaten, spit at, punched, kicked, and even killed are perpetually seared into our collective memory, and, despite the fact that we are a species that easily forgets, they serve as a stark reminder of the necessity of dissent itself and of the ongoing struggle of Black Americans not the harmed simply because they are Black. Their systematic and necessary refusal to play by a set of institutional and individual rules that perpetually wanted to enforce subservience to the dominant racial paradigm was an indispensable step toward the concretization of freedom and rights for a long-marginalized community. While the struggle and the means of dissent were different, the same could be said for the women's suffrage movement in the late 19th and early 20th centuries. In order to gain rights at even a merely *formal* level, women had to picket, protest, and, once in a while, literally fight[20] the men who were in power (in every sense of the term "power," both at the individual and structural levels). This formal recognition is simply around the most basic notion of right—one that confers *legal* recognition to the marginalized other and sees the said other as an equal agent at least in the court of law. The formal recognition often has a very long path to travel until institutional structures and individual social attitudes adjust to the level where we have *real* equality. In the Hegelian jargon, an alternate way to put it is that women's suffrage has yet to reach the level of the *Idea* since inequality persists well into the 21st century despite the initially formal recognition that was conferred in the early 20th century. Furthermore, from a historical lens there is perhaps no better example of dissent than the Haitian slave revolt that was occurring nearly simultaneously to the German Idealists articulation of freedom through the process of recognition.[21] It is to this that I will now turn before we dive back into Schelling's deduction.

## *Haiti and Dissent: A Case Study*

The Haitian Revolution (1791–1803/4) is a remarkable moment in human history. It is the only successful slave revolt during the various revolutionary upheavals of the late 18th and early 19th centuries, and, as Jeremy Popkin points out, "including the Haitian Revolution as one of the modern world's major revolutions requires us to rethink the very nature of such phenomena, and to recognize, for instance, that a revolution can develop without the appearance of a revolutionary party or movement."[22] That is, the Haitian Revolution explicitly emerges from the *dissent* of the various peoples of Haiti, showing how freedom is made manifest in light of brutal oppression and systematic, state-sanctioned slavery and misrecognition. No work of philosophy can quite do it justice, given the amount of historical digging necessary to unearth its complexities, and yet not to contend with it is a serious omission since there is no concrete struggle for freedom that is quite like the Haitian Revolution in human history. Relying on the accounts of historians such as Laurent Dubois,[23] David Geggus,[24] C.L.R. James,[25] and Jeremy D. Popkin, I will articulate a quick, general overview of the revolution in order to demonstrate the myriad instances of dissent which led to and shaped its possibility.

The story of the Haitian Revolution is a difficult one to tell even for professional historians (much less philosophers). The reasons are multiple: the vast majority of the documentation comes from those who had a vested interest in keeping slavery going; the leaders of the revolution, such as Toussaint Louverture, are complex, multifaceted figures who resist any straightforward narrative; and, finally, the telling of the story cannot be neatly untangled from the geopolitical climate of the late 18th and early 19th centuries. The final reason is in many ways true of any complex world event, and here it is caught up in the intersection between the expansion of colonialism, capitalism, and the general revolutionary fervor of the late 18th century. This fervor is responsible for bringing to the forefront the notion of *rights* in political discourse and praxis. Furthermore, its uniqueness is even more pronounced in the fact that Haiti (known as Saint-Domingue prior to the Revolution, but I will simply refer to it as Haiti from here forward) was a slave society rather than a society with slaves.[26] As Popkin[27] and Dubois[28] both point out, in 1789 there were between 465,000 and 500,000 slaves in Haiti, in contrast to the 31,000 whites and roughly 28,000 free people of color. The free people of color were almost entirely of mixed-race ancestry, and they occupied a position of power that sat uneasily between the white slave-owners and the majority Black population. The Black population came from large swaths of Africa, and the idea that it was somehow culturally monolithic is not seriously worth considering. It is comprised of dozens of different peoples, and what tied it together was an emerging set of religious and cultural practices that arose as a direct response to the oppressive conditions.

All slave-holding societies are built on a structure of domination and oppression, which follows directly from the horrific nature of the institution itself. Haiti was no different. The primary and exceptionally lucrative trade that was done in the former colony was sugar cane and coffee. The sugar cane plantations were especially demanding on the people working them. In fact, they were so demanding that "as many as a third of the slaves dies in their first year in the colonies. The average life expectancy of a slave after arriving in Saint-Domingue was no more than seven to ten years. Most slaves suffered from chronic malnutrition."[29] Furthermore, the slave-owners "worked their slaves to death, and replaced them by purchasing new ones"[30] instead of making any small changes that would improve their lives. Because of these conditions, the Haitian Revolution is not a single event, but rather a series of uprisings and back-and-forth fighting between slaves, white plantation owners, and the free people of color. Some slaves chose to side with their oppressors, as is always the case in complex historical processes, and free people of color were often torn between the lucrative nature of the slave trade, since many either owned slaves or had investments in the trade, and solidarity with the slaves. The slave population, which was almost entirely uneducated and chronically suffered from malnutrition, successfully fought off the French who were the original colonial power, the Spanish, and the English. Alliances were formed and broken all along, and the eventual success of the Revolution was paved with much suffering and violence. Since this is a work of philosophy rather than history, I would like to zero-in on the instances of dissent large and small that led to the Revolution itself and sustained it throughout. It is here that one witnesses its power in light of such brutal oppression.

Dissent reveals itself before, during, and after the Revolution in ways large and small, each significant in its own right. Dubois tells us that "for the plantation owners and managers, the slaves were laboring machines, cogs in a system meant to produce as much sugar or coffee as possible,"[31] and that this dehumanizing treatment was held in place through means of punishment and torture that are intrinsically horrific.[32] But humans are simply not machines, and such dehumanization necessitates dissent. The Revolution itself is in many ways the penultimate form of dissent in the Schellingian sense discussed above, coalescing eventually into an organized rebellion by Toussaint Louverture, but there were also *countless* instances of the phenomenon before and during the revolutionary process. These include but are not limited to: acts of sabotage, poisonings of especially harsh managers and sometimes plantation owners, self-harm and suicide by those who refuse to be slaves, abortion of infants that were to be born into slavery, and marronage.[33] "Maroons" were slaves who ran away, and marronage is "as old as slavery itself."[34] How does one fight a system in which one's humanity is stripped away? One answer to this question is the sheer refusal to participate in the system that is not of one's choosing. As Dubois further points out, marronage becomes both pragmatically and *symbolically* important in multiple ways:

> Maroons, by successfully flouting slavery, were also an inspiration and example for the enslaved, as well as antislavery writers. The 1791 revolt, however, emerged from the heart of the thriving sugar plantations on the northern plain…More important for the revolt were the practices of *marronage* at the edges of plantations, or in their towns, which had helped

sustain a culture of autonomy and the networks that connected various plantations. Like religious ceremonies and Sunday gatherings, the practice of running away laid the groundwork for an uprising that united slaves across plantations and in so doing enabled them to smash the system from within.[35]

By refusing to play a game not of their own making, the various enslaved peoples directly enacted the Schellingian "*I will not!*" In enacting it, they demonstrated their very universal humanity, a humanity that had been stripped away from them, a regained piece of freedom that eventually led to larger scale change.

Further instances of dissent which are found in Haiti are documented meticulously through the surviving primary sources by David Geggus. In dozens of letters dating back to 1785–1789 right before the Revolution takes off fully, slave managers and plantation owners describe large strikes and work stoppages accompanied through "temporary, collective marronage."[36] One letter dated 22 June 1789, states that "the Montaigue plantation was without its workforce for four months; it came back only after the steward was dismissed. Mr. Dumesil gave his plantation to the manager who had worked as an assistant to Mr. Bayon. The slaves gathered together and, in the most insolent tone, said they didn't want him."[37] The tone and structure of the letters unfailingly paints the slaves in a negative light. This is to be expected given that they are written by plantation owners and managers, and yet one sees that even in circumstance where the levers of power are held entirely by one group of people, the assertion of human freedom through dissent shows the managers the humanity and will of those dehumanized, and the collective power of labor withheld.

Geggus also gathers letters from a young widow who takes over a mountain plantation in order to show what he calls "day-to-day resistance on a mountain plantation."[38] What she describes are acts of theft (quite common due to the fact that slaves were chronically underfed and overworked), small acts of sabotage in the labor process, and marronage. Concerning a slave by the name of Azor, she complains that "beatings have no effect on him: he is incorrigible."[39] One can certainly understand why: if all was taken from you, what options do you have but to resist? What punishment could possibly be worse than slavery?

An independent investigating commission into the treatment of slaves in Saint-Domingue/Haiti comes to the same conclusion in response to the brutal killing of two slave women, arguing that slave-owners ought not to act with total impunity in punishing slaves because "if the violence of planters was not kept in check, and if slaves found no recourses from the administration, they would have no option but violent vengeance."[40]

As we of course now know, this is precisely what comes to be. The Haitian Revolution came about from bottom-up small-scare acts of resistance and dissent to a full-blown revolt. The full-blown revolt emerged organically from within various plantations, especially those that were tucked away in the mountains. It did not happen all-at-once, but was a long drawn out process lasting nearly fifteen years. Toussaint Louverture comes about as a brilliant and complex leader during this time, and he plays a central role in all narratives of the Haitian Revolution. Simply put, there is no way to tell the story without him and the ways in which the Haitian Revolution is entangled in the broader revolutionary context happening France and elsewhere.[41] Loverture took the disorganized instances of dissent and consolidated them into a centralized fighting force that *successfully* fought off the French, Spanish, and English. He did so again and again during a 10-year period before he was captured by the French, and he dies in a French prison on the 7th of April 1803.[42] Following his death, there are numerous fights until Haiti finally reaches independence in 1805 under the leadership of Jean-Jacques Dassalines, making the Haitian Revolution the *first and only* fully successful slave uprising in the modern period. In what is another first, the newly formed nation included in its constitution the abolition of slavery and race-based discrimination.[43]

Before this momentous achievement of dissent in light of brutal oppression is achieved, there is yet another substantive overlap with our study of Schelling: the invoking of the notion of the *general will* as an explanatory mechanism for what transpired in Haiti by firsthand observers. Reactionary groups in France and the colony were quick to point fingers at newly emerging philosophical ideas as the direct cause of the revolution. Dubois writes: "the front page of the *Montieur Général* of Saint-Domingue, a vehicle for the colony's plantation-dominated assembly, was a poem titled 'Philanthropy.' It identified a 'ferocious blood mania' called 'philosophy' as the 'invisible and perfidious arm' that was driving 'one hundred thousand rebel slaves.'"[44] While such a reductive explanation is most certainly not sufficient to account for a complex historical phenomenon, it is nevertheless the case that the language and ideas of the Enlightenment are being invoked by those on the ground. The most striking instance of directly invoking philosophical ideas to explain the extent of the revolutionary fervor that had gripped Haiti comes from the mouths of the insurgent leaders Georges Biassou and Jean-Francois. While negotiating with the General Assembly for granting the freedom of thousands of slaves,[45] they explicitly use the notion of the general will to explain to the white plantation owners why a simple return was a political impossibility.[46] Biassou and Jean-Fracois state: "a hundred thousand men are in arms . . . and you will realize from that we are entirely dependent on the general will, and what a will!"[47]

This invoking of the general will is fruitful for its demonstration of how philosophical ideas can concretely shape the world and also how they in turn are themselves shaped by world events. The message to the Assembly is straightforward: a few generals cannot hold back a populace. However, the phenomenon described is nevertheless deeply complex and philosophical. The weight of 100,000 voices completely united in a cause, and thus in the formation of a new set of political conditions and organizations, illustrates how a shared set of *general* principles across diverse individuals transcends the will of any one individual and becomes a *movement*. This movement topples, from within, the world's worst institution (at least in one location) thus making it a slightly better place, and the movement also allows us to directly observe a seemingly abstract phenomenon. It is to this phenomenon of the general will that we now turn.

## *New Deduction of Natural Right* Part 2: Freedom and the General Will

While dissent is a critical issue in political theory, especially given the status of the myriad political struggles working through the contemporary geopolitical climate, it is most certainly not the end of Schelling's discussion surrounding natural right. Given the aim of our study here, which is intended to be both an incursion of Schellingian themes into contemporary political discourse along with a (relatively) complete picture of his early political discourse, it is absolutely essential that we reconstitute the various, fragmented puzzle pieces and arrange them coherently in order to follow their implications through to their logical conclusion.

The fact of dissent, as we have seen in the above discussion, gives rise to freedom (always through struggle), but it also has further concrete ramifications that cascade because of its practical and logical necessity. For instance, echoing an insight that Schelling will follow to the Dark Ground in 1809, he states that freedom has an "unconditional causality"[48]—that is, a causality that is not constrained by a chain of mechanistic, domino-like causes, but rather inserts itself, *ad infinitum*, in the vast complexity of natural and social causal nexus, reverberating in either minute or significant ways throughout. When this unconditionality plays itself out in the human realm of morality it "becomes antagonistic…and *I begin to oppose my freedom to the freedom of others*."[49] Any reader of Locke, Hobbes, Rousseau, Kant, and other modern political thinkers will find this move unsurprising (or anyone who has existed among others for more than a few years, for that matter). At the empirical level, free actions have very real consequences, and billions of agents enacting free moves within a world system has both *structural* and *individual* reverberations. That is, my freedom ends up clashing with the freedom of others quite literally the instant that one steps into the public sphere. This is simultaneously one of the great joys and hardships of any system that resembles a democracy—what *I* want is almost never quite exactly what *anyone else* wants, thus necessitating an intricate balance between self and other in order to avoid the dreaded *bella omnium contra omnes*.[50]

The logic of the deduction leads in but a single direction—moral beings must assert their freedom in order to count *as moral being*,[51] and yet must at the same time come to a realization that the curbing of ones unlimited, unconditioned freedom is completely necessary to curb the chaos that ensues.[52] This chaos is curbed through the interplay between the Rousseauian general will and the will of the individual, leading Schelling to state that "since we must think that all moral beings as such have a will, this generic *will of all* must limit the *empirical* will of each individual in such a way that the will of all others can coexist with the will of each."[53] That is, in order to ensure that a peaceful coexistence is possible in the body politic, what Schelling is dubbing the "generic *will of all*" comes up with a set of institutional guidelines, laws, and general prohibitions by which concrete, *empirical* action is curtailed. Left completely unrestrained, we are at any moment capable of the greatest acts of kindness and cruelty, selfishness and selflessness, complete indifference to others, and everything in-between. It is precisely why Sartre tells us that we are "condemned to free"—with freedom comes endless, horrifying possibility.

This above concern leads Schelling to posit what to contemporary ears might come off as a somewhat arbitrary distinction: that between *morality* and *ethics*. Simply put, for the early Schelling (and for Hegel of the *Philosophy of Right*[54]) morality concerns individual interaction while ethics concerns the well-being of the whole or the state, characterized here as the generic or general will. Regardless of whether or not this sounds like a somewhat arbitrary distinction within the framework of 21st-century normative theory, in practice it has immediate and profound implications for politics insofar as it decisively entangles the individual and the social by positing a necessary interplay between morality and ethics all the while keeping them conceptually separate. Rather than making political theory a radically distinct normative inquiry from that of ethics traditionally construed, Schelling shows here that they are inextricably bound up in ways that cannot be easily untangled, or to put it even more strongly, the two cannot really be untangled at all because of the very nature and structure of freedom itself. Mundane daily decisions, ranging from the food I purchase; how I interact with students, friends, and family; whether I choose to stream my music or purchase a physical product; and on and on, end up having political implications and reverberations. The opposite is of course true as well. The decisions made on the purely political, macro level affect me in ways invisible and visible at every junction. The vast interconnectedness of the current structures of production, with supply chains intersecting nearly all corners of the world in a dizzying web that is virtually impossible to visualize (and understood only by experts in the field), mean that miniscule changes in law in Washington or Beijing have very real effects on the Midwestern farmer or the Apple factory employee.

It is for the above Schellingian reason that I must slightly part ways with the next step of his own derivation. Schelling argues that the ontological relation between the individual and general will is to be resolved from the standpoint of *individuality* alone, a move that is at odds with the very basic tenet articulated immediately above. He tells us that "what determines the general will is the form of the individual will as such (freedom), setting aside all content of willing. *Therefore the content of the general will is determined by the form of the individual will,* not vice versa."[55] Let us examine the implications of the following claim and some of the possible problems that will ensue if we adhere purely to Schelling's own presentation. Thus, in a somewhat Hegelian manner, I will attempt here to preserve what is true in the above insight while paying careful attention to avoid the potential pitfall of the overly individualistic nature of Schelling's account of the interplay between the general and individual will.

## *The Individual vs. the General Will: An Explanation and Assessment*

While there is no significant literature whatsoever, either in German or English, on Schelling's notion of the general will, this is not at all the case when it comes to Rousseau and Kant.[56] There one runs into the opposite concern—a vast and multifaceted debate into what each thinker had in mind concerning the nature and status of the general will. While a complete survey of the said literature is neither possible nor necessary given the scope of the current study, it is nonetheless indispensable to ground ourselves within these two thinkers insofar as they form the backdrop for Schelling's own theorizing. As Judith Shklar points out in her seminal work *Men and Citizens: A Study of Rousseau's Social Theory*, "the general will is Rousseau's most successful metaphor. It conveys everything he most wanted to say. It ties his moral psychology and political theory as no other words could."[57] Indeed, his *Social Contract* cannot be untangled without recourse to the notion of the general will, which, admittedly, is tougher to untangle that appears to be the case at first glance.

The general will is introduced by Rousseau in the context of the formation of the social pact or contract, which means that it is an emergent property of a social order that is never guaranteed. Indeed, the social order is a move away from the state of nature, which in the two *Discourses on the Origin of Inequality* is argued to be a state of pre-political innocence, an innocence that is lost through the formation of society. Through the social pact "*each of us puts his person and his full power in common under the supreme direction of the general will; and as a body we receive each member as an indivisible part of the whole.*"⁵⁸ That is, the formation of society is achieved through an initial contract where the individuals set aside their innate, idiosyncratic differences in order to function as an "*indivisible*" unit. This unit, unlike the one of Locke and Hobbes, explicitly aims at the common good of all as all rather than as separate individuals, this allowing Rousseau to make a distinction between the "will or all and the general will."⁵⁹ This distinction shows a fundamental difference between Rousseau and Schelling, given, as we will see directly below, that Schelling does not think that there is a separate general will over and above the sum total of all empirical wills. Rousseau further writes that,

> there is often a considerable difference between the will of all and the general will: the latter looks only to the common interest, the former to private interest and is nothing but the sum of particular wills; but if, from these same wills, one takes away the pluses and minuses, which cancel each other out, what is left as the sum of the differences is the general will.⁶⁰

This passage provides one of the clearest illustrations of what the general will is without a straightforward definition, yet there are unresolved interpretive possibilities. What we see is that if we add up all the disparate wills, then take away the idiosyncrasies, we are left with a *general* will, which binds the body politic with a strong, overlapping commonality. Yet a question remains: what *is* this general will?

The commentary on what this general will is (ontologically, practically, etc.) is fascinating in its own right and there are several possibilities to be flagged. One possibility is that the general will is a separate ontological entity that is somehow shared among human beings. This is a strongly Platonic interpretation that has its roots in a long line of religious notions concerning the general will which predate Rousseau.⁶¹ Another possibility is that the general will represents the elements in individual human wills which are themselves general—the elements that point to the common rather than individual good.⁶² Finally, in his article "The Substantive Elements of Rousseau's General Will," David Lay Williams argues that 20th- and 21st-century interpretations have fallen into "two broad camps: (1) those who treat the general will as a procedure for generating the substantive content of the general will, and (2) those who treat the general will as an expression of a prior commitment to substantive values."[63] That is, the generality is either found at the procedural level of generating overlapping consensus about issues that affect the body politic as a whole or the generality is that which binds the body politic in the first place. The concerns that Williams flags are primarily political ones that sidestep the more thorny metaphysical question of what the general will is *as such*, and, at least in this particular instance, I find that sidestepping useful because the notion of the general will is metaphorically pertinent even if there is no final settled interpretation on what it concretely is (although, as I will argue directly below when we examine the issue in Schelling, my preferred interpretation is to not multiply metaphysical entities and consider the general will that which is general across individuals in the body politic).

Moving away from Rousseau and looking at the Kantian picture, one sees yet another manifestation of the notion of the general will. While Kant is *deeply* influenced by Rousseau, equating his accomplishments in the field of moral and political philosophy to those of Newton in physics, it is unclear how much of this influence moves from Kant to Schelling when discussion of the general will is hard to concretely say. The reason for this is fairly simple— Kant's most sustained engagement with the notion is found in the *Metaphysics of Morals*, which is published in 1797, a year or so *after* Schelling's *New Deduction*. Nevertheless, a brief excursion into Kant is useful as a contrast case to Schelling's work. For Kant, the discussion concerning the general or "common" will occurs in the confines of his overall discussion of the conditions for the possibility of private property and universal right. He contends that ownership can only ever be "provisional"[64] under the conditions of pre-civil or state of nature society, and that it is the *common* will which has the coercive, collective power that is necessary for enforcing property disputes. In this sense Kant follows Rousseau's setup in the *Social Contract*. As Kant puts it,

> Now, a unilateral will cannot serve as a coercive law for everyone with regard to possession that is external and therefore contingent, since that would infringe upon freedom in accordance with universal laws.

So it is a will pitting everyone under obligation, hence only a collective general (common) and powerful will, that can provide everyone with this assurance.—But the condition of being under a general external (i.e., public) lawgiving accompanied with power is the civil condition. So only in a civil condition can something external be mine or yours.[65]

As Kant argues here, ownership in a state that is not civil or political—the fabled state of nature—is not and cannot be actual ownership. A unilateral will that dubs x as mine cannot truly have a mechanism of enforcement since it can always be countered by another will that is universally free. In this sense, Kant is Hobbesian, for the state of war of all-against-all results from unilateral wills fighting over scarce resource. Kant, however, distinctly breaks with Hobbes' solution of a single "leviathan" having the most power to override any single will, for that too is unilateral. Instead, we submit only to a *common* or collective general will in order to insure reciprocity between various parties. Original ownership in a pre-civil state is inherently common[66] for the simple reason that the resources of the planet are *shared* across an interconnected globe[67] and only divisions within a political framework can guarantee that individual things can be seen/respected as mine. Concerning the metaphysical or ontological status of the general will, Kant is silent. One can only speculate that given the massively deflationary account of metaphysics that we have in the first *Critique* cools Kant on this form of speculation even as he re-introduces God, freedom, and the immortality of the soul in the second *Critique*. I believe it suffices to say that the general will in Kant is the condition for the possibility of private right and ownership. With that we transition to Schelling's notion of the general will.

Moving back the distinction between morality and ethics articulated in the above section, Schelling further contends that "the problem of all ethics is to maintain the freedom of the individual by means of the general freedom . . . to harmonize the empirical will of all with the empirical will of the individual."[68] Schelling correctly diagnoses one key piece that is at the heart of all political life: how do we maintain the good and freedom of all, of the collective, that is, while simultaneously not trampling on individual agents? There are two logical possibilities based on the very structure of his account, and due to the nature of his deduction here, they are embedded in what is perhaps the thorniest chicken and egg dilemma of modern political theory—what comes first logically and ontologically, the individual or the community? The first possibility is the path that he himself takes here (and to a certain extent in the *Stuttgart Seminars*, where he runs an explicitly anti-Statist argument[69]): the general will is *nothing other* than the empirical sum total of individual will, and, as such, the whole ought never to bear down on the individual or the danger of trampling on freedom is omnipresent. The second possibility is decidedly more in the "communitarian" camp, a label that is often placed on thinkers such as Aristotle and Hegel (although obviously retroactively).[70] The second possibility entails that the individual is but an offshoot of the community, so to speak, and that the community must in fact have ontological priority over the individual insofar as it must preexist and shape the individual will. Thus, the individual will is an emergent property of the general will. While Schelling clearly and explicitly rejects the second possibility in the *New Deduction of Natural Right*, he will in fact align himself much closer to the second position in the *System of Transcendental Idealism*, as we will discover in the following chapter. While he does not maintain the Rousseauian/Kantian language and formulation between individual and general will in that particular text, he explicitly argues that recognition entails an intersubjective, communal framework as the condition for the possibility of individual subjectivity and willing (he nearly always places primacy on the will over subjectivity).

Given the discrepancy between the earlier and later formulation, a discrepancy that Schelling doesn't acknowledge, we must rethink the basic political ontology that is at play both here and in the *System of Transcendental Idealism*. We must ask who or what it is that serves as the unconditioned: the individual or the intersubjective communal? While I tend to fall closer to the Aristotelian and Hegelian position that the community has an ontological priority (for reasons that will become clear in the following chapter), acting as the condition for the possibility of individuality and subjectivity, I would contend along with Schelling here that there is a hidden (or perhaps not so hidden) danger to the notion of individual freedom as it emerges in the more communitarian context. That is the very real danger of trampling on individual freedom for the sake of the greater and common good, a danger that *must* be taken seriously. We can think here of how this phenomenon plays out in the context of marginalized individuals in the confines of strongly communal cultures.[71] Take for example a young homosexual woman living in a strongly religious community—a community that expects her to conform to the traditional standards of her people, which would often include marriage to a man and having children. To say that she would feel the weight of the general will, whether conceptualized as the sum total of individual wills or a separate ontological entity, crushing her individual freedom is an understatement. Stories such as these are seldom pleasant and altogether common. As such, Schelling's point concerning the need of harmonizing the collective will with the individual such that the former does not crush the latter stands quite strongly. Furthermore, despite my communitarian lean, one that is admittedly tempered by concerns from classical liberalism, I am nonetheless not entirely comfortable with positing a separate ontological entity that I would dub the general will that exists outside the collective community. A judicious use of Ockham's razor shows that what can be explained by the dialectical interplay of communal and individual need not add a further layer of complication by an appeal to a third, separate entity. As such, a small tightening up of Schelling's own account, with recourse to the *New Deduction* and *System of Transcendental Idealism* will provides a relatively complete account of the theoretical issues at stake.

We must think here of issues that in some instances transcend the will of the individual; issues where the common good, as common good, is *clearly* at stake (like our collective duty to the environment, issues of the distribution of state-wide resources/wealth, and structural racism). There it could be the case that *both* individual and collective freedom will be literally destroyed if one is only concerned with the freedom of the individual. The structural components cannot adequately address problems on a mass scale if restricted only to the concerns of the individual. (To be fair to Schelling here, *The New Deduction* is attempting to deal explicitly only with the problem of the unconditioned essence of individual freedom, but the worry nonetheless stands.) Despite the overly individualistic initial grounding of the Schellingian account of the general will, he is aware of the basic problem that emerges between my will and the "will of *all*."[72] Here it is indispensable to quote him at length to articulate the overall account that is at stake. Schelling writes:

> Only by conceiving of all will as *absolute* can I conceive of the will of all others as being restricted by mine, and mine as restricted by the will of all others. Therefore even the restriction of the individual will by the general presupposes the original unrestrictedness of the will.
>
> …
>
> Only by restricting my will within the limits of the will of all others, and the will of all others within the limits of mine, can I think the will itself as absolute. And the problem of the absolute will, as established by morality, is resolved in ethics *through the universal concordance of the will of all individuals.*
>
> …
>
> Therefore the *individual will is restricted by the general will only inasmuch as it becomes absolute owing to this very restriction, and the individual will is absolute only inasmuch as it is restricted by the condition of the general will.*[73]

The above sequence in the deduction amounts to a cohesive explanation on Schelling's behalf of the necessary interrelationship and interplay between individual freedom and the freedom of all. While the original will is "unrestricted," capable of infinite choice, this unrestricting does not reach the level "absoluteness" until it has been filtered through the general will. The reason for this is quite simple—freedom outside of a social context is a pure abstraction. That is, the individual will is free only in the most technical metaphysical sense, but it is only when freedom enters[74] the sociopolitical sphere (what Schelling dubs the empirical) that we can speak of *actual* freedom, a freedom that has a causal moral efficacy in determinate human affairs. Thus, rather than thinking of freedom as being restricted by society, it should be thought that it reaches its *absoluteness* (its true autonomy and reality) only when it is tempered through the general will. Freedom, then, for the early Schelling (as well as the Schelling of the middle authorship that arguably begins with the *Freedom Essay*) is inherently a *political* concept. This renders the Habermasian claim that Schelling is not a political thinker to be a problematic one at best or flat out mistaken at worst. The above sequence of the deduction inherently demonstrates that his lifelong concern with freedom, his profound obsession with it even, is not merely the speculation of an abstract metaphysician, but rather the explicit acknowledgment that freedom plays out in the human world only with the realization that one curbs their freedom, and others do the same, in the political sphere, making this portion of the authorship largely in line with developments of modern political thought.

## The Relationship between Morality and Ethics (*Sittlichkeit*)

The next portion of the argument in the *New Deduction* introduces a proto-recognitive framework, grounded here on the side of willing rather than from consciousness as such, and fleshes out the interrelationship between morality and ethics (i.e., duties that we have to one another *qua* private citizen vs. duties that only emerge at the macro level of political engagement. Given that Hegel uses this language both in his early unpublished political work and later in the *Philosophy of Right*, and given their close working relationship at this point of their respective lives, it is not out of the realm of possibility that they were developing these ideas in conversation with one another. However, there is not enough textual reference to each other's work at this point to more concretely substantiate this idea). Schelling begins the next portion of the deduction by stating that "since I can think of myself as an individual only insofar as another freedom is opposed to my freedom, I can also assert *my* will *as* will only in opposition to another will."[75] Continuing from the notion of the necessary connection between the individual and social, Schelling is clearly articulating here that the very idea of *individuality itself* is inherently *social*. Since I can only think of myself as a self only insofar as I find my freedom in opposition to the freedom of others, I come to see myself as an individual *only* in a social context. I do not begin as a well-differentiated individual—individuality is a direct result of my free interactions and oppositions within the body politic. These interactions lead the individual out of the realm of interpersonal responsibility (morality) and toward the realm of *social* responsibility (ethics). If we loop back to our discussion of dissent in the first portion of the chapter, we see here that for Schelling *dissent* isn't an aberration—a manifestation of failed political praxis—but rather the very constitution of the political as such.

The manner and content of Schelling's articulation of the relationship between morality and ethics owes a great debt to Kant and Fichte's distinction of theoretical and practical philosophy. As we know well from Kant's first *Critique*, freedom is not given, and in principle cannot be given, to theoretical consciences insofar as there is no intuition of freedom. As such, freedom is proven practically in the second *Critique* as the very possibility for morality as an axiomatic postulate, for without freedom it is inherently nonsensical to speak of personal duty and responsibility. Fichte goes a step further than Kant insofar as he completely reverses the very relationship between theoretical and practical philosophy, arguing all throughout the vast permutations of the *Wissenschaftslehre* that it is in fact *practical* reason that lays the foundations for the possibility of doing theory in the first place. The reason for this is that for all of their eventual disagreements (stemming largely from their divergent views on the status of Nature and the scope of transcendental argumentation) both Fichte's philosophy and Schelling's philosophy begin when the subject *freely* and decisively jumps from the serious of cascading natural conditions in order to contemplate the very possibility of said conditions.[76] The blurring between theoretical and practical philosophy in the *New Deduction* allows Schelling to directly connect the science of politics with the science of ethics. The nature and status of rights there ends up coinciding with the Kantian notion of duty: "I *ought* to do what is practically actual, and what I ought to do is obligatory; it is in line with *duty*. Duty is that which simply *is* because it ought to be[77]. . . *everything is duty that is in line with the matter of the general will.*"[78] This particular formulation, or, rather, re-formulation of the Kantian moral framework *explicitly* blurs the political with moral, extending the categorical imperative to the level of the general will in a similar manner as later found in the *Metaphysics of Morals*.

The above theoretical move has an inherent logical and practical plausibility given the very articulation of the categorical imperative—to act in such a way that my maxim can become universal law is, in fact, to *govern myself* based on a precept that is discerned by an individual will made general. As we have also seen above, this also stands largely in line with a certain reading of Rousseau, a reading that is adopted by Kant, by which the general will is the kernel of the individual will that coincides only with the interests of the whole body politic (or common good) rather than the narrow self-interest of individual agents. The general will in Rousseau also serves the function of giving the state the laws by which it governs itself, thus analogously serving as a categorical imperative at the macro level. Thus, my duties are given to me not from my own idiosyncratic or arbitrary self-imposed rules, but rather from the rules that are vetted by a *universalizing, communal* framework.[79] While I have certain misgivings that *morality* functions neatly under Kant's formal conditions, being of the inclination that form and content can never be neatly untangled, my misgivings are largely and *drastically* alleviated when the same procedure is used for the deduction of rights.

If we think of rights as the most basic or minimal moral standard, cutting across the vast messy structure that is indicative of morality as enacted in our everyday interpersonal affairs, I can think of no better way of articulating basic rights. That is, they make possible rule governed behavior established at the level of the general will that cuts across the nuance and difference that characterizes morality.[80] If we retroactively invoke the recognitive framework that I will develop in the next chapter, which we already saw an inkling of in his articulation of individuality as a process of acknowledgment of the will of the Other, we may *begin* to theorize about how a right emerges. Rights and rights discourse have a historical genesis during the late medieval period in the nexus when medieval, renaissance, and modern thought exist uneasily next to one another in Europe.[81] They are theoretically articulated in a set of philosophical discourses, as most prominently found in Hobbes, Locke, and Rousseau, and enter into the historical fray when actual agents *demand and fight* for rights in what is often a violent and chaotic process (think here of the French and American Revolutions, although the fight can also be symbolic or nonviolent as well). These rights are either recognized, not recognized, or sit uncomfortably within a recognitive purgatory when there is a give and take between various parties and power structures, after which they enter into a codified formal framework. This is an ongoing and often messy process, as certain rights need to be rethought depending on what concrete problem that needs to be addressed. For instance, as we have already seen in the women's suffrage movement, the right to vote was won for white land owning men much earlier than for women, and there are currently ongoing struggles and moments of dissent due to rampant voter disfranchisement in various parts of the world. One thus universalizes at the level of the general will, which is the neat, tidy theoretical image of the historical mess that is alluded to above and that can only be truly captured when one delves into history proper rather than theoretical philosophy, and the *general* will is what binds *me the individual* to the established set of rules. It may "bind" in a variety of ways: legally, top-down coercively, voluntarily, culturally, and so forth. Regardless of how the process happens in its concrete sociohistorical manifestation, the argument that Schelling is articulating clearly demonstrates how, at the level of the general will, our duties bind us—they confer an obligation to act along the parameters established by the general will, which itself is a matter of public deliberation and delineation of the very rules that govern society, or, as he phrased it above – "*everything is duty that is in line with the matter of the general will.*"[82]

With the intertwining of ethics and morality put in place, Schelling moves to re-evaluate the earlier claims made in the deduction, explicitly admitting that the assertion of strict individualism was "problematically assumed,"[83] and further stating that "will as will can become *individual* only in the context of the *general* will, just as the general will is *general* only in the contrast to *individual* will. Without this context there would be only an absolute will, which could be called neither individual nor general."[84] We now have a tri-partite distinction about the will—it can be individual or particular, general, or absolute. Schelling clearly insists here, and I believe correctly, that the general will ought not be confused with what he dubs an "absolute" will. While he does not explicitly define the absolute will, one need only slightly extrapolate from his overall corpus and early thinking on Absolute Idealism to know that the referent point would be a will that belongs to God or the totality of existence (at this point he is still very much embedded in a pantheistic framework, which he begins to chip away at after the *Freedom Essay*[85] by his insistence that at least one portion of God, the ground of God, must be radically beyond any and all human categories, thus taking inching more in the direction of apophatic theology and away from pantheism). This absolute will is undivided and one, but also represents an important distinction insofar as it breaks with one possible interpretation of the general will—one that will hold that the general will is an ontologically separate entity from the individual will. By putting the absolute will in its own category, Schelling indirectly clarifies that this cannot be the case. The individual and general will are in a dynamic dialectical interplay, but at no point can it be the case that the general is to be conflated with an absolute will.

This brings us squarely back to the discussion above about the interplay between the individual and general will, with an all-important added caveat of Schelling's own admission that his initial presentation is not quite as neat as initially proposed. However, the fundamental difference between that which has already transpired and that which will take place from here forward directly pertains to, and is transformed by, how morality and ethics relate to one another. Their interrelationship function in the following manner, according to Schelling:

> *Ethics* solves the problem of the absolute will by identifying the individual will with the general will, *the science of right* by identifying the general will with the individual. If both had completely solved their task, they would cease to be contrasting sciences.[86]

The distinction that Schelling is alluding to above is often conceptualized as a debate between *positive* and *negative* rights in political thought, and Schelling too uses the language of negative and positive rights.[87] While rights discourse, corresponding here to what Schelling dubs ethics, functions according to *negative* principles, delineating a set of prohibitions the general will ought *not* subject upon the individual will, duties or morality in fact perform the opposite function. That is, the science of duty is one of our *positive* obligations to others.[88] Unfortunately, Schelling drops this discussion as quickly as he brings it up, but, given its centrality in all subsequent extrapolations of liberalism, it must be picked up yet again in order to get a full sense of the issues at stake. As such, I will bracket the discussion here in order to pick it up in all of its relevant detail in the final portion of the book, where what is left undeveloped here gets its full expression in Schelling's subsequent derivation of freedom in the *Philosophical Investigations into the Essence of Human Freedom*.

## Schelling's Deduction of "Original Right"

In the second and final portion of Schelling's analysis of the nature of rights, he shifts his focus toward how "right" as a moral and political concept emerges in the first place. He thus begins with a distinction made by Kant and blurred by Fichte: that of the relationship between practical and theoretical philosophy (as well as Kant's distinction between synthetic and analytic propositions). Schelling states:

> Just as theoretical philosophy ascends through a series of syntheses to the highest possible synthesis, so in turn does *practical* philosophy descend through a series of *analyses* to the absolute *thesis,* and just as the procedure of theoretical philosophy is synthetic, so the procedure of practical philosophy is analytic.[89]

Rights, then, are the fundamental building block of all subsequent political interaction, forming the most basic nexus around which subjects assert their agency. They must be thought of as analytic rather than synthetic due to their foundational or basic nature, emerging and crystalizing through the practical process of the analysis—an extrapolation from the messy world conditions back down to a core kernel of moral truth inherent in various rights.[90] Schelling further posits that rights "*form*" the individual will as distinct from the general.[91] That Schelling would argue in such a manner ought not to be surprising to any reader of classical rights-based discourse. Furthermore, it strikes me as being essentially correct—rights, or something like them, are the only possibility of preserving individual liberty from strong incursions from the general will and the state as a whole, which *always* contain within them the possibility of crushing the individual.[92] Individual rights, derived practically, represent the manner in which this protection is possible.

Unfortunately for the contemporary reader, the method by which Schelling decides to address this sentiment in the *New Deduction* represents[93] a rather opaque portion of what has thus far been a generally clear and cogent account of modern political theorizing. However, unpacking it remains essential to our study, even if hermeneutic elements have to be brought in in order to shed light on the original formulation. Schelling subdivides the formulation of "original right" into what he dubs the "form" and "matter" of the individual and general will.[94] The notions of form and matter are one of the original discursive mechanisms to slice and dice the nature of reality in the Western philosophical tradition, as they are found at the very inception of philosophical thought itself and emerge and re-emerge in a multiplicity of disguises until the present. In the context of the current study, Schelling states that the interrelationship between the form and matter of original right is as follows: "*right* as such, as to its sheer *form,* is identical with right as to its *matter,* because the matter of right is determined by the form of right, not vice versa."[95] This is perhaps the most cryptic remark that Schelling makes in the text for the simple reason that with it ensues a glaring conceptual difficulty: if the form or structure of right is in fact *identical* with the matter or content, why would it be the case that the *matter* is determined by the form? The relationship of *identity*[96] would in fact imply that form and matter collapse together, and thus cross-determine one another in a manner that would defy any easy prioritization of one over the other. Given that my general aim throughout this work is to give *both* a coherent account of Schelling as political thinker and to mine his work for solutions to our most pressing political concerns, I believe it imperative that I am as hermeneutically charitable as possible to Schelling's account here.

As such, the most charitable read would entail the following relation between the form and matter of right: given the fact that the matter or content of concrete manifestations of right claims within the political (and moral) sphere can manifest itself into an endless, and perhaps infinite, variety due to the variability and specificity of individual actions, we cannot reasonably rely on the *matter* of right to constraint the form. Reliance on the side of matter, even if form and matter are ultimately identical (or intricately woven together) at an ontological level, would not allow us to coherently extrapolate from the endless variation of the empirical in order to get to the core truth within right—that which would allow us to articulate relatively simple universal standards. Instead we must hold in mind that the general structure or form of right shapes the matter or content. This would follow from Schelling's own insistence on the "analyticity" of his general approach. One begins with the overall, large and messy picture, and analytically extrapolates down in order to find the core truth.

The way in which Schelling ultimately squares the overall analysis is by identifying the form of right with *freedom* itself, still keeping to his now infamous dictum that freedom is the alpha and omega of *all* philosophy (or, in this instance, the fundamental analytic truth that is found when one unpacks all practical theorizing). As such, coinciding directly with the interpretation provided above, Schelling argues:

> The form of my will as willing is *freedom*. And freedom pertains to the will absolutely, inasmuch as it is always the *subject*, never the *object* of any determination, that is, inasmuch as the will is not determined by the *matter* (the object) of its willing, but the matter by the will itself.[97]

This serves as the theoretical bridge between the form and matter of the will. *Freedom* (which is often interchangeably used by Schelling as "the unconditioned") is not constrained or shaped by the matter of right if it is still to remain freedom *as such*. To be formed is to be molded, shaped, constrained, and determined into a particular configuration, thus immediately undermining the very notion of what is meant by freedom (since all of this would make the unconditioned conditioned). Thus, it is freedom itself that does the forming rather than the other way around.

However, and this is a most significant however as it demonstrates that Schelling is never so naïve as to think that there is anything simple about freedom, freedom itself is *never* a pure or simple abstraction. It manifests itself in concrete action in a world full of agents asserting their freedom, clashing over a dizzying array of exponentially complex issues, leading Schelling to further posit that

> Inasmuch as freedom, considered strictly as what it is, cannot be an *object* in any sense, it can never be the *object* of any act that could do away with it. However, the matter (the object) of my freedom can become the object of an opposing freedom, that is, it can be negated as the matter of *my* will.[98]

If we take here the notion of the *materiality* of *materialization* of one's will in its most literal configuration, we can theorize along with Schelling the concretization of freedom. My freedom exists in a direct and non-abstract manner *only when* it manifests itself in action set against the backdrop of countless other agents making their freedom known through their action. Thus, as he somewhat opaquely alludes in the opening moves of this portion of the *New Deduction*, the form and matter of the will do in fact intertwine in a manner that cannot be easily untangled except by philosophical abstraction—they intertwine in the world itself.

The concluding paragraphs of the *New Deduction of Natural Right* circle back to the relationship between the general and individual will, but they do so in such a terse and fragmented manner that they frankly do not add much to his original formulation. Furthermore, much of the discussion has already been covered more systematically earlier in the text and we have already worked through in part two of this chapter. As such, I will now transition our discussion toward the notion of recognition as it is developed in the *System of Transcendental Idealism*. While this particular text was written in the late 1700s nearly in tandem with the *Naturphilsophie*, and published in 1800 *after* the *Naturphilosophie* had already been largely worked out in at least its general parameters, I will somewhat break with a strictly chronological presentation of his political ideas for the simple reason that the recognitive framework he develops in the *System of Transcendental Idealism* forms a neater continuum with what has already been developed here.

# Conclusion

With this we will conclude our analysis of the first of two texts where Schelling explicitly and directly addresses political theory as such.[99] Our discussion here has coalesced around *two* key themes emerging within the text, both of which intertwine quite coherently: the notion of dissent, vital to the very articulation and concretization of freedom in the political sphere, and the relationship between the individual and general will. These two ideas serve as the bedrock or ground upon which the subsequent discussion of Schelling as political thinker will be built upon. To *dissent* is to demonstrate one's political agency, one's very efficacy as an embodied subject in the world. Quite similar to Hegel's, and Axel Honneth's subsequent reformulation, of *"struggle"* in the recognitive process, dissent is the foundation for the freedom of the will of subjects who have been traditionally marginalized and systematically devalued by long-term misrecognition—people who have been denied and/or deprived or their rights, freedom, and agency due to their race, gender, ethnicity, sexual orientation, religious standing, and so forth. Without the ability to rise up, protest, or even *revolt*[100] in instances where the oppressive forces are so pernicious that no other option is viable (as we saw in the case in Haiti), political change becomes quite literally impossible. Likewise, without some form of dissent freedom is turned into an empty abstraction—whether affirmed or denied—in the metaphysician's armchair, debated endlessly but never manifesting itself in reality. To dissent, then, *is to be human*, to be a subject, in all of its messy unfolding in the political sphere. We have also witnessed how the notion of the general will, which the German Idealists had seen unfold firsthand next door in the French Revolution, plays out in Schelling's early work. While Rousseau's and Kant's notion had a decidedly communitarian flavor in its original setup, Schelling weaves between his individualist account early on in the *New Deduction* and a more communal understanding toward the end of the text. This final understanding never gives up the idea that the general will ought not to trample the individual, and this idea should never be ignored in our political theorizing and our political practices.

The next piece of the Schellingian political is his unique articulation of the notion of recognition in the *System of Transcendental Idealism*.[101] Despite the relatively brief amount of space that Schelling devotes to recognition there, what makes his contribution exceptionally unique is the ontological ground in which he situates subjectivity and intersubjectivity is itself *unconscious*. Thus, anticipating Freudian developments that will not be fully fleshed out until close to a century later, Schelling offers a twist on the recognitive story that Fichte and Hegel are (rightfully[102]) more famous for. By demonstrating that consciousness and self-consciousness contain within themselves, by logical necessity, elements of the unconscious, Schelling paves a path toward showing that recognition is always a somewhat fragile phenomenon, carrying within itself unconscious processes and hidden biases that so often result in misrecognition. This is not to say that recognition is not a potent tool for analyzing political conflict—far from it, in fact—but rather that by incorporating an ontology of the unconscious as developed by Schelling we can in fact uncover a far *richer* account of the exactly why misrecognition is prevalent in modern political life. It is toward this account that I now turn.

# 2

# *The Unconscious Roots of Consciousness*

# *Recognition in the* System of Transcendental Idealism

## Introduction

The notion of "recognition" and its subsequent permutations has become an umbrella term which examines an ever-expanding cluster of concepts in political thought—concepts which look to capture what at times feel like an exponential growth curve of complexity in late 20th- and early 21st-century existence. At its most deceptively simplest, recognition is the notion that one can become a subject and political agent *only* by being acknowledged by another, while simultaneously reciprocating (or failing to reciprocate) the said acknowledgment. As such, it is a potent mechanism for theoretically parceling out and explaining concrete human struggles regarding rights, race, gender, sexual orientation, and so forth. Beginning in the late 1980s and early 1990s, thinkers such as Charles Taylor and Axel Honneth, who are both inspired by what can be dubbed a neo-Hegelian revival in political thought, began to introduce and argue for a recognitive approach that incorporates sociology, psychology, and philosophy as a means for addressing the above specified issues. Their work has dovetailed into an impressively wide variety of research by philosophers, political scientists, and sociologist, including a substantive critical backlash.

Honneth's work alone spans various volumes, including: *The Struggle for Recognition: The Moral Grammar of Social Conflicts* (easily his most influential work), *The I in We: Studies in the Theory of Recognition*, *Redistribution or Recognition? A Political-Philosophical Exchange* (written with Nancy Fraser as an interlocutor), and *Recognition: A Chapter in the History of European Ideas*. This set of work has inspired an ever-widening commentary[1] that is in principle impossible to capture into a single volume alone, and much less so in a *single chapter* whose aim is decidedly more modest—to see but one permutation of recognition theory from the standpoint of a hereto neglected thinker, and to demonstrate its unique contribution to an already existing and wide-ranging debate.

The list of detractors to the notion of recognition is no less impressive in its own right, and quite indispensable for getting to the fullness of what the concept entails. Recognition, and recognition theory as a normative standard for political action, has been questioned by thinkers from a wide variety of perspectives, ranging from classical liberal to Marxist to post-structuralist, to name but a few. Among them are Patchen Markell, Kelly Oliver, Lois McNay, and Nancy Fraser (who is simultaneously both sympathetic and also critical of certain economic facets of the theory, as witnessed in her debate with Honneth in the abovementioned *Redistribution or Recognition?* volume). They have criticized the idea of recognition and its real-world implications for failing to account for the detrimental effects of a lack of access to material resources, instead choosing to focus too heavily on identity (Fraser and McNay, for disparate reasons); for having a too narrow and reified notion of identity (Markell and McNay, again for different reasons); and for failing to consider that there are elements of human subjectivity that are simply inaccessible in and through the recognition process (Oliver).

Conspicuously absent from all of these major accounts, be they for or against recognition in general (or even in-between, as is the case for many of the critics), is any discussion of *Schelling*'s unique contribution. This is also largely true if one looks at the more historically oriented literature, which focuses nearly exclusively on the work of Fichte and Hegel. With the exception of Emiliano Acostas' account referred to in the first chapter and Robert R. Williams' short reconstruction in *Hegel's Ethics of Recognition*, almost no literature is devoted to Schelling's important, albeit admittedly brief, foray into recognition in the *System of Transcendental Idealism*. Given this lacuna, one of the central aims of this chapter is to demonstrate how the Schellingian notion of recognition, which situates the conditions for the possibility of consciousness in the *unconscious*, represents a missing piece of the historical puzzle that has thus far been connected and reconnected in a complex web by the wide variety of thinkers specified above (although it is most certainly not limited to those thinkers).

While this demonstrates a contribution to the scholarship surrounding recognition in general, my own critical aims have never been satisfied by filling in a neglected gap, no matter how crucial that might be. Rather, I aim to show something more theoretically and practically substantial. By situating recognition in the dark ground of an unconscious nature, Schelling presents us with a potent new theoretical tool for thinking and rethinking what it means to be recognized and misrecognized, and how this process is inherently messy in its historical unfolding. Thus the overall aim here is to integrate and work through multiple sub-strands of argumentation with the *System of Transcendental Idealism*'s account of recognition as the thread that holds it all together. We will first begin our analysis with a brief foray into the general recognitive project as it was being articulated by Fichte and Hegel, who bookend Schelling's own account and are widely seen as the first and last word on recognition in this particular period of time. It is important to note here that given the rapid development and time frame in which Fichte, Hegel, and Schelling were working through their various theories, the lines of influence between the three get so blurry that it is virtually impossible to tell who was at the forefront of these innovations. For instance, despite the fact that Fichte's *Foundations of Natural Right* is the first text to widely speak of recognition (there are some echoes of the notion in Rousseau, but nothing to the extent that is found in Fichte), Schelling was working within similar parameters in *New Deduction of Natural Right* at exactly the same time (and in fact *slightly* earlier by about a year), and Hegel's unpublished work from that period as well as the Jena *Phenomenology* are likewise full of recognition all throughout. As Williams points out, "although Hegel found the concept of recognition in Fichte, he did not first discover intersubjectivity by reading Fichte's *Grundlage des Naturrecht*. Before he discovered the concept of recognition, Hegel had arrived at an understanding of human being as social, and self-consciousness as involving intersubjective mediation."[2] The same applies to Schelling: we see him first developing a social model of the conscious self in the *New Deduction*, which comes before Fichte's account,[3] and then he explicitly develops a recognitive model in the *System of Transcendental Idealism*. Secondly, we must see how recognition develops in the *System of Transcendental Idealism*, which will include a general overview of this particular work with an eye toward the penultimate claim (at least from the standpoint of this analysis and chapter) that transcendental subjectivity is contingent upon transcendental intersubjectivity, which in turn is contingent upon the unconscious workings of nature as such. Thirdly and finally, we will examine how Schelling's view of recognition can demonstrate a concrete connection to structural issues of race and racism, thus staying true to German Idealists' dictum that theoretical and practical philosophy can never be neatly untangled.

## Part I: Fichte and Hegel on Recognition—A Brief Sketch

While it is most certainly the case that we ought to challenge the Hegelian picture of a progressive development in German thought toward the culmination of a dialectical, Absolute Idealism as it is found in Hegel's own system, given that it represents a decidedly one-dimensional story that is explicitly at odds from Hegel's own methodology, it is nonetheless the case that no thinker ever develops in isolation, Schelling included. This is especially true for Schelling during the time in which he composed the *System of Transcendental Idealism*, a period of collaboration with Hegel, and the beginning of the end of his relationship with Fichte. This historical note aside, it also happens to be the case that while Fichte and Hegel spill a significant amount of ink and influence an entire literature surrounding recognition, Schelling's discussion is largely confined to one substantive portion of the *System of Transcendental Idealism*. As such, no account of recognition in Schelling can be quite complete without seeing the larger philosophical, social, and historical context in which it is situated. We will thus begin with a (very) brief overview of recognition as it is found in Fichte and Hegel, and then transition into an in-depth examination of Schelling's unique contribution.

# Part I-A: Fichte

The Fichtean account of recognition develops explicitly from his political work as a means of addressing some of the deficiencies of beginning with the positing of an empirical ego from the transcendental one in his 1794 version of the *Wissenschaftslehre*. The initial formulation, where a single principle of "self-positing" is conceptualized as the sole ground for all subsequent philosophical inquiry, can be read as problematically solipsistic since one appears to be trapped in the activity of their own ego alone. This formulation thus gives way to an innovative account of intersubjectivity in the *Foundations of Natural Right*, which is woven from four fundamental postulates or theorems:

1) A finite rational being cannot posit itself without ascribing a free efficacy to itself.[4]

2) By thus positing its capacity to exercise free efficacy, the rational being posits and determines a sensible world outside itself.[5]

3) The finite rational being cannot ascribe to itself a free efficacy in the sensible world without presupposing the existence of other finite beings outside itself.[6]

4) The finite rational being cannot assume the existence of other finite rational beings outside it without positing itself as standing with those beings in a particular relation, called a relation of right.[7]

The beginning movement remains the same as that of the 1794 version of the *Wissenschaftslehre*: one cannot begin philosophizing or positing our own existence as a moment of radically self-apparent knowledge without doing so in a free move. The free move is the moment where the subject realizes their second-order consciousness by reflecting on the series of intentional states and realizing that the mere reflection shows a moment of detachment from the causally conditioned series. This leads the way to a second move which also mirrors the initial formulation.[8] Here, the finite being bumps up against a world which conditions the series of conscious experiences. That is, in order for the "I" or ego to exercise its free efficacy in any meaningful manner, there must be a "not-I" or object to exercise it upon. Even more simply, in order for us to be able to think of anything there must be things to think of. As Husserl will phrase this process later on, subject and object co-constitute one another, or if one like to go backward instead, we can think of the Neoplatonic dictum that thinking and Being cannot be neatly untangled for thinking can only be thinking *of something*.

The next two moves are where Fichte parts with his initial formulation and where he truly drives home the primacy of *practical* over theoretical reason. In order for *me* to have efficacy in the sensible world, I must "presuppose" the existence of other free beings. Why could that possibly be the case? Could I not be just as efficacious with no one to impede my agency? The answer is decidedly "no." The very concepts of freedom, agency, a world, and so forth are in fact themselves conditioned by a previous set of more primary conditions. There must be a social framework in which I am "summoned"[9] by others who preexist me, thus making transcendental intersubjectivity the condition for the possibility of transcendental (and empirical) subjectivity. These others teach me all that is necessary to make philosophical questions meaningful in the first place, and without them my free efficacy can never be reflected back to me such that I am capable of seeing it as free. In a space where humans are not social, the mediums of language and thought would be either impossible to articulate or useless. Once I realize that the condition of the possibility of the self is in and through the Other, I also realize that I am *inherently* in a political relationship with this Other, what Fichte dubs "a relation of right" directly above. The reason for this is because when I exercise my freedom in the world, that freedom now intertwines, interacts, and clashes with the freedom of others. As is the case with Hegel and Schelling, freedom is not an abstract construct of an abstract ego, but rather the freedom to act in an actual world among others where actions have direct repercussions. Fichte thus makes the transcendental ego *political*, showing the radical and often misunderstood nature of German Idealist thought.

## Part I-B: Hegel

Hegel is a philosopher of recognition *par excellence*. As Robert Williams argues throughout *Hegel's Ethics of Recognition*, there is a compelling case to be made that his entire authorship can be read as a series of meditations on the notion of recognition (albeit certainly not reducible to this notion). We find the idea in nearly all of his work beginning from his unpublished manuscripts, to his *Phenomenology of Spirit*, *Encyclopedia Philosophy of Mind*, *Philosophy of Right*, and so forth. It is therefore inherently impossible to do the notion of Hegelian recognition justice in such a short space. Given our narrative here, which primarily covers the earlier manifestations of German Idealism in general and Schelling in particular (ending in roughly 1810), I will instead focus our gaze on what is without a doubt the most famous manifestation of recognition in Hegel[10]—the Master/Slave dialectic. The Master/Slave dialectic (or more accurately Master/Servant or Master/Bondsman dialectic, since Hegel primarily uses the term "*knecht*") occurs in the *Phenomenology of Spirit* among three vectors. Consciousness, as desire[11] for self-understanding, looks to fulfill its desire for selfhood in a moment of destruction. Looking to assert my agency against the world, I consume the object which stands against me, and in the moment of consumption/destruction I fail to achieve recognition. The object is gone, leaving nothing to reflect my subjectivity. As such, "*self-consciousness attains its satisfaction only in another self-consciousness.*"[12] That is, one can in order for the self to be acknowledged as a full self, it must be through another consciousness and never from an object. When the self encounters this Other, either there is a moment of "pure" recognition or the infamous antagonism of the Master and Slave/Bondsman.

The moment of *pure*[13] recognition is one of mutuality, and the first vector of Hegelian recognition. I see myself reflected in you, you see yourself reflected in me, and we acknowledge each other as fully functioning selves and thus let each other freely be. The story could very well end here, but has not been the historical reality of recognition, which, more often than not, manifests itself in the world as *misrecognition*. Thus the need of the next vector. Self and Other engage in combat in order to assert their selfhood and agency, showing themselves to be self-conscious agents rather than mere consciousness in the world. "As each risks his own life, each must likewise aim at the death of the other, for that other no longer counts to him as himself."[14] When this fight to the death happens and one self triumphs over the Other, the destruction of the Other immediately foils the elevation of the first self to actual self-consciousness for there simply is no one to reflect my subjectivity and selfhood back to me. Thus the second vector leads to one party eventually unwilling to risk death and surrendering their agency for servitude.[15] The surrendering of agency is never truly possible, however. In the moment of Mastery, the Master doesn't receive full recognition from the Slave since they will not accept it—they see the Other as beneath them and not worth of giving this recognition. After all, they surrendered and thus are no longer on equal footing. The Servant or Slave likewise gets no recognition from the Master, but their agency is not squashed. Instead, in the final vector of this portion of the development of self-consciousness in the *Phenomenology*, the servant sees themselves reflected in their *work*. As Hegel writes, "through work, this servile consciousness comes round to itself."[16] That is, the servant sees themselves as self-consciousness in and through setting aside their immediate desire (that moment that begins the recognitive process) and focusing on that which they produce. This is echoed later by Hegel in the *Philosophy of Right* when he begins his account there with the self externalizing and objectifying itself by mixing their labor with the land, leading to Abstract Right. Before moving on to Schelling's account, it should at least be noted that the moment of labor and self-recognition through it, as well as the moment of Abstract Right, is ultimately and decidedly *not* the *telos* of Hegel's narrative. Recognition is made real in the realization of the self as a social being in the Spirit or lifeworld of a concrete people, *both* in the *Phenomenology of Spirit* and in the account of *Sittlichkeit* in the *Philosophy of Right*. This is a moment of "reconciliation" that is "a reciprocal recognition which is *absolute* spirit."[17]

# Part II: Schellingian Recognition

The facet of recognition that is perhaps murkiest in both Fichte and Schelling is the order of presentation of the unfolding of the recognitive process itself. That is, the written method of extrapolating the *logically* necessary movements by which consciousness reaches awareness of itself as self-consciousness is *ontologically reversed*. Although we begin with ideal or transcendental consciousness in order to uncover the necessary conditions which make its emergence possible, we uncover with each forced move the need for *practical* preconditions that made the transcendental moves necessary in the first place. A simpler way of stating the above problem is that while the philosopher is presenting each of the steps toward recognition and intersubjectivity as if intersubjectivity is the outcome of subjectivity, the *opposite is in fact the case*—as Husserl also later discovers, one cannot have subjectivity without intersubjectivity. Thus, although I as the phenomenologist am presenting each step of the process in what appears to be a solipsistic vacuum in which individual I-monads run into one another for the first time, what I eventually uncover in the logic of this process is that the steps I have taken are only possible in and through a social context. Consider the following propositions or axioms as explicated by Schelling:

> *First Proposition. Absolute abstraction*, i.e., *the beginning of consciousness, is explicable only through a self-determining, or an act of the intelligence upon itself.*[18]
>
> *Second Proposition. The act of self-determination, or the free action of the intelligence upon itself, can be explained only by the determinate action of an intelligence external to it.*[19]

We see the above-characterized move playing out in Schelling's order of presentation. The first proposition is one of abstraction—"*absolute abstraction*"—a motion that takes us away from determinate individual conscious existence and toward that which allows us to speak of consciousness, as such, in the first place. As is the case in Fichte, this involves the realization, a primordial awakening of sorts, where human beings realize that they are conscious only in and through second-order consciousness.[20] That is, I determine or delineate myself as conscious subject through my own activity by which I separate the stream of intentional consciousness from the I which is capable of *actively reflecting* on this stream. One could say that consciousness came about first, which would most likely be the correct empirical and ontological picture, but from the epistemological standpoint, the condition for the possibility of knowing that I am conscious does not lie in consciousness, but rather in self-consciousness, which is the only "thing"[21] that allows me to wrest myself from the stream of activity in order to simultaneously realize my own existence and that of the activity in the first place.

What follows in the transition between the first and second propositions above is a logical step that is made not merely by Schelling but by *all*[22] the post-Kantian Idealists: a deep-seated realization that the conditions for the possibility of subjectivity do not lie within the confines of the individual ego alone. That is, in the transition between "*absolute abstraction*," an abstraction that in principle could not be any more abstract,[23] and "*self-determination*" we come to see that the only way we could determine ourselves in the first place is in and through an Other. The requisite conditions for us being able to perform second-order self-reflection are ultimately not to be found in the activity of ourselves alone, but rather in the free activity of an intelligence external to us. As Schelling puts it above, the conditions for self-determining "*can be explained only*"[24] by an Other-determining. The reason for the strong "*only*" lies in the fact that theoretical and practical reason are completely entangled, such that the only untangling possible is one meant for the purpose of clear elucidation rather than a real distinction, to borrow a term from our medieval predecessors. Ultimately, as we will see at the end of the analysis here and in much of what preceded in the previous chapter, I can demonstrate free efficacy in the world in the *practical* sphere of concrete human activity (which is always-already *political* activity), and it is this sphere that conditions my own ability to come to grips with myself as a free self-conscious agent.

Schelling himself notes that the deductive nature of the transition between the absolute abstraction performed by the I itself and the conditioning of the I by another I is initially somewhat mysterious for the simple reason that it seems to simultaneously ground the impetus of an action in a self as well as on Other:

"we see at all events *that* a determinate action of an extraneous intelligence is the necessary condition of the act of self-determination, and thereby of consciousness; but we do not see *how*, and *in what manner* such an external act could be even the indirect ground of a self-determination in ourselves."[25] That is, how is it that we are the ones who determine our own action, thus being the impetus of our own willing, and at the same time need an Other to make said willing possible in the first place? As pointed out directly above, the answer to this difficulty lies in the nature and structure of *practical* rather than theoretical reason. From the ideal standpoint of theoretical reason, the I posits and determines itself, but this idealization does not neatly carry over in the realm of the practical, and we thus must contend with the interplay between ideal and real, theoretical and practical.[26] Schelling writes:

> By the act of self-determination I am to arise for myself *as* a self, that is, as a subject-object. Moreover, this act is to be a free one; that I determine myself is to have its ground wholly and solely in myself. If the act is a free one, I must have *willed* what comes about for me through this act, and that it must come about for me because I have willed it. But now that which arises for me through this act is willing itself (for the self is primordial willing). I must thus have willed the willing before I can act freely, and the concept of willing, like that of the self, likewise first arises for me only through this act.
>
> This manifest circle is eliminable only of willing can become object for me prior to willing. This is impossible through my own agency, so it will have to be simply that concept of willing which would arise for me through the act of an intelligence.[27]

To delineate, to come forth or to show myself to be a person, which simultaneously entails that I am subject (self-consciousness) and object (body), I have to *will* to do so. However, in the very earliest manifestation of this willing, what is coming forth from the self is not yet a self as such, but rather the "primordial willing." I am now stuck in the strange position of having to have willed *before* the determinate establishment of a stable self, which calls into question how I could have willed before willing itself is established and how this can be dubbed a free action. After all, for it to be a *free* will, there is an implication that I wield the will rather than it wielding me, and that there is a self who performs this wielding in the first place, and yet neither a self nor the will are yet manifest to do the necessary work.

The way out of this dilemma lies in a twofold process. First, we must take seriously the Schellingian notion that the "self is primordial willing." That is, like Schopenhauer who is clearly influenced by Schelling despite his loud protestations that he is an obscurantist, Schelling is arguing that at our *very core* we are not first and foremost rational agents but rather pure or primordial will—a bundle of unconscious drives. What this entails is that the process that tears us from our unconscious slumber is not found in our individual reflection but rather in an external stimulus from an intelligence that is not our own, an intelligence that calls us to *act*. Secondly, dovetailing from the preceding point, to avoid the problem of having willed before we have in fact will, the call to action is not first and foremost to be found in us but rather in an *external* intelligence will "demand"[28] an action from us. This leads Schelling to pose a question that will bring us to his argument for recognition: "how then, in general, can intelligences exert influence upon one another?"[29]

It is at this juncture that Schelling's argument for recognition takes its ultimate form. In the Fichtean formulation of the transcendental ground for recognition, the primacy of the practical over the theoretical was articulated through the notion of "summons," a call from social order that predates me and makes me what I am, which conditions the condition for the possibility of experience in the first place. Despite the fact that Schelling warns his reader at the outset of this section of the *System of Transcendental Idealism* that he will not be developing "a moral philosophy of any kind, but rather a transcendental deduction of the thinkability and explicability of moral concepts as such"[30] he nonetheless invokes the notion of an *obligation* as the impetus for recognition, echoing Fichte's summons. What we thus have is a notion of the social at the heart of transcendental inquiry, a notion that is repeated in different iterations by Fichte, Hegel, and Schelling, each of them clearly seeing that without the social dimension of recognition one's transcendental idealism is perpetually doomed to the charge of solipsism. However, this is no mere attempt to avoid a potential objection to one's theoretical work, but rather a deep-seated realization that ideas such as "subjectivity," "willing," "freedom," and so forth are mere words unless they are situated in concrete *deeds*. One cannot will to act in social/moral sphere unless there is an external impetus to call upon the subject. For instance, it cannot be said that I have a duty to my students, a duty that most certainly includes but is not limited to my teaching, if no students were around to take my courses. I may have *desire* or even a *will* to do so, but as Schelling argues, that would be a will before a will. It is they who make the obligation possible in the first place, thus allowing the will to become instantiated in the first place.

Given that the conditions for self-determining lie in the obligation that we have to the other, what are we to make of self-determining as such? The notion of self-determining, and its subsequent articulation as self-determining in and through others, has its roots in the Cartesian epistemological project of a radical new beginning for philosophy through the activity of the I coming to know itself. However, the Schellingian project flips the *Meditations* on their head, or perhaps in this instance rights them on their feet, through the transcendental idealism of Kant and Fichte. The intellect acts upon itself in the sense that it *freely* reverts its gaze away from the external series of determinations or intuitions with which it is bombarded with on a moment-to-moment basis, and is able to posit that there is a self in the first place which can move along the series and question it (consciousness of consciousness, or "reflection" as it is more often dubbed by Fichte and Schelling), inquiring into what makes the series possible in the first place. The full set of transcendental conditions which make this possible are numerous and multifaceted, to say the least, and they are articulated by Kant, Fichte, and Schelling in a collectively vast body of work that is far outside the scope of this project.[31] The question which is of interest to us here, and one that has never been far from my mind since my initial encounter with this tradition of thought, is what makes this reflective move possible in the first instance? The answer has clear and profound political implications.

The step that allows us to understand and ground the possibility of reflection or second-order consciousness is decidedly *not* the pure Cartesian self-reflection of the *Meditations* which allegedly grounds our epistemological certainty; rather, it is free, practical willing, made possible through a complex act of "*mirroring*" via other intelligences who predate me: "for the individual, these other intelligences are, as it were, the eternal bearers of the universe, and together they constitute so many indestructible mirrors of the objective world."[32] Here echoing Leibniz[33] rather than Kant, Schelling invokes the notion that the world of both subjective and objective experience is made possible through a complex, infinite act of reflection between countless intelligences. If we think here of our early 21st-century existence, there are eight *billion* intelligences if one counts humanity alone, each of which reflects from its own position one tiny portion of the world, with the net result being a nearly infinite amount of reflection and refraction of *both* the subjective and objective conditions of existence from any one standpoint, which are in turn conditioned by their own idiosyncratic sociohistorical circumstances and objective material reality (for subjective and objective are never neatly separable for Schelling and German Idealism in general). We are thrown into this world through no choice of our own, and simply cannot ignore this complex mirroring no matter how hard we may try to do so. It is the Other who gives me a language, a culture, a way of life, and all of these things are ever-increasingly brought into direct interaction between a vast multiplicity of languages, cultures, and ways of life. I can thus only situate myself in and through the Other.

The Leibnizian influence on this manifestation of recognition looms large and ought not to be ignored. By way of comparison, consider the following passage from the *Discourse on Metaphysics*: "every substance is like a complete world and like a mirror of God or the whole universe, which each one expresses in its own way, somewhat as the same city is variously represented depending on the different position from which it is viewed."[34] While what Leibniz has in mind here applies both to the primary intelligence or soul monad as well as to every other monad which is the building block of a more complex reality,[35] both the way he captures the notion and the metaphor of the city are extremely useful for elucidating precisely what Schelling has in mind as well. Thinking here of a city, both in its geographic/architectural divisions and its complex sociopolitical divisions based around race/class/income/ethnicity/ etc., the mirrored interactions between vast groups of people are reflecting mere tiny portions of each particular locale. Each locale is conditioned by the other locales, both in the sense that it is a part of a larger whole and insofar as people identify (or are sometimes forced to identify) by distinction to other places. For instance, working-class people have a strong tendency to live in working-class neighborhoods and see themselves as working class, which is a distinction that is only possible if and only if there are other classes. Within even that one particular subset, which cannot be neatly captured by any one single category, there are then more complex divisions and intersections based around race/gender/sexual orientation. What gives a city its uniqueness and complexity—elements that are often better captured in literature and art rather than purely philosophical prose—is precisely this complex set of mirrored and mirroring conditions.

It is this process of mirroring that provides the condition for the possibility of experience and, despite the Leibnizian influences, inaugurates the process of ultimately naturalizing the transcendental—a process that ultimately ends Fichte and Schelling's friendship, and one that I will turn to in the following chapter. Thus, Schelling writes:

> To achieve the original self-intuition of my own free activity, this latter can be posted only quantitatively, that is, under restriction; and since the activity is free and conscious, these restrictions are possible only though intelligences outside of me, in such a fashion that, in the operations of these intelligences upon me, I discern save the original bounds of my individuality, and would have to intuit these, even in fact if there were no intelligences beyond myself. That although other intelligences are posited in me only through negations, I nevertheless must acknowledge them as existing independently of me will surprise nobody who reflects that this relationship is a completely reciprocal one, and that no rational being can substantiate itself as such, save by the recognition of others as such.[36]

What this entails is that the self, conceptualized as "primordial willing" (to be contrasted with the rational self or one of primordial *thinking* that is much more common to the Western philosophical tradition), has the condition for the possibility of its own existence only through the recognition of others. As we have already witnessed at several junctures, despite the German Idealists' penchant for dense philosophical prose, the notion of willing is never understood as an abstract philosophical concept—it is rather *always* understood through the *doing* of concrete actions in the world as such, which receive their obligation from the external call of others. The need for an Other to ground the self is even so strong that Schelling goes so far as to maintain that even if no Other exists in the actual empirical realm, the logic of transcendental subjectivity is such that the Other is fundamentally necessary to make sense of the self in the first place. We can think here of the Aristotelian notion of virtue, whose logic requires a community for the simple reason that virtuous actions are meaningless if it is not directed toward someone.[37] Thus, what the other reflects back to me is not my sense of self as an abstract intelligence capable of theoretical work, but rather my *will* and my *agency* as a person with concrete real-world commitments.

The part which Schelling largely leaves out of what is admittedly a highly abstract presentation of the universal and necessary conditions for the emergence of both human subjectivity and the objective world which is its necessary correlate (thinking and being, subject and object, necessarily co-constitute one another), are the implications of what happens when the process of mirrored recognition does *not* in fact reflect my agency back to me in any stable manner. Distorted recognition happens because the "indestructible mirrors" that are responsible for the constitution of transcendental intersubjectivity are reflecting a world that is a pristine philosophical construct *only* at the purely formal or logical level, but the objective world is a historically[38] messy living, breathing entity populated by centuries worth of sedimented layers of misrecognition—misrecognition due to racial, ethnic, sexual, gendered, and other identities. Schelling's point does not concern identity, however, and I too contend that identity, while clearly important, is essentially misconstrued in contemporary discourse because it is thought of a static feature of a subject; rather, his point is about the necessary conditions which make human agency possible. Thus, misrecognition stifles our very primordial freedom and willing through reflecting back to us a distorted picture of who and what we are at the level of fundamental ontology.

## Part III: Recognition, the Unconscious, and Race

It is at this juncture that we must exit the realm of what Schelling refers to as "negative" philosophy during the final portion of his productive work, and enter into "positive" philosophy, albeit not precisely in the manner he used the terms. Positive philosophy takes existential circumstances into account in order to theorize in all of its truly messy glory. The history of the United States is a complex one, but two factors of it, our original sins, cannot be ignored: slavery and the systematic destruction of native peoples. So if we are to think of our present moment in the early days of the 2020s as being a snapshot of over three hundred million mirrors reflecting our subjectivity, agency, and the collectively shared objective world, filter that reflection through countless layers of historically sediment, we may begin to have a fairly accurate representation of how race and racism shape the collective psyche and intersubjectivity.

In the early colonial years the agency of various African peoples is stifled to near extinction in violent and dehumanizing ways that are nearly unimaginable from a contemporary standpoint (or perhaps purposefully left largely unimagined). What then followed is four hundred years of a collective narrative that at every instance perpetuates a story about the necessity of this dehumanization. Through examining political, religious, and philosophical argumentation (one need not even look further than the Idealists' own comments on race for evidence of such claims); through propaganda; through policy and everything in between, one begins to get a picture of just how race and racism, one of modernity's most pernicious inventions, have become such an inescapable component of our very subjectivity. Despite the fact both Fichte and Hegel have more broadly developed and sustained arguments surrounding recognition, it is Schelling who is supremely useful at theorizing the emergence of racism and the facets of it that make it so difficult to deal with. What Schelling adds to the discussion, and what makes him so pertinent from our contemporary position, is his notion of the *unconscious*.

The unconscious plays a central role throughout Schelling's corpus, and its status has been recently developed systematically in several scholarly volumes, including S. J. McGrath's *The Dark Ground of Spirit: Schelling and the Unconscious*, Tereas Fenichel's *Schelling, Freud, and the Philosophical Foundations of Psychoanalysis*, and Matt ffytche's *The Foundations of the Unconscious: Schelling, Freud and the Birth of the Modern Psyche*. Although Schelling tended to be quite reticent about directly stating his influences, the origins of the notion have even deeper roots in the German Mystical tradition, with thinkers such as Jakob Boehme, Mesiter Eckhart, and Friedrich Oetinger serving as important precursors to Schelling's own insights, which in turn are influenced by the Neoplatonism of Plotinus, Porphyry, and more indirectly Pseudo-Dionysius the Areopagite.[39] Despite Schelling's own arguments against Neoplatonism proper in books such as the *Philosophical Investigations into the Essence of Human Freedom*,[40] his own way of articulating metaphysical/ontological theses follows a Neoplatonic logic—one begins with layers of complexity in the empirical world and then recursively works to dead-end that complexity in "something" so utterly simple that it ultimately must transcend the very notion of simplicity itself (i.e., the "dark ground" in the *Freedom Essay* or the principle of the "identity of identity and difference" in the *Bruno* and *Weltseele*).

The move toward a radical grounding principle, an *Urgrund*, is done in order to ontologically anchor one's most fundamental philosophical claims, thus avoiding the occurrence of an infinite regress that would exclude the possibility of an ultimate explanation for how reality is structured and possible in the first place. In the case of *consciousness*, and slightly before the development of the full implications of the Identity Philosophy and the later notion of an *Urgrund*, the argument has the same basic structure/logic. Consciousness is a phenomenological ground zero—following Descartes, I know that I am thinking simply as a matter of sheer performance, and any attempt to cease thinking or to think of nothing only reveals further intentional claims (the *concept* "nothing," images, ideas, and so forth). When I examine thought qua thought, setting aside the claim of what kind of medium is capable of thought, I find that it *cannot* exist without *some* correlate—an *object* (defined here as any object of thinking as it need not have a physical manifestation). The next question is to determine the conditions for the possibility of consciousness, which is precisely the "Copernican Turn" in Kant, the turn which inaugurates German Idealism. This turn reveals the active nature of subjectivity, and a slew of preconditions that allow us to think in the first place (the transcendental intuitions of space/time, the twelve categories, and the transcendental ego). While developed out of the Kantian transcendental framework, the next step is one that is unique to Schelling. If consciousness is to be ultimately explained at all, it must have a foundation in the *world itself*. That is, in order to avoid the twin problems of solipsism/pure subjectivism and the dogmatic metaphysical idealism as found in Berkeley, one must examine *Nature* and the conditions which make Nature's emergence possible, for consciousness in the Schellingian framework, even when it is understood to be transcendental, must ultimately have a point of origin if it is to be fully explained.

If the conditions which make Nature possible in the first place are themselves somehow conscious, they ought to be readily available for inquiry through phenomenological investigation through introspection or reflection. Reflection, however, must dead-end in a place that is not conscious per se, in order to avoid yet another regress of consciousness of consciousness of consciousness, etc. This problem never manifests in consciousness as such since the phenomenologist has no experience of such an infinite regress, for what is available to us via phenomenological investigation is simply first- and second-order consciousness—the stream of objects/ideas given to me by the world and my consciousness of the said stream. Thus, the only step out of the following dilemma is that the ground for consciousness cannot lie in itself but rather in the *unconscious*. As McGrath points out, "the principle of sufficient reason stipulated that nothing is without a ground,"[41] and, furthermore, "the condition for the possibility of structure, intelligibility, and consciousness is the exclusion of something . . . that the whole structure depends on."[42] What the whole structure depends on is a principle that itself cannot be part of the structure as structure, but rather that which grounds the structure in the first place. According to Schelling, this principle must be the *unconscious*. Only through it can we ground consciousness in the first place.

The relevance to this position for contemporary discourse is quite significant. Simply stated, it demonstrates that our conscious processes as developed through the contingent workings of human history require a non-phenomenological grounding, and what this further entails is that misrecognition survives and thrives upon layers of sediment that are largely inaccessible to everyday second-order consciousness. This notion is certainly no longer radically new given that it is the foundation for psychoanalysis; it is, however, being reread here in light of metaphysics or fundamental ontology. Racism becomes not simply a psychological problem then, a matter of the individual attitudes that are enacted by atomistic agents, but rather an *ontological problem*. This makes it more murky and difficult to combat, but if the history of racism and resistance to it has shown us anything over the last half a millennium is that racism was always-already murky and difficult to combat. It was difficult to address when it was a part and parcel of the dominant zeitgeist during much of modernity, leading prominent and usually highly intelligent people to make stunningly racist claims (think Kant and Hegel here, for just two prominent examples from this time period); it was difficult to address when the zeitgeist ostensibly shifted away from explicit racism (in the United States, at least) and toward a de facto one before and following the civil rights movement; and it continues to be difficult to address now even as much of the world's *individual* attitudes, or at least the way these are reported, have in fact shifted away from explicitly endorsing any racist claims. Despite the explicit shift away, society nonetheless still struggles simultaneously with individual and systemic racism. How is this double movement possible? How is it that we can collectively[43] hold a certain position and yet racist praxis still continues? I propose that the Schellingian notion of the unconscious holds a portion[44] of the answer to these questions. We turn now to the unconscious in Schelling through a detour through Shannon Sullivan's *Revealing Whiteness: The Unconscious Habits of Racial Privilege*, a work which places the unconscious at the center of our quest to understand and combat the problems of racism.

Shannon Sullivan's *Revealing Whiteness* is not a historical text, nor one devoted to German philosophy. It is a contemporary philosophical reckoning with race and racism written from the standpoint of the pragmatic notion of *habit* and the psychoanalytic notion of the *unconscious*. The argument that I will be making here demonstrates how the notion of habit and habituation can be explicitly understood in and through the process of recognition—indeed, they can be thought of as practically synonymous in nearly all regards—and, furthermore, this notion of recognition is already caught up in the unconscious for Schelling, allowing us to connect and ground several disparate strands of argumentation in one overarching narrative. As such, I will again demonstrate how our supposedly unpolitical thinker turns out to be untimely in another regard. Schelling's notion of recognition and its unconscious roots allows us to better understand misrecognition due to race and to show the difficulty in combatting this misrecognition. We begin with an overview of Sullivan.

Sullivan contends that much of racism has very little, if anything at all, to do with explicit racist beliefs, statements, and actions, although the reality of these is not to be ignored. Instead, she argues, we must understand that due to the way that history has played out during the last 500 years or so, racism has become embedded in the very fabric of our reality. This embeddedness is to be understood in light of the pragmatic notion of habit. Sullivan writes:

> Understood pragmatically, habit is an organism's subconscious predisposition to transact with its physical, social, political, and natural worlds in particular ways. Habit is equivalent to neither routine nor a "bad habit," as the term is often used. Habits instead are that which constitute the self. Most of them are not objects of conscious awareness; human beings enact them "without thinking" which means that a significant portion of the self is nonconscious. One could say that habits compose the style in which an organism engages with its world, as long as "style" is understood phenomenologically rather than epiphenomenally. Habits are not like clothing fashions that one can pick up one day and discard the next. *They instead are manners of being and acting that constitute an organism's ongoing character.*[45]

We see here that habits are acquired the very moment we emerge into the world, and they are what fundamentally shape who and what we are. As we have already seen in our discussion of recognition, each of us is born situated in *a particular* place and time, which means that we inherit a multitude of elements from our culture and those around us. We inherit a language, idiosyncratic ways of using this language based on our social standing, certain practices (a religion, for example), and, most importantly, we inherit a way of *being-in-the world*.

Connecting this back up to the concrete ways in which history has shaped our world during the last 500 years one can argue that many of the habits that we inherit are essentially racialized and often racist habits (by racism here we denote largely a *structural* racism rather than a directly personal one). Sullivan draws this implication early on stating:

> what then might a pragmatist concept of habit mean in the context of race and white privilege? Because habit is transactional, in a raced and racist

world, the psychosomatic self will be racially and racistly constituted. Race is not a veneer lacquered over a non-racial core. It composes the very bodily and psychical being that humans are and the particular ways by which we engage the world.[46]

To say that habits are "transactional" means that they are not acquired or learned in isolation, but rather through the countless interactions we have had with other people. Under this understanding of the human being, the self isn't a fixed static thing, but rather a porous dynamic one. Others shape our way of being-in-the-world and we in turn shape theirs through the ways in which we live, think, speak, and so on. Viewed on a macro scale there are quite literally millions of ways that these interactions crisscross. Furthermore, under this framework, there is no underlying "real"[47] self, like a transcendental ego or Cartesian "I," that habits cover over. To put it somewhat differently, the self is made of habit all the way down. The habits fundamentally constitute or shape the self, which, in a racist world, becomes a racist self. Any solution to racism, then, will not involve peeling the layers of habit away in order to unveil a "pure" self that can then reacquire new non-racist habits. A solution must involve some form of re-habituation.

According to Sullivan, this transactional notion of habituation needs to be modified in light of psychoanalysis and psychoanalysis needs to be modified in light of the transactional account.[48] Her reasoning for this is relatively straightforward: Freudian psychoanalysis is too atomistic at the familial rather than individual level.[49] That is, Freud himself does not connect the wider sociohistorical context into his notion of the development of the unconscious, which is theorized under the oedipal complex that involves the triad of mother-father-child. This complex itself theorizes the family largely from within the confines of the newly emergent, largely bourgeois notion of the family unit that is a product of European modernity and decidedly not the historical familial norm. Furthermore, for Freud groups are formed voluntarily and subsequent to the initial family formation, which is a difficult claim to reconcile from findings in anthropology, psychology, and sociology that humans never truly exist outside of the social nexus. We are always-already thrown into group life. Nevertheless, the Freudian picture is an incredibly useful one for social theory and can be modified. Sullivan takes the notion of group formation in Freud, which precedes on the basis of displaced libidinal ties that naturally occur in the family, and connects the idea to the formation of a new ego ideal.[50] When a libidinal tie that is formed in the oedipal complex is displaced in a voluntarily formed group, usually a *leader* is seen as the ego ideal.[51] Yet a leader is not always to be found, so the ego ideal can also be replaced by an idea, and this idea, according to both Freud and Sullivan, can be *either* positive or negative.[52] In a world divided between self and Other, the oldest and most permanent division according to Simone de Beauvoir, the Other in the last several centuries has been a racialized Other. Thus the ego ideal becomes racialized and holds onto a racist ego ideal.

How precisely does this fit with the Schellingian notion of the unconscious and our overarching framework here? Ultimately, I believe that instead of modifying the pragmatist notion of habit and the psychoanalytic notion of the unconscious, we can instead dial right back to German Idealist notion of recognition and Schelling's notion of the unconscious, thus neatly bringing the various layers of inquiry into a single ground. What Schelling (along with Fichte and Hegel) provide is the direct mechanism by which human subjectivity is structured in the habitual manner described by Sullivan. The processes of recognition and misrecognition are *intrinsically and necessarily* transactional. One does not begin with subjectivity and a stable identity. Rather both are the results of ongoing historically messy interactions. Since the conditions for the possibility of subjectivity are intersubjective, the sociohistorical account of the emergence of subjectivity takes ultimate primacy even in a transcendental framework (which Schelling modifies quite heavily even in the *System of Transcendental Idealism*, and ultimately naturalizes in a way). As such, we can much better understand the emergence of notions such as race, ethnicity, identity, the nation-state that is the direct product of modernity, or the subject itself with a rigorous account of recognition. For instance, in the notion of the nation-state, the subject of recognition is an international legal order (not unlike what Kant proposes in *Toward Perpetual Peace*). There recognition and misrecognition guides not just international trade agreements, but also how people see themselves and one another. The emergence of the notion of race is likewise caught up and directly entangled in the nation building project of modernity, along with the colonial practices of much of the West.

Given the colonial project and the notion of nation building, lines of self and Other that used to be distinguished based on familial/tribal/religious lines began to shift toward notions of races. In order to justify what really has no justification (i.e., the plundering of the resources of the Other and their enslavement), the dominant European, and later American, powers engaged in a state-sanctioned misrecognition campaign. The Other was reduced to laboring animal, dehumanized and sold, and laws were placed in the books to legitimate the process and make it official. In the American context we can add the killing of entire Native cultures. By the time the arguments shifted in the opposite direction and society likewise shifts away from the explicit exploitative and oppressive legally sanctioned tactics, we have collective already lived through *centuries* of racist praxis. No amount of denial can erase this fact. Freud himself, while being too atomistic in places, knows that sociohistorical circumstances will always affect the individual. He writes: "the contrast between individual and social or group psychology, which at first glance may seem to be full of significance, loses a great deal of its sharpness when it is examined more closely . . . only rarely and under certain exceptional conditions is individual psychology in a position to disregard the relations of this individual to others."[53] While I would switch the "rarely" to "never," the point is well put. One cannot understand the individual consciousness without recognition transpiring in the social sphere, and one cannot understand this recognition without also understating misrecognition. Finally, this misrecognition can become a part and parcel of the unconscious and the two cross-influence each other. As Freud argues, the conscious and the unconscious are intertwined, such that things that are in the unconscious can be brought to consciousness (through therapy) and conscious elements can be repressed into the unconscious.[54] Given that this in an ongoing process, there is never a final moment of disentanglement, but rather just ongoing back and forth, such that people can be individually or collectively at one point aware and at another unaware of the way they have recognized or misrecognized the Other. This explains the continued persistence of racism in the world and the difficulty we have in combating it. What can be brought out and examined is repressed again, and, as Sullivan astutely argues, whether we like it or not it becomes habitual.

What all of this entails is that we must lean into the notion of recognition in the *normative* sense that the German term *Anerkennung* contains—a notion that is not as abundantly clear from the English translation. It is not simply that we recognize or not, or even that we repress and hold onto misrecognized racial dispositions (at the individual and structural level), but also about *how* we go about in making recognition itself into a normative ideal. In the more mundane sense of recognizing or misrecognizing we may fall into the potential trap of thinking of the process simply as a *descriptive* mechanism by which we understand how subject and identity formation takes place, making the whole thing into an ontological/psychological necessity that we can do nothing about. But that is not at all the full picture. We also have to say that we *ought* to foster ever-increasingly better recognitive frameworks by which we can collectively confront and atone for our past sins, so to speak, to not only understand how racism becomes embedded in the individual and social psyche, but also how from the very same framework it can be brought out and combatted, incrementally leading us toward better and better outcomes with the full knowledge that the category of "Other" can never be fully replaced in the human psyche. There are always elements of others that we will fail to recognize, yet we must strive to do so along individual person-to-person interactions, along formal legal processes, through education,[55] and so forth. As Schelling argues in the *Stuttgart Seminars*,

> Within us there are two principles, an unconscious, dark one and a conscious one. Regardless of whether we see to cultivate ourselves with regard to cognition and science, in the moral sense, the process of self-creation always involves our raising to consciousness what exists in us in unconscious form, to turn the innate darkness into light, in short, to attain a state of clarity.[56]

The Schellingian account of recognition and the unconscious, coupled with Fichte, Hegel, Honneth, and now hundreds of other contemporary researchers into the approach, can provide us with the tools to move forward and to set recognition as an ongoing normative ideal—a process with no fixed terminus point that ought to guide our political praxis surrounding issues of racial justice toward greater clarity. Last but not least of all, it is Schelling alone among the early proponents of recognition who couples it with a strong notion of the unconscious, thus giving us further insight and tools into this ongoing praxis.

# 3
# Naturphilosophie *as Political Theory*

## Introduction

In a quote that is so eerily prescient to the point of being haunting, Schelling both diagnoses the means by which we tamper with Nature at our own risk and lays the ground for our obligation to it. He writes:

> The purest exercise of man's rightful dominion over dead matter, which was bestowed upon him together with reason and freedom, is that he spontaneously operates upon Nature, determines her according to purpose and intention, lets her act before his eyes, and as it were spies on her at work. But that the exercise of this dominion is possible, he owes yet again to Nature, whom he would strive in vain to dominate, if he could not put her in conflict with herself and set her own forces in motion against her.[1]

Nature made it possible for us to peek behind the veil of organic creation, to work on it and reshape it in our own image—to instill our own purposes upon it—and yet our reshaping of its fundamental forces is ultimately a human vanity, and dominion is always an illusion. Whereas it would have seemed virtually impossible for us to unleash the forces of Nature against Nature in the late 18th early 19th century, it is now indisputably the case that we have done precisely just that, and continue to do so at an alarming rate, at the detriment of ourselves and this iteration of Earth's creative forces. What we owe to Nature is the question of this chapter, our guiding inquiry that will determine the scope and essence of our responsibility. In order to uncover it, we turn to the *Naturphilosophie*.

Schelling's *Naturphilosophie* (Philosophy of Nature) represents the lifeblood of his thought. Its importance for the development of German Idealism cannot be overstated, and, as Frederick Beiser points out, the development of Absolute Idealism itself cannot be disentangled from the philosophy of nature.[2] Beiser writes: "above the portals of the academy of absolute idealism there is written the inscription '*Let no one enter who has not studied Naturphilosophie.*' Without an understanding of at least the central doctrines, basic arguments, and fundamental problems of *Naturphilosophie* the absolute idealism of Schelling and Hegel is all but incomprehensible."[3] The aim here, however, is not simply to reconstruct the arguments of a Schelling's philosophy of nature for hermeneutic or historical purposes (although I believe that such work is indispensable to the dialectical praxis of philosophy), but rather to once again re-articulate and re-habilitate its central tenets in order to ask what I take to be the most pressing question of the early 21st century: "What is our political responsibility to Nature *as such*?" This question is absolutely loaded, having reverberations that echo forward and backward throughout this project and through Schelling's philosophy as a whole,[4] and, I contend, it is a conceptually thorny question, eluding any easy answers and always-already pushed aside in political discourse due to the inescapable, crushing weight of the material conditions of our current milieu. It is for that reason that we must continue to ask and re-ask the question, to perpetually insist that just because philosophers have in fact forgotten Nature, leaving its study to our colleagues in the natural sciences, this forgetting has come at a steep price.

Given what I take to be the centrality of the question of our responsibility to Nature, this chapter serves as the giant trunk of the metaphorical tree that holds our narrative together, or, if the reader permits me to mix my metaphors, the gravitational vortex around which the rest of the book revolves.[5] My aim and structure is thus threefold: as always, the first task is the hermeneutic reconstruction of the central doctrines of the *Naturphilosophie* itself; secondly, and perhaps most importantly, is the systematic drawing out of the political and ontological implications of the *Naturphilosophie* for our responsibility to

Nature itself, arguing throughout that this responsibility is direct, inescapable, and fundamental to what we are as a species at the most core ontological level; finally, I will end by showing how the earlier notions of dissent/recognition and the later deduction of *freedom* effect the analysis in the second portion, pointing to how this direct responsibility is fraught with difficulty due to the very constitution of human subjectivity and its fragile materiality.

# Part I: Reconstructing Schelling's *Naturphilosophie*

The challenges of painting a neat portrait of Schelling's thought on *any* particular issue are readily acknowledged. Prone to significant changes of what are core ideas, the reader and interpreter are at a constant risk of either getting overly bogged down in the concrete details of Schelling's labyrinthine twist and turns or, at the opposite extreme, of reducing him to a caricature by oversimplifying his admittedly difficult and contentious work. This is especially the case in the *Naturphilosophie*, an area where Schelling has written, and certain published, more than on any other notion. Given that my explicit aim throughout this work has been guided by a spirit of hermeneutical charity, I will largely avoid playing the interpretive game of pointing out the various places where Schelling "gets it wrong."[6] Instead I will focus my efforts in articulating a coherent picture of a world where the human and natural aren't split from each other, in direct opposition where we can subdue and tame Nature for our purposes, or point to our normative responsibility to it only by referencing back to us. As such, I follow Confucius' dictum in *The Analects*: "all that I teach can be strung together on a single thread."[7] The interpretive "single thread" here will be Schelling's dynamic, process ontology by which Nature is understood in light of its basic oppositional forces. All the rest can and will be deduced from this core insight. With this in mind, let us turn toward Schelling's texts.

The general interpretive strategy for understanding what Schelling had in mind in constructing a philosophy of nature largely falls along two trajectories: a transcendental trajectory and a naturalistic one. The transcendental trajectory played a key role in earlier interpretations of Schelling, arguing that the overall project of *Naturphilosophie* is a reversal of Kant's transcendental idealism—the conditions for the possibility of experience aren't simply features of human subjectivity, making and shaping our basic experience of the world, but, rather, they are embedded in Nature itself. That is, there are conditions for the possibility of Nature as such; categories which make the natural world itself possible. This reading then, makes the transcendental subject to be simply the highest product of a more primordial transcendental structure which has shaped the universe itself. As such, *Naturphilosophie* is transcendental idealism folding back on itself, spilling through and infecting the real.

The reading of Schelling as a naturalist has recently been articulated in the work of Frederick Beiser, Iain Hamilton Grant, and Ben Woodard (to name but a few).[8] As both Beiser and Grant meticulously document in their work, the naturalistic reading has as its support *ample* primary textual evidence to be found all throughout Schelling's writings on Nature. Rather than thinking of the philosophy of nature as a metaphysician's speculative fever dream, an attempt to ground empirical science in philosophical categories derived from the armchair rather than the backbreaking labor of the laboratory, one should think of its insights as emerging from the sciences themselves. In the introduction to the *Ideas for a Philosophy of Nature*, which at times wavers between transcendentalism and naturalism, Schelling himself clearly presents the foundation for such a reading: "it will be apparent from the Introduction that my purpose is not to *apply* philosophy to natural science, since I can think of no more pitiful, workaday occupation than such an application of abstract principles to an already existing empirical science."[9] That is, to take philosophical principles and force them upon the already existing structure of the scientific enterprise is fool's errand, making for *both* bad science and bad philosophy. Instead, one can think of philosophy of nature following what is essentially the reverse order, taking the insights painstakingly gained by the working scientist and incorporating them into the architectonic of a speculative idealism—an idealism which builds *from* these insights, thus *bolstering itself by the real* (hence the necessity for understanding the Absolute in light of the philosophy of nature, as Beiser mentions above).

My sympathies largely lie with the second reading of Schelling, since his own pronouncements throughout tend to heavily favor the notion that one builds from Nature itself and does not impose principles upon it by philosophical fiat. Having said that, I do not think that the two readings are completely incompatible with each other, and, furthermore, the naturalistic read does not absolve us from the task of metaphysics. In fact, naturalism itself, despite its protestations, is in many ways a metaphysically loaded notion, as I will argue below and as I have argued in my previous work.[10] What I propose here is what I will be referring to as a *dynamic process ontology*—an ontology that will borrow some of Schelling's transcendental statements and reconstitute/rethink them in light of his own admitted commitments to naturalism—thus emerging with a metaphysical picture of the fabric of reality that *does not* and *cannot* eschew the empirical. The basic argument is that the notions of *dynamism* and *process* in fact require at least *some* stable channels or avenues (this is the rethinking of the transcendental categories). In order for there to be flow, there must be a path, an avenue, a channel for the said flow to move through. "Pure" process or flow is in fact a meaningless notion, a mere puddle on a flat surface, uncontained yet stagnant. As Schelling points out in the *First Outline*, "*pure productivity originally passes into formlessness... productivity appears as productivity only when limits are set to it*."[11] Rather than completely ignoring the transcendental categorization of Nature, then, we then think of these categories as the channels or avenues that allow the dynamic unfolding of Nature itself, understood as the most basic laws of polarity that allow Nature to organize itself.

## (A) Nature in the *Ideas for a Philosophy of Nature*

Before launching into the *First Outline of a System of the Philosophy of Nature*, the text that I take to be the most relevant for articulating the process ontology that will serve as the guiding thread for my investigation into our political responsibility to Nature, I would first like to lay the groundwork by examining the *Ideas for a Philosophy of Nature*. This groundwork is important *both* because it shapes the subsequent discussion *and* because Schelling articulates what in retrospect appears to be a strikingly prescient insight into how modernity's forgetting of Nature has already sown the seeds of our current environmental crisis. The *Ideas* are the first significant crack in continuity of Critical Idealism, a point of rupture between the transcendentalism of Kant and Fichte and the later Absolute Idealism of Schelling and Hegel. Despite Schelling's reputation as a protégé of Fichte's, often exaggerated for the sake of drawing a neat philosophical line between Kant to Hegel, the *Ideas* opening moves demonstrate that Schelling's allegiance to a more "pure" transcendental idealism was *very* short lived indeed. He states:

> Originally in man there is an absolute equilibrium of forces and of consciousness. But he can upset this equilibrium through freedom, in order to restabilize it through freedom. But only in an equilibrium of forces is there health… mere reflection is a spiritual sickness in mankind. It makes the separation between man and the world permanent, because it treats the later as a thing-in-itself, which neither intuition nor imagination, neither understanding nor reason, can reach.[12]

While the context of the following quote makes it seem as if this is an argument that is primarily leveled at modernity's representationalist theories of knowledge, its implications have clear and direct implications for transcendental idealism as well (although it would be unfair to categorize Fichte as a representational theorist), as well the germs of the ideas concerning freedom and the identity between subject and object that will be found in Schelling's later thought.

What is it, then, that we can philosophically mine from the above insight? First of all, Schelling's romantic leanings are in display, as well as what appears to be an unacknowledged debt to Rousseau. For there to be an original "absolute equilibrium of forces and of consciousness" means that there was, according to Schelling, a point in humanity's existence where the unity between us and natural world was *absolute*; subject and object, self and other, were inoperative categories, keeping us in direct communion with Nature. Echoing core Daoist insights within a radically different philosophical and historical milieu, Schelling presents us with a mythical point of radical identity—humanity and world aren't in philosophical and material opposition; they are One. Secondly, the change comes about because of our philosophical awakening, where *reflection* begins to split us from our primordial immersion, waking us from an unimaginably long period of naiveté with us making a *free* split from nature in consciousness itself. Nature and humanity, then, cease to be One and become Two—the category of Other becomes endemic throughout the human sphere, a disease fostered by reflection. Reflection, in reflecting on the world, tears the universal from the particular, placing it squarely in the domain of consciousness and through a period of successive stages leads us to the Cartesian cogito, the apex of modernity's radical solipsism and rejection of Nature, a prison of representations of our own making.

However, because it was philosophy itself that builds the walls of this prison freely, it will be philosophy once again that begins to chip away at their edifice in order to bring us back to Nature.[13] The *Ideas* are thus among the first sustained effort in Western thought to freely tear down that which took millennia to build, to again bridge the gap between the Ideal and the Real. In order to bridge this gap, which modernity has turned into a veritable chasm, Schelling attacks the mechanistic edifice upon which philosophy has hitherto been constructed upon, thus making philosophy *historicist*, *genetic*, and *organic* in one fell swoop. "Philosophy, accordingly, is nothing other than the *natural history of mind*."[14] With this in place Schelling is inaugurating nothing less than a paradigm shift in philosophical research.[15] Philosophy here ceases to be an armchair exercise, and begins to incorporate within itself insights gained from natural science and history. That is, the task of the philosopher isn't to simply uncover the logical architectonic that underpins reality, pointing to the static categories of Being that have always been in place and will always be in place (we can think here of thinkers such as Spinoza, Leibniz, and Wolff), but, rather, a *genetic* project that attempts to catch a moving target—*Nature in its productivity*. As Dale Snow points out in *Schelling and the End of Idealism*, "the philosophy of nature had enabled Schelling to move away from the static, logical metaphysic to a dynamic vitalistic one."[16]

This dynamic, process account of Nature begins in the *Ideas* with an explicitly developmental claim, albeit one that alludes to the transcendental interpretation discussed above. Schelling tells the reader that he "shall provisionally presuppose that a philosophy of Nature *ought* to deduce the possibility of Nature, that is of the all-inclusive world of experience, from first principles."[17] Heavily echoing the language of Kant of the *Critiques*, Schelling beings the project with the aim to uncover the basic conditions which make Nature itself possible, and then working from the bottom-up to demonstrate how it is that these conditions structure everything from the basic law-like forces that hold the universe together to the apex of their development in human subjectivity. Thus, looking forward and backward throughout the account I am defending here, and moving past the philosophy of Nature for a brief moment, if we think of the fundamental ground of Being lying *not* in static, fixed substances and essences, but rather the most logically simple of processes—binaries or interrelationships between dueling positive and negative polarities—we can add layer upon layer of complexity, each of which in turn manifests itself into a different empirical phenomenon (e.g., gravitation, genetic structure, photosynthesis, consciousness, family, community, economy, and institutions). Each layer of complexity, deduced carefully by the philosopher of Nature from first principles, allows for the arising of increasingly complex phenomena, which in turn end up recursively affecting the lower levels of process in some instances. For example, in the economic realm, micro decisions which are initially extremely simple[18]—the direct exchange of goods in the form of barter—have gradually and inexorably led us to a *global* system that is so bewilderingly complex that it quite literally takes *billions* of humans to maintain, make sense of, and propel forward (perhaps directly back into the abyss of forces from which it originally emerged . . . ). Once established, the system then shapes and structures the smaller scale processes of exchange, like the seemingly simple act of me buying a cup of tea in the morning. This forms a feedback loop, now inextricably entangled, where it becomes in principle impossible to tear the micro from the macro (and vice versa) except for the purpose of elucidating simpler sub-points. This, I contend, is the picture of the world that is necessitated by Schelling's insights into Nature—insights that have far-reaching reverberations. Like the Great Dao, Nature in Schelling is in a perpetual flux, channeled through basic structures that underpin the process.

The basic structures at play in the *Ideas* are explained by Schelling in term of three "potencies." The notion of "potency" is interwoven throughout Schelling's corpus, from the earliest manifestations in the Philosophy of Nature to his late reflections on the nature of the divine.[19] At its basic, potencies describe the emergence of higher-order levels of organization in the world from more basic underlying forces, with each potency conditioning the possibility for the next in the manner described in the above paragraph. Unlike the Hegelian notion of *aufgehoben*, however, the Schellingian notion of potency does not have the sense that the higher-order potency subsume within itself the lower-order ones in the perpetual cycle of sublation. Rather, each serves as a grounding principle for the next, building layers of complexity upon each other. Here it is key to quote Schelling at some length. In the *Ideas*, he writes:

> In order to fulfill our purpose completely, we still have to mention in particular something of the inner relationships and structure of the Philosophy of Nature as a whole. It has already been recalled that the particular unity, just because it is this, also again comprehends, in itself and for itself, all unities. So too with Nature. These unities, each of which signifies a definite degree of embodiment of the infinite into the finite, are represented in three potencies of Nature-philosophy. The first unity, which is embodying the infinite into the finite is itself again this embodiment, presents itself as a whole though the *universal structure of the world,* individually through the series of bodies. The other unity, of the reverse embodiment of the particular into the universal or essence, expresses itself, though always in subordination to the real unity which is predominant in Nature, in *universal mechanism,* where the universal or essence issues as *light,* the particular as *bodies,* in accordance of all dynamical determinations. Finally, the absolute integration into one, or indifferencing, of both unities, yet still in the real, is expressed by *organism,* which is once more the *in-itself* of the first two unities (though considered, not as a synthesis, but as primary), and the prefect mirror-image of the absolute in Nature and for Nature.[20]

The above quote distills the overall framework of the Philosophy of Nature as it is represented in the *Ideas*. Working from the bottom and moving backward, we see all the key components from which to build a robust ontology of Nature. The *organism* serves as the "mirror-image" of the Absolute in Nature, but, in Schelling's own words, "not as a synthesis, but as primary."[21] That is, the most fundamental ontological structure of the natural is to be understood in terms of its *organizational* forces. These form the basic, necessary structures of reality as such, pointing to a picture of the world as organizational and dynamic at its most basic. As Grant points out, "rather than a projection of organicism 'downstream' in the scale of nature, organization is a power or *Potenz* of the 'self-construction of matter.'"[22] That is, the ultimate nature of reality is to be understood in an *organic* sense, but certainly not in any crude picture of the world and/or universe as some sort of colossal body, which would be a naïve kind of romanticism or proto-Gaia theory as is later found in James Lovelock. Rather, this basic structure unfolds along three layers or potencies in the totality of reality: the universal structure, the universal mechanism, and the organism. The organicism begins with the very construction, or to put it more transcendentally, it conditions the very possibility of matter itself.

Let us further unpack these three potencies in the *Ideas* before moving our analysis to the *First Outline of a System of the Philosophy of Nature*. Taking Schelling directly at his word, the *first* potency is to be understood as the embodiment of the infinite into the finite. The infinite here is the basic law-like structure of reality. This law-like structure necessarily permeates the universe in its infinite totality as the most fundamental set of laws/forces which hold it all together, leading to a direct proof of Grant's insistence on there being a need to blur, or rather rethink, the relationship between physics and metaphysics.[23] The infinite universal laws/forces do not just stay as they are however; they coalesce into *finite* bodies—galaxies, planets, black holes, plants, animals, and so forth—directly spilling out in to the multiplicity *bodies* we observe all around us, each of them operating and being held together by these primordial forces.

The *second* potency yields to the reverse trajectory of the first. Rather than moving from infinite to finite, from the law-like structure that will be articulated in great detail and nuance by physicists and astrophysicists (in a way that philosophy can never, in principle, capture) to the bodies which emerge from the said structure. We instead now move from the particular to the universal. That is, individual bodies pave the way toward *universals*, pointing to a necessary interplay between the universal and particular. In a beautifully speculative move which indeed ontologizes physics, Schelling describes the universal essence as "*light*." Although Schelling himself is being rather literal with the use of light as the "universal mechanism" of the second potency, for the very basic reason that without light very many actual organisms on the planet fall apart and have no way of sustaining themselves, we can also make use of the obviously metaphorical implications (found from Plato forward in Western metaphysics) of light illuminating, expressing, and bringing forth "the particular into the universal." That is, the *essence* of individual beings is being rethought here not in terms of the standard albeit somewhat crude reading of Platonism as putting forth a set of static, eternal categories or Ideas, cut off permanently from material reality in a two-world metaphysics due to the risk of contaminating the eternal with the ever-changing temporal, but rather "in accordance of all dynamical determinations."[24] The dynamical determinations and interactions are between the light illuminating and making possible universality itself and, along with it, the particularity of individual bodies. In Schelling's own terms, "we can go on to define all cohesion as a such as synthesis of identity and difference, of universal and particular, except that in the first kind the universal is objectified in the particular, which is thus itself posited as universal, whereas in the other case the particular is subsumed under the universal and accordingly is posited as particular."[25]

Found in the supplement to the first chapter of *Ideas*, the above quote weaves between the earlier *Naturphilosophie* into Schelling's subsequent development of an Identity Philosophy, but also provides a key insight into Schelling's ontology. The very essence of ideas and our access to them implies that there is a synthesis, a direct interplay, between universality and particularity. Predating Hegel's own account of this notion in the *Phenomenology of Spirit* and *Science of Logic*, Schelling is arguing that to rigidly parcel out the ideas of universality and particularity is to commit a mistake at *both* the ontological and epistemological level. One can only understand the universal insofar as it is manifesting itself in and through the particular, and universality itself is incoherent if it does not ground itself in particularity. Hence the need for a direct "cohesion" or "synthesis" of the two, understood at this juncture through the phenomenon of light.

Taking ourselves out of the philosophy of Nature for a moment and back into the messy realm of the political which this study is undertaking, this picture of reality has clear repercussions for our earlier account of recognition and for our understating of the phenomena of race/gender/identity/etc. The operative categories by which we cleave the world and the humans who are found in it find their grounding not in any of the abstractions of philosophical discourse or a separate realm of reified universality, but in the lived reality of concrete, living breathing processes of individuals and their dealing with complex geopolitical systems that are often not of their own making. Identity and difference, universality and particularity, are always-already caught up in the lived experience of individual agents in a complex matrix of distinctions that *only* makes send or have any cohesion when understood *relationally* rather than in isolation. That is, the universal "human" is found in the concrete particularity of individual humans who have disparate experiences structured by culture and the contingencies of *history*, as Schelling points out in the final portion of the *System of Transcendental Idealism*.[26] Furthermore, all human experience shares phenomenological and experiential factors such that pure individuality is also a fiction. If indeed experience was only individual and had no shared communal or universal elements, then it would in fact become impossible to speak of it in *any coherent fashion*.

The same can be said of the related categories of identity and difference. Pure identity does in fact collapse in Hegel's infamous night in which all cows are black, but even in the height of Schelling's Identity Philosophy, and certainly in the quote above, at no point does he think that "*pure*" identity can be understood or parceled out without the category of "difference."[27] So, *actual* identities (and not simply the category "identity") make sense if and only if they take differences into account (for instance, I in principle cannot understand the racial category of "whiteness" without reference to "blackness"), and pure difference is conceptually problematic, and perhaps even incoherent, insofar as I cannot even state that x and y are different from one another if there is absolutely no ground for comparison. As Bowie points out, "without some underlying absolute identity predication becomes impossible. If the relative differences are not transitively predicated by the Same, they cannot even *be* differences, because there would be no criterion of difference and differences could not even be in the relative way they are."[28] That is, pure difference would be unobservable as well as unspeakable since it would be so radically Other as to be rendered impossible to even conceptualize or recognize—difference needs at least *some* identity in order to operate. Thus, the categories of universality and particularity, identity and difference, as simultaneously operating on the most fundamental ontological level as well as that of practical social/political philosophy must cohere and synthesize in the way that Schelling envisions above.

Returning to the Philosophy of Nature as found in the *Ideas*, two points must be addressed as they are indispensable to our analysis of the practical: first, the vast interconnectedness and interdependence of all of Nature, and, secondly, the interplay between the Ideal and the Real (the hallmark of post-Kantian Absolute Idealism). The inherent interconnectedness of Nature has the perplexing quality of being a basic feature of reality that is both shockingly obvious under any analysis and yet perpetually forgotten. Its forgetting is apparent at the level of public policy (although glimmers of hope are emerging across the globe) as well as in the hyper-individualist underpinnings common to many Western political institutions. That it is forgotten is also in many ways unsurprising. The solipsistic Cartesian Theatre has the annoying quality of being intuitively plausible given the fact that many of us live trapped in the confines of our own psyches, often unable and unwilling to break through the barrier of the I and observe its radical contingency upon the We.[29] As such, for reasons that are complexly psychological, social, cultural, political, and the intersection of all of them together, many seem to remain trapped in psychical fortresses of their own making, only able to catch brief glimmers of the interconnectedness of self and Other, self and Nature, through a vast amount of theory (or perhaps a deep personal experience, although I have always found such insight to be fleeting).

Given that this is a work of practical and theoretical philosophy, the claim that the interconnectedness of Nature is shockingly obvious needs at least some defense. We are taught from a young age about the basic function of ecosystems being sustained in relative equilibrium (now often disrupted by the workings of humanity) in and through the interactions of millions of species. Aldo Leopold captures this point simply and beautifully in his discussion of the land pyramid in the *Sand County Almanac*. He writes:

> plants absorb energy from the sun. The energy flows through a circuit called the biota, which may be represented by a pyramid consisting of layers. The

bottom layer is the soil. A plant layer rests on the soil, an insect layer on the plants, a bird and rodent layer on the insects, and so on up through various animal groups to the apex layer, which consists of larger carnivores.[30]

What Leopold states here can be easily corroborated by nearly any biology and ecology textbook (or even simply by working outdoors for a period of time). However, even a simple exercise of meditative reflection reveals the truth of the claim. The lungs depend on breath that is external to us, the belly on food, and the health of the mind on interactions with other humans. If I simply decide to rearrange my living room, I cannot do it on my own. I require the help of others to lift and reposition cumbersome furniture. That same furniture requires resources found in the environment to be made, roads for it to be transported upon, which in turn take a vast amount of infrastructure. All of this is just on the human end, and the introspection slowly reveals evermore intricate layers of *necessary* interconnection. The interconnection between natural ecosystems is even more complex, and there is no way for introspection alone to capture it—science and philosophy together are a much better guide here.

Schelling must argue for the interconnection even more vehemently given the absolute predominance of mechanistic thinking that had nearly completely entrenched itself into science and philosophy during modernity—so much so that our thinking is still imprisoned by its basic postulates even while our empirical sciences have largely outgrown it. While some of the language that Schelling employs in discussing these issues is stuck within the framework of *his* contemporary scientific discourse (and the conventions of post-Kantian Idealism), a particular passage on the nature of *air* found in *Ideas* is very much worth quoting at length to drive the above points home. Schelling argues:

> Our globe is surrounded by a transparent, elastic fluid, which we call air, in whose absence no process of Nature flourishes, without which animal as well as vegetable life would be totally extinguished—as it seems, the universal vehicle for all life-giving forces, an inexhaustible source, from which both animate and inanimate Nature draw everything necessary to their welfare. But Nature has admitted nothing, in her entire economy, which could exist on its own and independently of the whole interconnection of things, no force which is not limited by an opposing one, and finds its continuance

only in this conflict, no product that has not become what it is solely through action and reaction, and does not incessantly give back what it received, and in a new form again recover what it has given back. This is the great artifice of Nature, by which alone she ensures the perpetual cycle in which she endures, and therewith her own *eternity*... Hence there is nothing original, nothing absolute, nothing self-subsistent within Nature... In order to maintain this perpetual exchange, Nature had everywhere to count upon *contradictories,* has to set up *extremes,* within which alone the endless multiplicity of her phenomena was possible.[31]

I believe the passage largely speaks for itself concerning the interconnectedness of Nature, so I would like to begin our analysis of the above paragraph in a lateral direction—we begin by examining the individual, free agent that has haunted political thought since Hobbes, Locke, Descartes, and the very inception of modernity. Said individual, living in the fabled "state of nature,"[32] would perish in a matter of minutes without the air necessary to perform all other basic bodily functions, showing the very first signs of radical dependence. This "individual" spills their labor into nature, transforming raw energy into the goods necessary for survival, showing one more obvious layer of dependence. Unlike the amazing capacity which the plant kingdom enjoys, being able to transform the basic elements of light and water into energy, the said agent requires significant chunks of matter, transformed yet again through our natural potency, in order to survive day to day. The story of course doesn't end but merely begins here—we quite literally *need*, in the strongest sense of biological and ontological necessity, perhaps even delving into strict *logical*[33] necessity, *others* for our existence. This includes the long dependence on our family for our survival, prompting Confucius, in a quite different philosophical framework and time period, to argue for three years of ritual mourning for our departed parents as symbolic, minimal payback for our first few years of complete dependence on their care.[34] Our own dependence on Nature is much more primary and profound than our dependence on our parents, and yet day in and day out we forget our debt.

Moving away from just the very basics, the need for an exchange of scarce resources, love, care of every conceivable kind (medical, social, emotional, etc.), and, as we have seen in much detail in Chapter 2, the need for *recognition* as the condition for the possibility of subjectivity itself. This, along with the fact that all complex phenomena rest upon relatively simpler potencies, demonstrates that the whole is so tightly interwoven that any denial to the contrary, be it at the level of politics, science, or fundamental ontology, is at best a conceptual fiction (admittedly sometimes useful for purposes of clarification and distinction) and at worst catastrophically destructive. Furthermore, as Schelling is clearly demonstrating in the quote above, this interdependence is an ever-flowing *process*, a clash of dueling polarities. One does not simply extract x from Nature without causing a deficit in y. We have been running a resource deficit for well over two hundred years, mercilessly extracting, exponentially growing, and hardly putting anything back into our small portion of Nature. It very well might be the case that the *only* political discussion we have in the next several decades will revolve almost entirely around this issue, with all other factors of injustice (of which there are many, to say the least) as subsidiary or derivative concerns under this omnipresent dilemma. This is not to say that many practical concerns surrounding misrecognition—racism, sexism, transphobia, and so forth—are somehow unimportant. It is simply the case that their fate is now tied to this particular vortex, and, furthermore, that their tentative solutions can only be addressed by how well we address the vast imbalance in the Natural order that we have caused—an imbalance borne out of our foolish, gnawing obsession with individuality and independence.

Weaving this point with the notion recognition and misrecognition presented in Chapter 2, we can first think of recognition as an umbrella concept that allows us to understand and help to alleviate several form of injustice.[35] While thinkers such as Nancy Fraser argue that the economic notions of distribution should be more carefully distinguished from the purely recognitive,[36] I argue along with Honneth that economic distributive factors also ought to be thought through the prism of the recognitive framework. For instance, think through the following scenario that is transpiring as I write this from COVID lockdown. One the most striking features of the pandemic lockdown is how it has shown to a public the vast chasm between what is deemed as essential work and the pay that is received for this work. While it is obvious that *all* humans depend upon our food producers and distributors for our *basic* survival, the current pay (as of 2020) for the average grocery store employee, for instance, is between 21,000 dollars to 35,000 dollars in the United States. Given the demands of the work and the fact that it is in fact absolutely essential, one still does not approach the threshold of a living wage. The pernicious narrative of late-stage capitalism, even in its "meritocratic" variety (yet another fiction), is that if they want to "remove" themselves from such pay conditions, then one ought to "educate" themselves—"go to college, trade school, blah, blah, blah." This is precisely the definition of misrecognition—we depend upon others who do such work at such a rudimentary level that we systematically fail to see them as subjects worthy of the fullest respect, and the fullest respect can only be met with a reasonable compensation for full-time work (along with the basic human rituals of decency while people are doing this work). The situation is of course ripe with irony, one that I am sure will be immediately forgotten the minute that lockdowns are lifted and we slip into old patterns of behavior,[37] as people who get paid vastly or are finding themselves in the category of Hegel's infamous master—effectively useless. Thus, both from the standpoint of recognition and that of Nature, we perpetuate a deadly political myth of self-sufficiency while unconsciously burying the obvious falsehood, made abundantly clear by Shelling above: *absolutely nothing in Nature, other than the Absolute itself, is self-subsistent, especially not us.*

## (B) The Ideal and the Real

Finally, to conclude our examination of the political themes in the *Ideas for a Philosophy of Nature*, let us unpack the relationship between the Ideal and the Real that is found in the text. The reason for tackling this relationship here is essentially twofold: first, it is a key piece to understanding Schelling's ontological edifice at this juncture of his work, and that edifice lies at the core of the argument that I am making throughout the chapter—that our *political* responsibility to Nature can be successfully and best grounded in a Schellingian ontology; and, secondly, despite Schelling's gradual movement away from his early idealism, political and social institutions nevertheless manifest as human Ideas made concrete. While this second point admittedly sounds rather Hegelian, it must be remembered that during this period of Schelling's authorship his and Hegel's primary insights have *significant* overlap.[38] Furthermore, while the divergence most certainly happens after the publication of Hegel's *Phenomenology* and Schelling's *Freedom Essay*, the second of which deconstructs the notion of system in philosophy, it should be remembered that Schelling was the first to articulate the basic positions of Absolute Idealism that Hegel goes on to develop in amazingly intricate ways throughout his post-*Phenomenology* career (at which point Schelling had subsided from the public's eye).

The ontological status of Ideas is in some sense the very heart that makes German Idealism beat. From the transcendentalism of Kant, its radical reformulation in Fichte's praxis-oriented *Wissenschaftslehre*, to Schelling and Hegel's transformation of both (with a heavy helping of Spinoza and German mysticism) in their Absolute Idealism, the idea of "Ideas" in many ways makes German Idealism *what it is*. Regardless of any of the above thinkers, but with a special eye toward Schelling, we can say that for the German Idealists Ideas are only *Ideas* insofar as they are directly tethered to reality— they are the very rational structure of the world itself, or, if one prefers it put slightly more metaphorically, they are the spiritual element of the vast, ever-changing, perpetually decaying and renewing material realm. As Grant points out, "Schelling's 'absolute idealism,' which embraces 'the empirical *and* philosophical,' consists in the dynamic elaboration of the identity of nature and Ideas."[39] It is for this reason that the rigid distinction between the material and formal, real and ideal, represent a false dichotomy. Rather, the two form an intricately and intrinsically interwoven dyad that can only be parceled out for the sake of discussion and clarification, but not for the sake of a real distinction. The "material" realm is, quite literally, entangled with a vast, idealistic, *conceptual* structure—DNA, atom, molecule, proton, neutron, quark, prime matter, corpuscle, string, and so forth—all imbued with meaning insofar as they constitute a realm rendered permanently inaccessible to everyday phenomenological experience without the *Idea*. It seems to be the case that this core insight of Absolute Idealism, the stirring of the Idea with reality as Plato poetically imagines the Demiurge doing in the *Timaeus*,[40] is one that somehow remains rather neglected. Furthermore, as Beiser showed above, *Naturphilosophie* is how Absolute Idealism begins in the first place. It is empirical science that delves into the proper understanding of the physical structure, while philosophy is concerned with the underlying *conceptual necessity*.

Conversely, Ideas would be utterly vacuous if they did not bump into or follow from the Real. A notion of Ideas or matter "all the way down" (empirical idealism or strict materialism) is thus rendered nonsensical. It is the deficit of dogmatism in its purest sense that reality is reducible one way or the other, and its falsehood is demonstrated performatively by the very act of theorizing, be it purely scientific or philosophical theorizing. Reality is *always* filtered through a prism of Ideas—or, more precisely—Reality is the very point at which Ideas and objects coincide. The very act of writing represents an attempt to capture the ongoing flux of Nature, to set it to a momentary standstill, to manifest the very *materiality* of the Idea. We find the foundation for the notion of the Absolute, and thus the relationship of Ideal and Real, scattered throughout the early Schellingian corpus, but he primarily develops these arguments within the Philosophy of Nature and the Identity Philosophy. We ought to further examine these concepts in the *Ideas* and then follow their movement in the *Further Presentation of my System of Philosophy*.

In the *Ideas*, Schelling states:

> The first step to philosophy and the conditions without which it cannot be entered is the insight that the absolute-ideal is also the absolute-real, and without this there is only sensible and conditioned, but no absolute and unconditioned, reality.[41]

And, furthermore

> The absolute is an eternal act of cognition, which is itself matter and form, a producing in which, in eternal fashion, it converts itself in its totality as Idea, as sheer identity, into the real, into the form, and conversely, in equally eternal fashion, resolves itself as form, and to that extent as object, into essence or subject.[42]

We see here one of Schelling's numerous attempts to break through the various dualisms that plague Western philosophy—dualisms that arise out of a nearly mechanical inevitability of a linguistic structure that bifurcates everything into subject/predicate. Perhaps the earliest of our dualisms is the

Platonic two-world metaphysics that splits reality into Ideal and Real, often granting primacy to the perfect, crystalline structure of the Ideal.[43] The key insight of Absolute Idealism, one that the 20th century seemed incapable of stomaching due to its speculative nature, is to merge the Ideal and the Real into a deeper unity. As we clearly see from the quotes above, the very notion of an "Absolute" or the *grand total* of reality as such, cannot abide by *any* strict dualism because to do so is to simply give up its status as Absolute. After all, the very term "Absolute" entails and designates a grand totality of *all there is*. (Both 20th-century Anglophone analytic thought as well as the various sub-branches of inquiry that are dubbed Continental gave up and often situated themselves against the notion of an Absolute. We can think here of everything from Russell's break with British Idealism to Foucault's death of grand theorizing to Derrida's *différance*. I simply cannot see concrete solutions, be they theoretical or practical, to our intertwined politico-environmental crisis without at *least some* grappling with the Absolute—the intertwined Whole.)

To state that the Absolute is either Ideality or Reality, or to tip the scales in favor of one over the other, is to lose sight of its Absoluteness. As such, ideal and real, form and matter, subject and object, and so forth, form a series of necessarily interconnected dyads wherein the existence and nature of any one logically entails the need for the other, without any strict separation at the ontological level. Objectivity is given to a subject, and cannot be properly grappled without uncovering the structures of subjectivity (the key claim of both German Idealism as well as phenomenology); materiality is structured by ideality; and prime matter is simply an illusion or a heuristic device. We speak of any one of these as purely distinct at the risk of losing both sides. Furthermore, it should be noted here that none of the above entails that reality itself is somehow an indistinguishable Parmenidian One—a realm of pure sameness. If that were the case, then all things would be indistinguishable in the first place, and the need to write anything or to convince someone of a point would be rendered either pointless, or, much more precisely, would be impossible in the first place because it would immediately introduce difference. As Schelling repeats many times, identity is *always* the identity of identity and difference, not pure sameness.

What, then, are the *political* implications of such a worldview? Are we merely caught up in the flights of speculative fancy that Marx and Kierkegaard will criticize and poke fun at shortly after the decline of the Absolute Idealism? What, if anything, does Schelling's notion of the Absolute (and the interplay between real and ideal) have to teach us about the political at this particular point of history in the early, increasingly chaotic, 21st century? I contend that there are key insights here for understanding both *institutional structures* as well as a demonstration that the critiques of idealism leveled by the likes of Feuerbach, Marx, and Engels are in fact a caricature of German Idealism.

Let us begin with the institutional political structures that shape nearly every facet of our existence while Schelling does not often theorize about the ontological status of human institutions as such,[44] his conception of the Absolute, and the interplay between Ideal and Real that emerges from it, contains exceptionally suggestive insights. The 19th-century critiques of Idealism having lost sight of the Real is immediately disproven by the very framing of the debate surrounding Nature. In positing the interplay between the Ideal and the Real in the Absolute, the grand totality of reality as such, Schelling hands us the tools to move beyond where he himself ends in the Philosophy of Nature. We can demonstrate how human-made structures emerge organically out of the intersubjective nature of consciousness, taking on the status of yet another *potency*, albeit not one explicitly theorized by Schelling in his own writings on Nature. Institutions—governments, corporations, universities, NGOs, international organizations, etc.—clearly owe their existence to the activity of human beings, and this activity is conditioned and made possible by the dynamic, organizational activity of Nature itself. The organization of this higher-order human potency is teleologically directed in a way that Nature simply is not, insofar as *we* imbue these structural entities with a direct purpose (that we often chose to ignore or forget or distort the purpose of our own institutions is an entirely separate problem). Once established, institutional structures also contain the interplay between the Ideal and Real that Schelling situates in the Absolute (as does every potency below that of human institution until we either reach the *Identity* or the early to mid-1800s or the dark ground of God in 1809. The Identity Philosophy would have to meet the initial conditions to be the identity of identity and difference, and thus cause a collapse of all distinctions at the level of fundamental ontology, and, in 1809, the dark ground of God is beyond all categories if it is to serve as a dark ground in the first place, which would necessarily exclude the categories of Ideal and Real). Thus, if we imagine a founding document such as a constitution, its Ideality is strikingly obvious—it is quite literally *Idea*, directly captured on a page, but one that is meaningless without the corresponding governing structures which confer its reality. These structures would be a chaotic mess incapable of being even called "structures" without a guiding or organizing principles, an Idea.

So what, though? What is the point of demonstrating this point at this particular level of philosophical abstraction? First of all, we see how *political structures are yet another* emergent property of the organization that runs throughout Nature itself. These structure are neither reducible to those who run them, nor are they divorced from them (and they are *most certainly* not reducible to Nature as such, except insofar as it is the necessary condition for their emergence, albeit insufficient as it is conceivable that humans never reached the point of second-order consciousness that is required to make these structures possible). This allows us to capture the general Marxist point regarding the importance of structures in our theorizing, showing that said structures have an internal logic that sediments over decades and centuries, while at the same time avoiding the potential pitfall of a thinker such as Althusser[45] who comes dangerously close to a kind of fatalism about the possibility of structural reform except perhaps by whole-scale internal disruptions in economic systems. Secondly, it is also in fact the case that structures take on an existence of their own divorced from the agency of the individual agents who are tasked with running the structure, be it a university, government office, or corporation. A single guiding organizational document and the economic framework which makes institutions workable (whatever that may be) are never really divorced from one another. These structures can run in perpetuity after settling into what can only be described as calcified praxis (the later Sartre's "practico-inert") that over-determines the actions and thoughts of those living and working in them. Thus, if we loop back to Chapters 1 and 2 here, and then think forward toward the final chapter of the book which will deal with the ontology of freedom, we can flesh out a relatively complete picture of what a Schellingian political worldview would look like based around his dynamic process ontology.[46] The condition for the possibility of consciousness lies in Nature, which is in turn conditioned by more primary dueling forces of polarity. Shaped by dissent, recognition, and freedom that consciousness establishes a potency left relatively untheorized by Schelling—the potency of political and institutional structures, which in turn have reverberations *all the way back down to Nature*. That is, we are simultaneously shaped by Nature as we currently over-shape it in the Anthropocene.

Given the above, certain structures, which are always-already a confluence of Ideal/Real, take on a life of their own. Let us for a moment think through how certain structures would function and look like when they are *racialized*. Whether "race" itself is real, socially constructed, or even somehow completely unreal (whatever that would mean given the fact that its effects are very real regardless of its ontological or metaphysical status) is in some ways beside the point in a Schellingian framework. The dynamic interplay between Ideal/Real guarantees that a reductive either/or position is incapable of capturing its theoretical complexity or its lived reality. Under a *purely naturalized* picture of reality, one which I do not think Schelling completely ever subscribes to given his commitment to various kinds of philosophical discourse steeped in ontology/metaphysics, race can in some way be thought of as not being completely real. That is, there is nothing in the Idea or blueprint that we call DNA that marks off race *qua* race. Many of us share DNA in ways that are not at all neatly mapped to our geographic or cultural background, or our phenotype. And yet, from the same naturalized, scientific standpoint, it is also the case that humans exhibit certain features over others due to our DNA—skin and hair color, to use the two crudest mechanisms by which we have racialized the world, but also genetic predispositions to certain health conditions that are very much detrimental to certain populations of humans if ignored.[47] As such, the Ideal and Real here are quite difficult to neatly untangle. Likewise, when we look at race from a *purely social constructive* manner, here too we see a fundamental entanglement. Our Ideas guide our praxis, and the praxis in turn guides our Ideas, all the while we situate this praxis in the chaos of the Real. From this particular viewpoint, regardless of whether or not race is embedded in biology or fundamental ontology, it nonetheless exists as a *human* phenomenon arising out of colonial praxis and sustained by currently existing institutions.[48] Race here is a social construct, an Idea that has nothing to underpin it other than the Reality of the social, which of course very much has a tremendous weight of its own as far as our daily existence is concerned.[49]

Thus, whether we find the notion of race embedded in the potency of biological nature or the higher-order potency of the sociohistorical which would not be possible if we were a different kind of biological organism, the copula of Ideal/Real follows us both in the upward and downward trajectories. At the institutional level, such as the private and public structures that emerge historically in the American context, we have a societal build based upon a philosophical Ideal known as a constitution, but also an economic Reality of slave labor that is directly at odds with this Ideal. A *substantial* amount of effort was spent justifying the existence of slavery as an institution since society, if it is even *remotely* reflective, has to recognize the steep incongruity between the Ideal of equality fought for in the constitution and the ownership of human beings. This recognition, as we have seen in the previous chapter, has the troublesome feature of being simultaneously conscious and unconscious, and thus continues to be fragile and tentative. At one point it was mired only in misrecognition. What are the results of this misrecognition? A set of institutional practices that at one point functioned to perpetuate inequality are ostensibly changed, at least on paper, after the civil war and yet remain stubbornly rooted in the older set of practices which were explicitly racist. As such, the very Ideas that make an institution what it is in the first place get a rebranding, for lack of a better term, but the material praxis (the Real) that they came out of and which they helped to shape in the first place, remains largely the same. Hence the burden of institutional racism that is now being attacked by a number of prominent politicians on the political right as some kind of fabrication.

Ideality and Reality thus merge at the institutional level, *but*, and this is key, they are *always* merged at all levels of inquiry and are in continuous dynamic interplay. Thus, ideologically motivated agents (in whatever shape that ideology might find itself) and theoretical Ideas have the chance to influence and exert their Reality and this Reality in turn shapes Ideas in innumerable ways. This ever-flowing feedback loop gives rise to the hope that while structures are in practice slow and difficult to change, change is in fact always possible, and quite often inevitable given the fact that Reality insists upon itself. For instance, if we think here of climate change, no matter our opinion on the matter it is now abundantly clear that something must be done if humanity as we know it is not to perish (the success of the action is of course another matter entirely). What is particularly fruitful about the Schellingian framework is its showing of the direct connection of the human and the Natural, demonstrating concretely that they form a living continuum all the way from the basic bond of forces to the contingency of the sociohistorical which is only possible from the lower order of potencies. Schelling allows us to theorize Nature, institutions, historicity, freedom, recognition, and the relationship between all of them in a matter that is systematic without being beholden to any one particular system. We finish our study of the political implications of *Naturphilosophie* by examining the work that I take to be the most suggestive and fruitful for contemporary concerns: *First Outline of a System of the Philosophy of Nature*. It is this work that will allow us to tie together the various strings of inquiry that have been running throughout this chapter, and to situate us in the final, politically indispensable interrogation of freedom that will be found at the end our study.

# Part II: Further Reconstruction of Schelling's

## *Naturphilosophie—First Outline of a System of the Philosophy of Nature*

The *Ideas for a Philosophy of Nature* is a key piece for understanding Schelling's early moves away from his brief foray into a Fichtean notion of transcendental philosophy, his accompanying methodology of interrogating the Ideal and Real simultaneously with Kant's critical turn in mind, the development of Absolute Idealism, and Schelling's own development. Despite its adherence to what are now antiquated findings in the natural sciences (although they were at the cutting edge when he penned the work), it is also a key document for understanding the history of fields such as chemistry and biology. It is admittedly somewhat tonally uneven, especially since the final version of the text retroactively inserts the metaphysical framework of the Identity

Philosophy, developed immediately subsequent to the *System of Transcendental Idealism*.[50] However, as I have been demonstrating and arguing throughout this chapter, the *Ideas* contains significant advancements in the ontology of the German Idealist critical project that are absolutely indispensable for a new re-examination of Nature as such—a re-examination that is desperately needed at this particular historical juncture. To the present moment, Schelling remains one of the only greats in the Western framework who is willing to theorize Nature in its glorious concreteness, and the *Ideas* remains, and I believe will continue to remain now that Schelling has been rediscovered, a key text for doing such work. Furthermore, as I have also demonstrated thus far, its central line of ontological and metaphysical speculation has cascading repercussions well past what Schelling himself envisioned, spilling well into the realm of the political with its insights into the relationship between humanity and Nature, identity and difference, the Real and Ideal (along with the ontology of institutions that follows from this philosophical outlook), and so forth.

While I think that Grant is correct in pointing out that *Naturphilosophie* is a concern that never truly disappears for Schelling,[51] following him well into his final years where he turns toward a more traditional Christian doctrine and a concern with positive philosophy (rather than critical or negative philosophy that is the hallmark of the early authorship), in its earliest manifestations I take the *First Outline of a System of the Philosophy of Nature* to be the definitive document on the topic.[52] I hold the *First Outline* in such high regard because it is there that Schelling articulates the clearest version of *the core* insight of *Naturphilosophie*: mainly, the distinction between Nature as *productivity* and Nature as *product*. It is this core insight that leads to the final arc of my argument here, showing the true *radicality* of our *political* responsibility to Nature; a responsibility which we are spectacularly failing to honor at the present moment. It is toward this notion that I now turn.

In the translator's introduction to the English version of the text, Keith Peterson observes that "the critical apparatus that the philosophy of nature brought to bear on the modern scientific project demanded not merely a theoretical or epistemological shift, but a reformulation of the relation between human beings and nature, often entailing novel political or ethical commitments."[53] This book as a whole, and this chapter in particular, is one of the first of hopefully many attempts to make use of the Philosophy of Nature to do *precisely* what Peterson suggests. The distinction between productivity and product will be the primary hermeneutical lens through which this goal will be accomplished here. Schelling derives this distinction through several systematic principles, beginning the work with what is clearly an ontological point concerning the nature of the "unconditioned," that which grounds reality itself (and a notion we saw from a different angle in the first chapter). He states:

> *The unconditioned cannot be sought in any individual "thing" nor in anything of which one can say that it "is." For what "is" only partakes of being, and is only an individual form or kind of being.-Conversely, one can never say of the unconditioned that it "is." For it is* BEING ITSELF, *and, as such, it does not exhibit itself in any finite product, and every individual is, as it were, a particular expression of it.*[54]

Echoing Heidegger's later distinction between being and Being, Schelling here begins his inquiry with fundamental ontology—Being *qua* Being or Being as such cannot be either sought or found in any particular being or thing because individual beings obtain their existence through Being itself, so to try to find the unconditioned in beings is to *reverse* the ontological order of the world. One cannot find ultimate reality in its finite products. Likewise the use of "is" to designate Being itself makes the mistake of attributing an unwarranted term to reality at its most fundamental level. Individual things or beings obtain their "is ness" from Being itself, but we cannot say that Being *is* anything without destroying its status as both Being and the unconditioned. For to state of any x that it *is* y is to condition one by means of the other.

The opening move of the *First Outline*, then, demonstrates clearly that it is not a reverse empiricism which begins with Nature and its individual products, laws, and principles, extrapolating backward in order to deduce universal philosophical propositions, but rather a *fundamental ontology* in the truest sense. That is, it begins with the classic Aristotelian notion of Being *qua* Being and then proceeds to work forward, integrating empirical findings and insights into itself. As such, one can either call it a naturalized ontology, or perhaps better yet, an ontological naturalism. My tendency is to think of it as the latter for the simple reason that naturalized philosophy has echoes of logical positivism and the quest to reduce all inquiry to that which empirical science can demonstrate, and I do not for an instant believe that this is what Schelling had in mind (that would be both anachronistic and simply out of line with the overall aims of Absolute Idealism that he was still committed to at the time he wrote the *First Outline*).

While Schelling starts with the question of Being itself and carries it throughout the duration of the text, he very quickly breaks from the standard conception of Being that is found prior to the Kantian critical project, which largely uses logical analysis to slice and dice reality into either *static* categories or beings, and instead builds upon an edifice of *activity, process,* and *force*. His spiritual predecessors in this endeavor are Heraclitus in the West and Laozi in the East—thinkers who theorize Being in terms of *relationality* and *becoming*.[55] For Schelling, to truly philosophize about Nature means to

> heave it out of the dead mechanism to which it seems predisposed, to quicken it with freedom and to set into its own free development—to philosophize about nature, means, in other words, to tear *yourself* away from the common view which discerns in nature only what 'happens'—and which, at most, views the act as a *factum, not the action itself* in its acting.[56]

Furthermore, added in a helpful elucidatory footnote to the above, "In the usual view, the original productivity of nature disappears behind the product. For us the product must disappear behind the productivity."[57] I believe that these opening moves of the *First Outline* are perhaps among the most radical, and often ignored, advancements in German Idealist thought. In one fell swoop Schelling rethinks the very nature of transcendental idealism, flipping it on its head and extending it all the way throughout Nature, and then performs *yet another* even more important reversal insofar as he transforms what transcendental idealism even means from the inside out—no longer merely a doctrine of epistemological categories and intuitions that make subjective experience possible, it becomes the dynamic edifice that makes Nature as such possible. The truly radical move, however, is to make the whole "thing" *active*, to put into words the very flow of reality itself, *setting aside the product or being in favor of the productivity!*

This initial move of focusing on the productive element in Nature rather than the finite products which are continually created and easily destroyed leads Schelling to posit a second principle: "*Absolute activity cannot be exhibited by a finite product, but only by an Infinite one.*"[58] We can think here of a Spinozism made dynamic (which is precisely where Schelling gets a part of his inspiration). The very starting point of the *Ethics* defines substance as "that which is in itself and is conceived through itself; that is, that the conception of which does not require the conception of another thing from which it has to be formed."[59] Substance for Spinoza is the grand totality of all of reality—God himself, coextensive or perhaps identical to the universe/Absolute. Independent of any particular thing, product, or being, this substance is the substratum which allows all else to be. As such, Spinoza's substance is also not exhausted in any of its modes or products, which is precisely what Schelling is arguing concerning the unconditioned. However, and this is absolutely a key however, the Schellingian substance does not sit still, nor does it fit under the usual Western rubric of what counts as a substance.[60] In putting activity at the heart of substance, Schelling completely changes its very basic nature, and this must perform his own entirely new set of deductions.

Schelling himself notes that the deductions must flow in a new direction from the usual confines of pre-critical metaphysics because there are clear logical and ontological consequences that occur when moving from a metaphysics of infinite Being (Spinoza's God or substance) to one of infinite *becoming*. The first consequence is that an absolute activity "*must appear as inhibited ad infinitum*"[61] and, secondly and more importantly for our purposes here, "*Nature* EXISTS *nowhere* as product: all individual productions in Nature are merely apparent products, not the absolute product that always BECOMES and never IS, and in which the absolute activity exhausts itself."[62] Nature as such cannot be understood in terms of the substance metaphysics that has been the perennial hallmark of Western metaphysics. IT is decisively *not* "the individual man or the individual horse,"[63] as is the case in the Aristotelian framework that dominates philosophical discourse even well into Modernity; it is not the greatly pared-down Cartesian dualism which reduces all substance either to mind or body, subject or object (plus God); it is not even Spinoza's infinite substance, for this one stands still from the standpoint of the whole, being guided only by ironclad logical necessity. It is instead the very organizing forces that make the individual man or horse possible (or *any* being possible). The sheer radicality of this move is somewhat difficult to overstate. Schelling is indeed "untimely" in the Nietzschean sense. This untimeliness is demonstrated both by *what* he articulates—the destruction of Nature if we continue to think of it as dead mechanism, the importance of freedom at all levels of philosophy and life, the need to establish positive existential principles, and so forth—and *how* he articulates it. Not only does he naturalize metaphysical speculation, he also sees that this naturalization folds back on itself, leaving behind another potency of metaphysics: one heavily informed rather than divorced from the natural sciences.

Returning to Schelling's original claim, when we theorize nature *philosophically* and do not merely rely on the sciences to do all the work for us, we observe throughout the grand totality of reality a system functioning on *self-organizing* principles which never seem to exhaust themselves in any individual product. This is true of both macro and micro phenomena, and Schelling characterizes it in terms of dueling polarities of positive and negative forces resolving themselves in finite products through connecting in a whirlpool. While it is unclear if he is being literal or metaphorical with the whirlpool metaphor (it seems the latter), current finding in astrophysics, including recently captured images of the formation of planets and many previous images of galaxies, demonstrate in a visual medium that the notion of the whirlpool was in fact not far-fetched even from a quite literal standpoint. Regarding this notion, Schelling states:

> A stream flows in a straight line forward as long as it encounters no resistance. Where there is resistance-a whirlpool forms. Every original product of nature is such a whirlpool, every organism. The whirlpool is not something immobilized, it is rather something constantly transforming-but reproduced anew at each moment. Thus no product in nature is *fixed*, but is reproduced at each instance through the force of nature entire.[64]

Given the above quote, what is clear is that not only has Schelling moved away from substance metaphysics in general, he has also moved the individual parts of the whole away from any static conception that may be found in metaphysics. As such, his view on the ultimate nature of reality is much more compatible with findings in contemporary physics, chemistry, and biology (his chief three inspirations), as well as our phenomenological constitution of a world that is in perpetual flux yet so vast as to appear nearly immutable on the grand scale (it is definitely not immutable however). Nature, then, never exhausts itself in any one of its products for the simple reason that it itself is the productive forces, and it makes no difference whether these products are the size of a single cell or an entire galaxy, and it has process and movement built into its ontological[65] core: "Nature does not tolerate any *final product,* nothing permanent and fixed for once and for all. The direction of all natural activity will aim toward *mean products...,* toward materials which are absolutely composable and absolutely indecomposable at once, and *permanent processes* will appear in Nature."[66]

The next logical question that must be excavated is why the "*permanent processes*" or movements sustain themselves in perpetuity. The answer here remains essentially the same throughout Schelling's writings on Nature: dueling polarities. Let us examine this point in some detail before we end with the political implications of the Schellingian picture of Nature/reality. These dueling polarities subsist both conceptually and actually throughout Nature, dialectically in interplay with each other without the Hegelian *aufheben* that would have higher-order polarities subsume the lower, for the lower-order ones lie as the ground for the higher in Schelling, thus serving as a foundation for the higher that cannot be broken apart or subsumed without sacrificing the whole. Schelling phrases the above point initially as a "problem"[67] —a problem of how "*to deduce a dynamic graded series of stages in Nature* a priori."[68] To reiterate yet again, the *a priori* structure of Schelling's deduction *does not* make the project the armchair musings of a Romantic thinker, which is how the project was often received after the decline of Absolute Idealism. As *all* recent commentators of Schelling point out (Snow, Beiser, Grant, Matthews, and Woodard, to name a few), Schelling is *steeped*, at the level of the working scientist, in the latest developments available to him in physics, chemistry, and biology (the last two still in their relative infancy at that point of time). The *a priority*, then, lies at the need for a universal structure that will hold the whole together.

Schelling's "first principle" for deducing the abovementioned whole (and for solving that which was presented as a "problem") contains within the overview for the entire argument for the *First Outline*. He writes:

> *The activity of the organism is determined through its receptivity.* The organic activity is, therefore, through and through dependent upon the influence of external (material) causes. But matter can only act on matter, and only according to inexorable laws. Therefore, both the action of external causes on the organism and the functions maintained throughout it occur completely and entirely according to laws of matter. Matter acts on matter either through repulsive force (thrust) or through attractive force (gravity). The influence of external causes on the organism is explicable neither by the later nor by the former type of effect alone, and neither is the activity of the organism animated by it—thus, it is explicable only from both taken together, or from the reciprocal action of both of those forces. This reciprocity produces what are called chemical phenomena. The influence of external causes on the organism, as well as on the organic activity, is itself consequently *of a chemical sort.* All functions of the organism follow from chemical laws of matter, and life itself is a *chemical process.*[69]

Contained within that argument are all the hallmarks of the Philosophy of Nature, as well as important elucidations and clarifications of the worldview that Schelling has in mind. First and foremost, we see the need for a conceptual pairing of activity and receptivity at the very outset—as was the case throughout the *Ideas*, the notion of a *pure* activity is inherently meaningless without its dialectical copula of receptivity. After all, *what* is it that's acting? *Where* is the activity directed to? *Who* is it aimed at? "Pure" activity would be like a small child who in the midst of vigorous play runs this way and that, without any obvious purpose to achieve, it exhausts itself and collapses. That is, "pure" activity would be pure chaos exhausting and collapsing into itself.[70] Activity can only be understood in and through its dialectical copula—*receptivity*. Weaving back to the guiding metaphor of how to read transcendental idealism in light of Schelling's radical reformulation of it, the metaphor which has guided my thinking on this chapter in particular but also Schelling's general predisposition as a thinker, activity must have a pathway that it is working through and toward if it is not to dissolve in either complete chaos or complete stagnation thus losing its very status of "activity."

The second element necessary for understanding the quote above is that the active universal forces are received in *matter*, but matter itself is only possible through the force of attraction and repulsion (thrust and gravity, respectively). If we think here of gravitation/attraction and thrust/repulsion as the more concrete physical manifestations of activity and passivity, it becomes immediately evident that adherence to any particular one over the other, or any prominence of one over the other, would entail that the world either collapses in on itself in pure darkness that would result in gravity run amok or disperse into eventual oblivion through the repulsive forces. This would hold true both via *a priori* metaphysics or *a posteriori* physics, and it is precisely here that metaphysics and physics cannot be all that far apart. That is, we know from physics that if the initial conditions of the Big Bang were slightly off then either the then-emerging particle soup would have collapsed in on itself or it would have drifted apart too quickly in order to coalesce into more complex particles, compounds, planets, and so forth. Furthermore, if it turns out to be conclusive that the universe is indeed drifting apart at an ever-faster rate, as current models in astrophysics suggests, then the force of repulsion (as Schelling would conceptualize this phenomena without the recourse to 21st-century astrophysics) will eventually "win" leading to a cold, dead universe. From a logical standpoint, especially of the dialectical sort that is upheld by much of German Idealism, one cannot conceptually untangle repulsion and attraction because their very meaning is co-constitutive. One cannot speak of thing being repulsed from one another without the frame of reference of them being attracted, and vice versa. Each concept entails and gives rise to the other even if the Hegelian picture of sublation or the Fichtean notion of synthesis is not operative. That is, the concepts do not need a higher-order concept to transform them and hold them together in order for them to form a dialectical copula in the same manner that tall/short have no higher-order concept that sublates or synthesizes them, yet one cannot speak of there being something "tall" or "short" independently.

Third and finally, the above dueling forces coalesce in matter in increasing levels of organization and complexity through chemical processes. Chemistry, then, is the higher-order organization that serves as the condition for the possibility of life itself. This condition for the possibility of life itself is in turn conditioned by the dueling polarities, which, as we have found in much greater detail after Schelling, is part and parcel of the very nature of the atom and the domain of physics. Thus, the interplay between polarity runs the gamut of macro and micro, instantiating itself simultaneously through the whole and through the various parts of Nature.[71] However, it should be noted that Schelling is carefully and meticulously *anti-reductive*: "organic and inorganic nature must reciprocally explain and determine one another."[72] That is, one does not explain the workings of chemistry by moving back down a potency to the level of physics, or, if we want to take it even one step further, back to the very *conceptual* (philosophical and metaphysical) level of necessary interplay between polarities. Despite the fact that self-organization runs through the whole of Nature, or even reality as such, *this* higher level of organization *is* not reducible to the lower layers, and must be studied *both* in their respective domains and in how they interact and effect the lower layers (and vice versa). It would be ineffective and counterproductive to attempt to explain physics by recourse to metaphysics, or to explain politics by looking at chemistry, but, that fact aside, the project of *Naturphilosophie* is one of seeing how the show is *inextricably* tied together, which is often attested by research in the various subdomains. For instance, while I can't reduce politics to chemistry (it would be an absurd project), it is still the case that chemistry and politics do in fact overlap in the form of medicine and public policy concerning everything from drug approval to the use of pesticides. As such, as a philosopher I must rely on the expertise of the biologist and chemist for insight into their respective domains, all the while keeping in mind the fundamental ontology which grounds or underpins the whole enterprise, and this ontology is *always* informed by the actual finding of the empirical sciences.[73]

What this ontology entails, in Schelling's own terms, is that "Nature is organic in its most original product, but the functions of the organism cannot be deduced otherwise than in opposition to the anorganic world. *Excitability* must be posited as the essence of the organism, by virtue of which alone the organic activity is really hindered from exhausting itself in its product that, therefore, never *is* but always *becomes*."[74] Nature, then, has *becoming* at the very heart of its Being, such that any conception that attempts to fix it in place with static metaphysical categories (be they the Aristotelian, pre-critical ones that dominated realist thought well into modernity or the Kantian-Fichtean ones reserved for subjectivity alone) fundamentally misunderstands what it *is* at its innermost core. With some obvious exceptions in place—exceptions such as Heraclitus, Bergson, and Whitehead—this manner of conceptualizing both metaphysics and ontology is an obvious outlier in Western thought (the story is much different in the East). It places *movement* at the very heart of reality, seeing organizational structures that perpetuate the flux as the necessary conditions which make Nature possible. At no point can we posit a static, mechanistic view of the world because to do so is to lose the very explanatory framework of how Nature functions in the first place. Mechanism runs in a strictly linear fashion from A to Z, and no matter how complex this mechanism may be, it *cannot* truly explain self-movement and organization at the grand scale of Nature as a whole. The infinite, cascading domino effect of a mechanistic Nature cannot show us how we obtain and set up the dominoes in the first place or how they came to be organized in such a manner that they fall so neatly. The only explanation that is provided by the Moderns is that God does the heavy lifting. One can think here of Descartes, Malebranche, and Leibniz, to name a few of the greats, each needing the divine to explain everything from how the world is possible in the first place to how I can type these words given that mind never strictly interacts with body.

## Part III: The Politics of *Naturphilosophie*

While Schelling himself never quite draws the political (and ethical) implications of the picture of Nature he has developed in the *Ideas* and *First Outline*, they are in fact clearly contained within it and have *staggering* implications to what our responsibility to Nature actually entails (how to actually implement the implication is a question for public policy that, frankly, has no easy answer given the current ideological calcification of hyper-capitalist modes of production across much of the globe). The aim of the final portion of this chapter is to draw out and delineate these implications, as well as to tie the somewhat disparate strands of argumentation concerning the relationship between *Naturphilosophie* and the *polis* that I have been weaving all throughout. This includes the notions of radical interdependence; the relationship between the Ideal and Real (which has been discussed at length in the section concerning the *Ideas*); the extrapolation upward from the most intellectually complex natural organism (us) to its institutions; and, finally and most importantly, the key argument of a Schellingian point of view inspired by the *Naturphilosophie*—the *direct* and *primordial* responsibility that humans bear toward Nature as such. This direct responsibility flows with a logical necessity from the very ontological structures that permeate reality—from the subatomic to the human to the planet itself. Since the first three aspects outlined above have already been discussed in detail, I will instead begin with the final point and use that as the gravitational center that pulls the rest into a coherent worldview—one in which philosophy finally remembers Nature.

The forgetting of Nature in mainstream philosophical discourse (Environmental Ethics excluded), especially in Modernity and forward, ends up becoming so embedded in the psyche of humanity that for the contemporary thinker it becomes almost a given. Philosophers forgot Nature so long ago and so well that we forgot how this happened in the first place despite the fact that we are reminded daily of immanent and ever-unfolding ecological damage. For this reason it is important to see precisely how it was forgotten. While there are hints of this happening in the early Christian and medieval traditions, insofar as "man" is seen as the height of creation and Nature is there for "his" use, there is still a strong counter-current since Nature too would be seen as a part of God's creation (it is also the case that the technological advancements of the period were such that no one would have been terribly worried about Nature at that historical juncture). It is even the case that some classical Christian thinkers such as St. John Chrysostom, Symeon the New Theologian, and Maximus the Confessor argued heavily against our overuse of Nature. The reason for this is fairly simply: Nature is the domain of the divine, effectively lent to us for temporary use given our finite status; our abuse of it is seen as an affront to creation itself. "The things and possessions that are in the world are common to all . . . in terms of ownership they belong to no one,"[75] writes Symeon. In the book *Man and the Environment*, Anestis Keselopulus points out the radical implications of the thought of someone like Symeon:

> Despite his monastic state and radical renunciation of the world, his interests are not confined to the concerns of the monastery, but extend to the life of lay people and the community at large. On the basis of the Gospel teaching, he is sharply critical of the social order of his day which represented misuse of creation and material luxury. Ten centuries before the present ecological impasse, he points out the connection of environmental problems with the social and economic problem in our use of the world and material goods. *The ecological crisis is an expression and generalization of the social problem.*[76]

For early medieval thinkers, especially ones coming from the East, our responsibility to Nature is part and parcel to our responsibility we have toward one another. One cannot easily separate ecological problems from ones of economics and social policy. This couldn't be more pertinent today, and it also puts a certain strand of early and medieval Christian thought closer to ancient Daoism and Native American philosophies rather than Western European intellectual orthodoxy.

Even for the Western medieval thinkers who do not theorize Nature *qua* Nature heavily, which is admittedly quite a few given the predominance of Aristotelian physics/metaphysics and a strongly religious bent, Nature is still full of *living substances*—trees, animals, insects, etc., are still *ensouled* creatures, different from humanity *only* in their lack of a rational soul. This general position essentially becomes philosophical orthodoxy from Aquinas forward in the West, and it is also found in thinkers, such as Ibn Rushd (Averroes), in the Middle East, who predate and inspire Aquinas' own position. Thus, it is in modernity and the period of the Enlightenment where Nature is rendered into dead matter, stripped of living soul, and increasingly cleaved away from humanity. Since Aristotle is inherently correct in calling us the political animal, this cleavage is not only an existential one, where we are alienated and sequestered from the rest of living reality, but even more perniciously a *political* one. The public discourse concerning our political responsibility to Nature is, until the instant that I write this, *predominantly* and almost exclusively concerned with how long we can continue into perpetuity the way of life built upon our Enlightenment foundation. Hence the public policy focus on green technology and job creation (not that these are bad things, but simply that they completely ignore what I will argue are even more basic duties). That we might have a further responsibility occurs to almost none but environmental philosophers and scientists.[77] The first is a tiny, tiny minority in a relatively tiny discipline, now largely sequestered away from the broader public discourse except in our interactions with students. The second group has been shouting into the wind for decades, but it is also caught up in the structural complex where science is the engine of capital, not a vehicle for radical change.

Our current system is the direct result of the convergence between metaphysics, science, and political economy that emerges from the Enlightenment break with ancient and medieval thought. Among the first to make Nature into mere matter to be used for humanity's ultimate purposes is Francis Bacon. In a semi-autobiographical passage, Bacon notes his underlying motivation for doing philosophy and science:

> of myself I say noting, but in behalf of the business which is in hand I entreat men to believe that it is not an opinion to be held but a work to be done, and to be well assured that I am laboring to lay the foundation, not of any sect or doctrine, but of human utility and power.[78]

That is, the aim of the working scientist and philosopher, the two of course being completely intertwined at the moment Bacon penned those words, is to make discoveries that are good *for us*—discoveries that increase our *power*. Now, it ought to be noted here that Bacon is writing these words at a period where the current human reality of first industrialization and then de-industrialization, heavy amount of robotic automation, artificial intelligence, gene editing, and so forth couldn't even have been science fiction. He lived during a much simpler epoch where science was in its relative infancy, and humanity remained at mercy of Nature (it still is at its mercy, but many of us like to pretend otherwise). Regardless, it is often the case that what is initially envisioned as a noble aim—the improvement of humanity—can over time be distorted into a zero-sum game where Bacon's own warnings on how far utility and power can take us become ignored for short-term gain.[79] In a passage in the *New Organon* that is both terrifying and easy to distort, Bacon further cements this position while given a warning that has been repeatedly ignored. Regarding the types of power one may wield, he argues:

> Further it will not be amiss to distinguish the three kinds and as it were grades of ambition in mankind. The first is of those who desire to extent their own power in their native country, which kind is vulgar and degenerate. The second is of those who labor to extent the power of their country and its dominion among men. This certainly has more dignity, though not less covetousness. But if man endeavor to establish and extend the power and dominion of the human race itself over the universe, his ambition (if ambition it can be called) is without a doubt a more wholesome thing and more noble than the other two. Now the empire of man over things depends wholly on the arts and sciences. For we cannot command nature except by obeying her.[80]

While one can see here that Bacon is more subtle than to advocate a world in which Nature is a mere resource for our use, arguing in the end that we can only command through first obeying, the end result and the *telos* of his worldview ends up being the same regardless. The only noble pursuit of power is the conversion of the universe (the universe!) into a "thing" for our use. The *telos* of the Enlightenment is one of imperialism over Nature, aided by arts and science.

While being among the first that will adopt the modern worldview, Bacon is not the primary architect of modern philosophy. That mantle ever belongs to Descartes, whose obvious genius led to some theoretically dark places; places that have had longstanding repercussions for radically reshaping a vast amount of discursive praxis, and whose implication he too had no way of truly foreseeing.[81] Cartesian metaphysics, via the backdoor of epistemology, divided the world into two primary substances (and God)—mind and body. Mind belongs to humans alone, as we are the only ones who can perform the *cogito* (as far as we know), while body is *mere mathematical extension*. Thus, Nature as a whole, including innumerable living organisms is radically reduced into extension, making life itself nothing other than a complex mechanism. In the *Discourse on Method*, Descartes states:

> through this philosophy we could know the power and action of fire, water, the stars, the heavens and all the other bodies in our environment,

as distinctly as we know the various crafts of our artisans; and we could use this knowledge—as artisans use theirs—for all the purposes for which it is appropriate, and thus make ourselves, as it were, *the lords and masters of nature*.[82]

To some extent, we have indeed become "lords and masters" of Nature, but mastery is often as short lived as we are and is currently poised to fail us spectacularly if the illusion of it cannot be broken.

Spinoza sees all the obvious (and many of the non-obvious) problems with the Cartesian philosophical worldview, and as a consequence pushes rationalism into a much more coherent direction. He finds a way to neatly resolve the problems made by dualism, he unifies humanity to Nature, and he fundamentally reworks the notion of substance. However, we must remember two important points here, the first being historical and the second theoretical. Spinoza was virtually forgotten in Europe until the Pantheism Controversy, thus making less of a mark on the development of the enlightenment than thinkers such as Descartes and Leibniz on the continent and Locke and Hume in Britain (and subsequently the United States). Secondly, Spinoza reduces all of Nature to a single substance, governed by the inexorable, strict rules of mechanism. In this picture of reality *everything* is governed by the tyranny of the Principle of Sufficient Reason to such an extent that it becomes easy to throw one's hands up in the air and give up in light of one's immensely diminished agency (a point we will turn to in the following chapter). Spinoza, though, becomes a key touchstone for rethinking a host of philosophical issues for Schelling and Hegel (and many of the Romantic thinkers), such that he must remembered as an important corrective, and perhaps largely a general exception, to the Enlightenment view of reality which puts humanity on a pedestal upon which it has no business of occupying.

Despite the massive influence that they still hold over my own theorizing, it nevertheless is the case that Kant and Fichte fare only but a little better than Descartes and Bacon when it comes to their conception of Nature. Nature as it truly is, as opposed to how it is given to the subject, is relegated to the realm of the *noumenal* for Kant—a vast reality perpetually made inaccessible to the transcendental ego trapped in its own representations.[83] While Fichte drops the *noumenal* (as do Schelling and Hegel), he retains the explicit focus on the subject. He does so to such an extent that Nature for him remains perpetually the "not-I," a theoretical-practical *posit* needed to account for his proto-version of intentionality. He too ends up moving in the direction of Descartes and Bacon concerning the status of Nature, writing "that the powers of nature must be subjected to human ends"[84] in his 1806 *Lectures Concerning the Nature of the Scholar*, and, in the 1798 *System of Ethics*:

> if humanity is to make any considerable advance, then it must waste as little time and power as possible on mechanical work; nature must become mild, matter must become pliant, everything must become such that, with only a little effort, it will grant human beings what they need and the struggle against nature will no longer be such a pressing matter.[85]

That is, Nature is simply seen as something directly and diametrically opposed to the workings of the transcendental ego, which alone is free and the sole arbiter/ground for philosophical reflection, and its value is only to be found in its *use*. In what ends up being a very public break with his one-time collaborator, Schelling criticizes Fichte in rather stark terms in the *Statement on the True Relationship of the Philosophy of Nature and the Revised Fichtean Doctrine*: "for what in the end, is the essence of his opinion on nature? It is that nature should be exploited, used and only exists in order to be exploited; his principle, according to which he views nature, is the economic-teleological principle."[86] Despite the polemical tone of the critique, Schelling is correct in his evaluation of Fichte's view of Nature—for Fichte, Nature is dead mechanical matter or mere resource at best, and, as evidenced by the quote from his *System of Ethics*, an external tyrant at worst. Nature remains mere resource, its purpose to satisfy humanity alone as if we are the only living thing on the planet that ought to be taken into consideration. In many ways this is the direct fallout of Fichte's *Wissenschaftslehre*, which takes the primacy of subjectivity and its intentional structures as the only possible starting point of philosophy. If all theorizing and practical action is ultimately grounded in the activity of the ego or I, as Fichte repeatedly contends throughout his entire corpus, Nature will become sidelined.

Even Hegel, who has a robust and well-developed philosophy of Nature of his own in the form of the second volume of the *Encyclopedia of the Philosophical*

*Sciences*, ends up arguing in a similar vein as Fichte does in the *Philosophy of Right*. Hegel tells us that our break with Nature is a manifestation of our freedom and the elevation of humanity away from its initial immersion into Nature, which, unlike Schelling, he sees in decidedly negative terms. Hegel argues that "a condition in which natural needs as such were immediately satisfied would merely be one in which spirituality was immersed in nature, and hence a condition of savagery and unfreedom; whereas freedom consists solely in the reflection of the spiritual into itself, its distinction from the natural, and its reflection upon the latter."[87] While Hegel has Rousseau's state of nature argument in mind here rather than Schelling, the implications of the argument remain consistent. Humanity becomes free only when it throws off the shackles of Nature as an external, imposing tyrant and lives as the Aristotelian political animal. To claim that Hegel forgets or ignores Nature as such is unfair, but that he ends up here is telling of his own general philosophical concerns, which, like those of Fichte, are human-centered.[88] In the end liberation is one *from* Nature, and the dialectic removes us progressively further and further away from it. Our political responsibilities are quite clearly articulated in Hegel, and they are invariably directed squarely to the human realm alone. *Sittlichkeit* (Ethical Life) encompasses the political good of the universal whole that is the state, mediating between the private good of Civil Society and the universal needs of the people as a whole. For Hegel the state is the objectification of *Geist*, and Ethical Life is where consciousness ultimately understands itself as self-consciousness, thus allowing *Geist* or Spirit to realize itself both in its objective and subjective dimension. Both subjective and objective Spirit are direct manifestations of humanity and humanity alone.

This leaves us with Schelling, the only thinker other than his Romantic contemporaries and colleagues who did not forget Nature, and quite possibly among the first in the West to catch a glimpse of the very tangible horror that this forgetting has brought us: the Anthropocene. How, then, are we to conceptualize *our* political responsibility to Nature within his theoretical framing of its essence and status? I propose *two* interrelated strategies. I call the first our *direct and primordial* responsibility to Nature, developed explicitly by relying on his ontology and by the many suggestive passages discussed throughout this chapter. The second and slightly more indirect path to conceptualizing our responsibility to Nature lies in the theory of recognition that has thus far only been used to articulate intersubjectivity and our responsibility to one another. I will rely on the framework set in place in the second chapter to direct and extend recognition in a novel direction which will allow us to think, somewhat metaphorically, how we and Nature (a continuum or being/becoming rather than strictly separable entities) are also caught in a recognitive feedback loop. Let us look at the direct route first.

## (A) The Direct Route—Our Primordial Responsibility to Nature

The primary innovation of modern political theory, one that has had a clear impact on the way we organize governmental and international organizations for the last several hundred years, is that of a *right*. In its initial development at the hands of Hobbes and Locke, rights are clearly and exclusively a *human* phenomenon, embedded and expressed through the kind of creature we are "naturally." Both Hobbes and Locke play on a similar variation of the notion— one has a right to anything that we mingle our labor with, which ends up clashing with the rights of countless others who have the exact same right in a milieu of scarcity. Hence the need of a state or "leviathan" to keep us from the chaos of millions of humans exercising their most basic of rights. So, we voluntarily relinquish our absolute, natural right for the relative peace and stability of a state, be it the democratic iteration that is advocated by Locke or the monarchical one Hobbes favors. The final years of the 20th century saw the theoretical attempt to expand rights discourse and rights themselves past their original grounding in the nature of humanity and toward animals[89] and the rest of the environment.[90] For instance, Tom Regan has argued that the only way to coherently attribute and defend *any* rights claims without losing what a "right" is in the first place is to extend them to animals as well as humans. His argument centers on the fact that one cannot coherently distinguish between infants and very young children, the severely mentally handicapped, those in comas, and animals in any meaningful way. Since we would like to say that people in the first three categories obviously must have rights, so too must animals. Christopher Stone extended a rights-based discourse to the environment in the early 1970s by arguing that parts of the environment, like corporations, can be given the status of legal person in order to be able to defend these parts from encroachment.

However, as it pertains to the environment, the core feature of rights-based discourse is that it takes what historically began as a decidedly human-centered concept and extrapolates it to apply it to the environment *indirectly*. As we have seen in the narrative above, which is just a drop in the proverbial bucket when it comes to the anthropocentricism that has long dominated Western thought, modernity perpetuated the most radical disconnect imaginable between the human and natural—humanity stands in stark opposition to Nature as a unique entity for whom Nature is to be overcome or used as a resource. A right, which can be understood as a *minimal* norm of interaction, is torn away from the original context in order to be added to Nature. As we have seen in Chapter 1, humans exercise and assert their rights by acts of micro and macro *dissent*. From the original revolutions across the United States to France to Haiti, to the women's suffrage and civil rights movements, rights have been asserted through recognition and dissent. As Axel Honneth points out,[91] what has occurred historically is a gradual expansion of rights in the 18th century forward, beginning to white landowning men to people of color to women to more and more inclusive rights (at least in some parts of the West). At every single historical juncture there has been what Schelling dubs calls dissent and what Honneth calls struggle for said rights. People have quite literally *fought to the death* to have their basic rights recognized, and have often failed in the fight. Nature itself obviously cannot do the same thing in the same manner.[92] We can be rest assured that Nature will "fight back" insofar as feedback loops are built into it: the more we blindly use Nature, the more unstable it becomes in the short term, thus exponentially growing in likelihood that vast parts of it become uninhabitable and deadly to humans. That is, Nature too will dissent in its own way, potentially claiming much of humanity, along with innumerable other species, along with it (in this scenario I also anticipate that the infinitely creative forces of Nature will once again bounce back and restore a different iteration of life on Earth, but I assume that won't be much comfort to many of us). However, it seems prudent, to say the least, to avoid this scenario if at all possible. Schelling's ontology of Nature gives us the perfect means for articulating just how and why we have a *primordially direct* relationship and responsibility to Nature.

Human beings are especially prone to the error of thinking, caused almost certainly from our possession of second-order intentionality, that we are *discrete individual* entities, easily delineated from the objects around us and from Nature itself. Of course by all appearances and for largely practical purposes, that is in fact largely the case. I am certainly not the pen I write with or the desk on which I do the writing. However, both the empirical sciences and Schelling's *Naturphilosophie* demonstrate that this ontological separation is an illusion on the most fundamental level, perhaps fostered by the evolutionary survival mechanism of our species which absolutely needs a ready-made schematic distinction between self and other, subject and object, safety and danger. While I would contend that there is a spark of individuality fostered by unique experiences and sociohistorical circumstances, and perhaps even a primary monadic self buried deep down "somewhere," we are nevertheless completely intertwined with trillions of microbes that permeate our body and make countless biological processes possible; we consume pieces of Nature to keep yet another piece of Nature (i.e., us) going; we need the Other for the very development of the self (as recognition and intersubjectivity repeatedly demonstrate); we quite literally fall apart and lose all sense of self when isolated from others (as has been shown by even tiny periods of solitary confinement in prisoners and immersion in sensory deprivation chambers); and so forth. While *some* independence is clearly essential to our mental well-being, we must conclude that actual individualistic independence is among the most pernicious of fictions penned by the modern spirit. As we will see in the following chapter, for Schelling of the *Freedom Essay* this abstract individualism is in fact the root of evil itself, the usurpation of all else into an isolated self. This, however, is the legacy of modern political thought as it begins in Hobbes and Locke (the picture is quite different in Rousseau, who demonstrates communal tendencies); a legacy which insists upon the notion that the individual and individual alone is the bedrock of society. Based on this opening presupposition the West has built a body politic that is in many ways hyper-individualistic. We have cut off our direct involvement and dependence on Nature through technological and social means, thus fostering the illusion of independence for several centuries, but it is now imperative that we learn humility and accept our radical dependence upon one another and Nature itself. In order to do this we absolutely have to rethink the metaphysics of Nature, and that is precisely what we have been doing all throughout here with the help of Schelling.[93]

Based around the Schellingian view of Nature articulated in this chapter, we now have the basis for showing that we are not a radically distinct substance from the rest of Nature, but rather only a relatively distinct entity that is part and parcel of Nature's productive processes. Schelling's proto-evolutionary process metaphysics blurs the distinction between the human and Natural that has been the default position of Western philosophical thought, and especially so in the realm of political theory. Humankind is unique insofar as it alone on this planet has linguistic capacities and second-order consciousness, and this ought to be used to give a voice to Nature, to show that not only can we not exist without it, but that its boundless creative forces are intrinsically worthy of preservation. Nature is most decidedly and assuredly NOT a set of resources for the use of a *single* species on the planet. In this tiny corner of the universe it is the site of the perpetual unfolding of Being itself, a miracle that we witness daily and catalogue exhaustively in scientific discourse. *Both for the sake of our continual survival and for the sake of Nature as such we must allow the creative forces to continue*, especially given the fact that we have individual and collective agency to disrupt as well as to keep them going in their current manifestation. We must fight to preserve it at the level of public policy by insisting on a shift in perspective as monumental as that which happened during modernity's insistence that all individuals have rights, a thereto unheard of proposition. The new insistence will be a rethinking of what *we* are in respect to Nature. If Schelling is correct, and I believe that he essentially is, we *are* Nature, but all of Nature is most definitely not us. What does this mean and what does it entail?

Schelling states all throughout the early corpus that we are the most complex piece of the creative forces of Nature. The reasons for this are fairly straightforward and seemingly evident—we form complex societal structures, we have a dizzying variety of languages and cultures, we have self-evident second-order consciousness, we have the ability to understand and manipulate

Nature itself to a staggering amount (still growing in ways that would have been unimaginable to Schelling), and so forth. Thus, let us grant Schelling's premise that humanity is the most complex piece of Nature, still in a continuum with all else rather than completely different in kind, but nonetheless different in many ways from the rest of animal world. The transcendental conditions that make our subjectivity, and thus all this complexity, possible are not simply an explanatory heuristic, but rather a necessary piece of us that arises because of the underlying necessary developments of Nature (we are talking *a posteriori* necessity here). Given that any small amount of complexity in Nature lays the ground for much higher-order complexity, the transcendental conditions are not removed from Nature at all and are instead a part and parcel of it. As such, they are transcendental in a sense that is quite a bit different from what Kant himself had in mind, for whom they are simply the conditions for the possibility of subjective experience. What that entails is that we are but a single mere component of creation itself, envisioned here on the processes that Schelling develops and articulates throughout the *Naturphilosophie*. We are the component that marvels back at creation and can see more and more of its inner working, which, it turns out, is a frightening ability fraught with danger (both for us and for Nature). In its hubris, built into it by its very power, the self or the subject has lost on a mass scale a simple detail that was for the vast majority of human existence so obvious that it need not have been theorized about—the self or subject is in every conceivable way entirely dependent on Nature. Nature, however, does not share this quality with us. Despite the damage we are currently doing to it, Nature *qua* Nature—that is, the very creative processes and forces that make entities possible rather than the collection of entities—is not dependent on us. Like the Hegelian "master" we are under the impression of independence and victory, and like that same "master" we are only now learning the truth of our radical dependence; a dependence on each other and on Nature. I contend that this dependency relation entails such respect, perhaps even such *worship*, that it makes our responsibility to Nature of the most primordial kind at the collective level of the body politic. It is at the root of every other responsibility because without it there simply would not be any other responsibility and because it teaches us something that we seem to be categorically incapable of learning—"mastery" is always an illusion and that independence always hides dependence. When we finally learn this we can have a clearer picture of what responsibility truly looks like, first and foremost toward Nature itself and then toward each other (philosophy is quite good at theorizing the second if not at actually following through on its own theories).

Furthermore, much of discourse in political theory concerning rights, as well as much of ethical discourse, is predicated on a fairly strict separation of the human from the non-human. Whether that was justified by our having a "rational soul" (Aristotle and Aquinas, for instance), as soul in general (as is the case for the monotheistic religions as well as many of the polytheistic ones), or simply just rationality (Descartes, Kant, and on and on), the result is strikingly similar if not the same—we have political and moral responsibility to humans, which we often ignore, and to nothing else. Insofar as we have any responsibility to the non-human, it is filtered through the way in which it impacts the human. It is indirect at best. A simple example is the way we speak about tuna or other fish. We fish at such a rate that at our current pace tuna, as well as many other species, will become extinct in a matter of decades. Instead of speaking about this as a tragedy (which it most assuredly is for we are speaking about the loss of an *entire species*) we instead seem to treat it as a mere inconvenience to our culinary preferences. Labeled as a "protein" on many a menu, along with other organisms such as chicken and beef, we discursively and materially reduce it to mere resource for human consumption, and an interchangeable one at that, in its abstract euphemistic universalization as "protein." This is but one example among countless others in the Anthropocene. It is for the above reason that Schelling pokes fun at Fichte in *The Statement*, writing that Fichte is categorically incapable of appreciating a tree unless it was first turned into a chair.[94]

Schelling's ontology, now backed in its broad parameters by findings in the physics, evolutionary biology, and the environmental sciences, demonstrates that the strict separation between the human and non-human is in fact a presupposition that looks rather dubious. By taking what is a difference in degree and making it into a difference in kind, humanity has brought itself potentially to the brink of collapse. It is simply *not* good enough to for us to insist in the preservation of Nature for our needs alone, although I do not discount those needs (with the strong caveat that they are much, much more basic than what the West believes them to be). Of course we need natural resources in order to survive, but counterintuitively and ironically the human-centered approach is currently undermining our long-term survival and flourishing. Thus, a first step in any struggle is the change or reinvention of a perspective. We absolutely must rethink what Nature as such actually is and how we are beholden to it on a massive scale. Despite the fact that Schelling's presentation is somewhat uneven in his various works on *Naturphilosophie*, and his ontology being representative of a minority position in Western metaphysics, he nevertheless remains among the most relevant of thinkers for showing our *inherent* connection to Nature; a connection which entails a direct political responsibility. This connection is demonstrated not along any naively romantic sense, but with the logical rigor that is now backed by findings in the sciences that Schelling could not have possibly conceptualized (for instance, the primacy of force for the creation of matter, evolutionary processes that are self-organizing, the interdependence of species and need for biodiversity for the preservation of certain environments, and so forth.)

In radically blurring the division between the human and Nature, I have opened Schelling and myself to a potential objection—since we are just another parcel of Nature, is not all that we do, including the mass consumption of the environment for purely human use, in some sense natural? That is, the more "basic" or primary function of Nature in the form of dueling forces and polarities serve as a grounding factor for the more complex organizational forces and entities that result from them. The more complex organism has developed culture, government, technology of an increasingly amazing sort (so much so that it begins to appear as magical), and so forth. Ultimately, then, there is no final or real distinction in essence/kind between a mushroom and nano-tech. *All* is natural insofar as it is an emergent property of one of Nature's most complex organisms (us, as far as we can tell). I will grant the premise as it neatly follows from the account, but I do not grant the conclusion. While we cannot strictly separate the human from the natural, we can and already have separated those elements within the natural that are now actively undermining the viability of the organisms and even the creative forces of the *whole of Nature*.[95] The environmental sciences have already catalogued the various ways in which this has happened and continues to happen, and the work is readily available and readily ignored by anyone with access to the internet. Adding to this element, it must be acknowledged that the dominant economic ideology of the last two centuries—capitalism—is the insatiable beast with infinite heads that requires infinite growth. Yet, the fact is that we find ourselves on a finite planet.

How to implement such a re-orientation in thinking is difficult to say the least. Institutions calcify, ways of life different from the ones we currently have are difficult for many to imagine, logistical factors such as the production and transportation of food and other resources are now obscenely complex, and people balk at talk that requires them to change anything of their current way of life. Furthermore, a re-orientation in thinking is a long way removed from a re-orientation in *doing*. As such, a re-orientation in thinking is only a small step, and perhaps it will be forced upon us through no choice of our own when the material conditions change due to an increasingly unstable climate.[96] Given that those of us who are older and are less likely to change, I believe that the change will and must come from those in the younger generation (and there is reason to be optimistic on that front since they simply can no longer ignore the issue). A book such as this one is just one *tiny* contribution to what must amount to be a complete paradigm shift if we are to take our responsibility to Nature seriously. I must confess that I find various proposals from Deep Ecology, which overlaps with some of what I am arguing here, and movements such as eco-primitivism to be ultimately inadequate. While I think that personal radical reduction in one's consumption is perfectly morally acceptable and a viable path for *some*, the problem of what we owe Nature is a structural/political one first and foremost, and, as such, not solvable through individual action. Unless a catastrophe of mass scale forces the issue, people will likely not want to go this route anyways. We must, then, green our technology and our basic living conditions as a necessary but insufficient step. This requires massive *political* planning, and only such massive political planning can solve the issue (and, as Marx and Critical Theory have amply demonstrated again and again, the economic and the political are inextricably intertwined such that corporate action *is* inherently political).

As has been the case historically and continues to be the case, technologies of a vast industrial scale have caused the majority of destruction and misuse of Nature. Individuals as individuals have relatively little say in their use and development (although I certainly do not want to dismiss individual freedom and responsibility for change as that is an important, albeit smaller, facet in tackling this political problem). Even if one or two billion people choose to live as if they have the direct responsibility to Nature that I articulate here, the underlying structural problem remains—the economy as it is requires further growth and consumption, further ignoring of our basic responsibility, so the net effect is only partially reduced. It is for this reason that I think of our responsibility to Nature and the environment to be an inherently *political* rather than purely moral problem. I take morality to be largely about interpersonal decisions on a smaller scale, and the political is a matter of collective responsibility. Collective responsibility requires mass organizational efforts that transcend any individual action, and the responsibility to Nature is most certainly a problem of mass organization. However, despite this fact, it is still very much the case that individual change is also necessary. In their ability to *dissent* and *recognize* individuals still hold agency. The shift in perspective of seeing Nature for it is ontologically, metaphysically, and scientifically, and responding accordingly based on this shift in perspective, also entails the need for ethical change as well. At least some of us retain control of what we consume, how much we consume, our travel patterns, and so on. These changes too are necessary but insufficient. Only by combining the structural with the individual can we *merely begin* to uphold our direct responsibility to Nature.[97]

## (B) The Indirect Route—Recognition and Dissent

This brings us to the final portion and argument of this chapter, one that combines the finding of the recognitive structure of intersubjectivity developed by Schelling in the *System of Transcendental Idealism* with the process ontology of the *Naturphilosophie*. As we have seen in the *Ideas*, *First Outline*, and *System*, Schelling's transformation of the Kantian "transcendental" is quite substantial. While he retains the original and general notion that transcendental is "the condition for the possibility of," he stretches it in a direction which Kant would not have approved, and Fichte most assuredly did not as it caused a break in their collaboration and friendship. The manner in which Schelling performs the transformation is in making all of philosophy genetic. He also wants to see what in fact conditions the conditions for the possibility of experience. Whereas for Kant the transcendental points to the limit point of human reason, that which has to be in place to make sense of experience in the first place, for Schelling that is most certainly not the case. As we have seen here, the transcendental is not at all antithetical to the natural for Schelling, but rather itself emerges along the genetic developmental lines of the dueling polarities which make Nature possible in the first place. As such, Schelling naturalizes the transcendental all the while transcendentalizing certain elements of the natural. In doing so he paves the ground for Absolute Idealism. In a move that echoes Plato's demiurge stirring the Ideas all throughout material reality in the *Timaeus*, Schelling does the same for transcendental notions. The way that I have been conceptualizing this move is to think of the transcendental categories as the relatively stable channels or avenues upon which the processes that make Nature possible flow. In doing so, he transforms critical philosophy and inaugurates what is perhaps the final frontier of Western metaphysics— one that moves away from *a priori* rationalism as well as the full-blown transcendental idealism of Kant and Fichte.

This move allows us to rethink how recognition theory would develop upon an alternate, albeit related, path of the Fichtean transcendental framework in *Foundations of Natural Right*. Since the theoretical underpinning to this piece of Schelling's argument has already been addressed in the second chapter, the question that remains here is a different one: we must see here if there is anything in the recognitive process that can potentially address our political responsibility to Nature. I remain committed to the position that recognition is *the primary* mechanism by which subjectivity develops, and, furthermore, a full picture of this is only possible by a wider look at Fichte, Hegel, *and* Schelling (along with Husserl later on, especially in the *Cartesian Meditations*). Here, however, we are focusing on Schelling. Following this approach in general, human beings would not be subjects if they were not recognized as such, while they must simultaneously reciprocate this recognition/acknowledgment. All of this happens in real time in a messy way since there are various sociohistorical conditions that foster better or worse recognition. For instance, centuries of anti-Black racism in the United States, including "scientific" racism that became prevalent in the 19th century (justified by pseudo-sciences such as phrenology), have made misrecognition both endemic and deeply buried in the American unconscious, which is precisely why it is so difficult to eradicate at both the individual and structural level. While I think that the notion of recognition ought to be for the most part sequestered to the notion of human subjectivity and the various identities that develop from a historically and materially situated subjectivity, I also take seriously the German Idealist and later phenomenological claim that subject and object are not in fact strictly separated, but rather fundamentally intertwined. To borrow a phrase from Husserl, subject and object co-constitute one another. Schelling takes this even further in *Naturphilosophie* and the Identity Philosophy insofar as he insists all throughout this period that they are linked at the level of fundamental ontology. Furthermore, we have added to this a genetic naturalized account of their emergence, such that subjects do not and cannot stand in direct opposition to Nature or the objectively real. What does this do for recognition in the *Naturphilosophie*?

I contend that we can now stretch the concept of recognition just slightly past its intended social sphere as the explanatory mechanism of subjectivity/intersubjectivity, and in a more metaphorical way think through recognition between humanity and Nature. Consider the following argument. If the condition for the possibility of rights and freedom rests upon a recognitive framework, which I have argued in Chapter 2 as well as elsewhere, then we must ask the next quite classically Schellingian question: what are the grounding, universal conditions that make recognitive process possible in the first place? The answer should be clear from everything that has been established thus far—the condition for the possibility for the recognitive processes are grounded in processes that are *unconscious*, which, in turn, owe their existence to Nature itself. As such, *Nature* is not peripheral to political and moral questions. It is in fact ontologically impossible to even formulate such questions without Nature. As an emergent property of the processes of Nature, humans ought not to and in fact *cannot* sideline questions of justice, fairness, and even recognition as being set purely in the domain of human affairs, since the very possibility of human affairs presupposes a Natural framework. One of the factors that has evolved from our insistence on being somehow "separate" from Nature is that we have ceased to *recognize* Nature as Nature. We do not see ourselves in it, and, at the risk of stretching the recognitive framework, Nature will *fail* to recognize us and will in fact *dissent* (this process has already begun). Without invoking a self-conscious *telos* in Nature or anthropomorphizing it, it will nonetheless quite literally and systematically kill us through our very own actions that have built feedback loops into it. Thus, one piece of Nature, failing to recognize *itself* for what it is in the first place (i.e., a piece of Nature), builds the seeds of its own destruction with its own hands. As I have already specified above, I do not ultimately think that Nature as Nature will be damaged on the scales of deep time in which it exists, and I also suspect that even if the worse happens some of us might still make it (although prophecy is tricky business), but this is not particularly comforting or even all that relevant for the basic responsibility that we are avoiding *here and now*. In order for that responsibility to be addressed we have to rethink who and what we are, and re-imagine what our societies ought to look like on a massive scale. At this particular juncture nothing else will do and the task ahead is a supremely difficult one with no guarantees built in.

# Conclusion

What this chapter has demonstrated is that while Schelling himself never articulates what our political responsibility to Nature would ultimately look like, the very structure of that argument is already embedded in the *Naturphilosophie* and clearly echoed in the quote that begins this chapter. The normative implications are evident and have been demonstrated all throughout here through our reconstruction of the uniquely Schellingian ontology developed during this period—a process ontology that moves away from the metaphysics of substance that had long dominated Western thought, and has tendency to either completely sideline or ignore Nature itself in favor of static categories. As we have also seen, and as Schelling himself clearly demonstrates through his own *praxis* at the time, this ontology *absolutely must* take insight from the empirical sciences, and conversely, it shows that the sciences themselves are loaded with metaphysical presuppositions (which is not a bad thing in the slightest).

We have seen how the interplay between various dualities that are often kept separated in much of philosophical discourse—Ideal and real, subject and object, self and other, identity and difference, human and Natural—have cascading repercussions for political theory. These repercussions have been followed all throughout this chapter to demonstrate the various political concerns ranging from the connection between institutions to individuals to the primordial responsibility we have to Nature itself, a topic that I believe is the single most pressing issue of the 21st century. What we owe to Nature is quite literally *everything*. We are but *one* component that emerges from the creative forces and processes of Nature, and when we separated from Nature through reflection we brought with us a forgetfulness of this primordial fact, and have thus used Nature as mere resource for much of recorded history (glaring exceptions are found in Daoism, Native American and other Indigenous thought, Buddhism, especially the work of the great Zen Master Dōgen, and Environmental Ethics). Furthermore, in discussing the notions of Ideal/Real and identity/difference, I have shown how they move past their intended metaphysical domain in Schelling's *Naturphilosophie* and toward cultural, social, and political institutions. More strongly than that, the interplay between these categories allows us to think of a metaphysics of institutions that is non-reductive and emergent from simpler levels of organization, adding layers of depth and complexity that takes a life of its own with the passage of time. This life is often fraught with inequality and misrecognition of the Other, which becomes simultaneously structurally sedimented and buried in the unconscious of a people. It makes recognition difficult and dissent absolutely indispensable for changing the evils of racism, sexism, and environmental destruction. We turn next to the final piece of the puzzle, one that is at the heart of *every* political discourse: *freedom*.

# 4

# *The Politics of the Neoplatonic Ground of Freedom in Schelling's* Philosophical Investigations into the Essence of Human Freedom

## Introduction

Thus far we have followed and extrapolated Schelling's various incursions into the political through his work on the *New Deduction of Natural Right*, *System of Transcendental Idealism*, *Ideas for a Philosophy of Nature*, and *First Outline of a System of the Philosophy of Nature*. At each step of the process we have seen Schelling establish strong political *oughts*: first, one has a right due to the unconditioned that haunts Schelling's work from inception to end—that is, freedom. This right manifests itself quite often through large and small acts of dissent; second, one ought to recognize the Other *qua* Other, with the added caveat that this recognition is always fragile, tentative, and sometimes hopelessly lopsided due to the messy nature of the unconscious; thirdly and finally, one ought to protect Nature due to a primordial responsibility to it and because we are a part of Nature. This is necessitated by the very kind of creature we are. Now comes the most perilous turning point for the narrative that has been so neat thus far. The dreaded omega that bites the snake on its own tail—that is, freedom. Being perhaps the philosopher most in tune with the primacy and chaotic manifestation of freedom, Schelling will show in the *Philosophical Investigations into the Essence of Human Freedom* precisely what it means to be free. It is this that disrupts and makes all the more difficult the various oughts that have been established so far. Freedom, as Schelling will show, is the freedom to do good *and* evil, not good *or* evil, and that is the hardest lesson to remember in political theory, which always has the proclivity toward the utopian (even for me, despite the fact that I know better). In this sense, too, Habermas was mistaken in claiming that Schelling is not a political thinker. After all, what would it even mean to do political theory without taking freedom into account?

*The Philosophical Investigations into the Essence of Human Freedom* (henceforth *The Freedom Essay*) is without a doubt one of the high points of 19th-century philosophy. By its very structure, tone, and argumentative method, it breaks with much of classical Western metaphysics and takes its influence from generally neglected thinkers. Jacob Böhme, Franz Baader, and Friedrich Oetinger, all heavily steeped in mystical thought, as well as Proclus, Porphyry, and Plotinus, all classical Neoplatonic thinkers, figure heavily in the background of the work. Leibniz's *Theodicy* haunts the work throughout as well, especially given the topic of how to reconcile the obvious evil humanity perpetrates on itself and the world in general with the existence of God. Gone is the systematic purely philosophical mode of presentation, replaced by more suggestive and metaphorical prose. Despite relative neglect upon publication, the book has rightly come to be seen as a high point of Schelling's authorship, a radical work which upends and transforms German Idealism from the inside out. While not a text on political philosophy as such, its concern with freedom has implications for political thought that are quite profound and deep seated. It is the aim of this chapter to draw out these implications and thus complete the puzzle of what a relatively complete and systematic Schellingian political philosophy would ultimately look like. As such, the method of proceeding is to first move through a reconstruction of the overall argument in the *Freedom Essay*, followed by a political deconstruction. In our political deconstruction I aim to demonstrate how Schelling offers fresh insight into *three* key issues—the relationship between negative and positive freedom, further worked through the interplay between freedom and necessity; the reality of *evil* in the body politic which manifests itself at the level of individual agency and systemic structures (as Fichte, Hegel, and Schelling demonstrate, the individual and socio-structural are inherently interconnected through their dialectical interplay); and, finally, a contention with a politics that is non-teleological (i.e., a politics which breaks with the Enlightenment's faith in linear progress by factoring with it freedom, evil, and a historical contingency that shows the inherent fragility of all human projects).

## The Ontological Structure of the *Freedom Essay*

Schelling's notion of freedom cannot be disentangled from the ontological edifice on which it rests. That is, to understand how and why he theorizes freedom in that manner he does it must be made clear what is at stake metaphysically. While my account of Schelling's political ideas has proceeded largely in chronological order, beginning with the *New Deduction*, jumping shortly thereafter to the *System of Transcendental Idealism*, and then covering a few key texts in *Naturphilosophie*,[1] what I have skipped in this order, except for various allusions, is the Identity Philosophy period. The Identity Philosophy, as exemplified by works such as *Bruno* and *Der Weltseele (On the World Soul)*, is Schelling's most sustained attempt at a radical Spinozistic, and perhaps even Parmenidian, monism; an attempt to capture and collapse *all* other categories and Ideas into a single primordial Being or God. Without delving into the specifics of precisely how Schelling gets to this monism, which would easily fill another manuscript, it suffices to say that the ultimate category of his investigation is one of *Identity*. In pure Identity all beings or entities or processes of Nature are simply manifestations of Being *qua* Being, which in turn is characterized as the Identity of Identity and Difference. It cannot be *pure* Identity for the simple reason that if all things were in fact so radically identical then Being itself would persist with absolutely no predication whatsoever, making the simple action of writing itself performatively impossible. After all, how could I predicate anything of Schelling's thought or even Schelling himself if all was One? There would be no distinction between any of us or anything whatsoever. Being would never have left itself, speaking somewhat crudely, and would thus not have allowed me at this temporal point to use the imperfections of language to articulate anything about it. Self, Other, Nature, Idea, God, or any of the favorite topics of philosophical discourse would all have been simply Being and the philosopher or scientist would never even have arisen in the first place to categorize and understand its individual manifestations. Indeed, pure Being properly understood would not even allow for the possibility of any individual manifestations without complete disruption to its fundamental unity (which is Plato's main point in the *Parmenides*). However, it is simply not the case that we operate with that particular manifestation of radical unity. Being gave rise to beings, thus giving rise to multiplicity and difference. So, true *Identity* cannot be simple or "pure" Being, but rather the identity of itself and that which differentiates it.

By the time of the *Freedom Essay* in 1809, it becomes clear that Schelling is not satisfied with *either* his presentation or with his conclusion concerning the nature of Identity. Freedom itself is the sticking point. In a system of pure Being, becoming and freedom are washed away at the most fundamental ontological level. To borrow from a common idiom often uttered in English (and rarely all that helpful as advice despite the fact that it contains a kernel of truth): "it is what it is." However, the *Freedom Essay* is not a complete break with the Identity Philosophy period, but rather a course correction. I contend here that the ontological structure of the work is Neoplatonic at its core, albeit what Schelling provides is a Neoplatonism that has been transformed by critical philosophy and newly discovered findings in the natural sciences. While Plotinus is explicitly invoked only *once* in the essay,[2] Böhme, Baader, Spinoza, and Kant loom large throughout.[3] Furthermore, German Idealism *and* German Theosophy (one of the key inspirations behind the essay) owe a heavy debt to Neoplatonism.[4] As Werner Marx points out, "in Neo-Platonism the conviction arose that the conjunction between Being and thought, nature and mind, this 'system,' must find its final foundation in something that is absolved from finitude that reigns over both of these realms. Schelling also stood in this tradition."[5] Given that this is the case, an extrapolation of the general Neoplatonic edifice is hermeneutically useful for untangling Schelling's distinction between Being and the ground of Being (*Urgrund*)—the very distinction that captures Heidegger's imagination over a century later. In order to interrogate the connection to Neoplatonism, we begin with a brief excursion into its founder Plotinus.

## A Neoplatonic Interlude

In the classic Neoplatonic picture of metaphysics "the One" serves as a placeholder for that which cannot truly be named. Thinking and writing about the One is necessarily limited, since the One is outside of the process of both discursive and intuitive thought; regardless, Plotinus spends much time in trying to articulate some sort of conception of the One. For the most part, he closely adheres to the notion that we cannot truly say anything about the One because all of reality is radically different from the One, but we must nonetheless try to articulate it in some way since it is the principle from which everything emerges. In *Ennead* III.8, titled "On Nature and Contemplation," Plotinus examines the relationship between Intellect and the One. Intellect is the first reality to emerge out of the One since otherness, and hence multiplicity pertains to Intellect. Intellect "is not the first, but what is beyond it must exist (that to which our discussion has been leading), first of all, because multiplicity comes after unity."[6] Thus, there cannot be a sort of infinite Intellect which is the creator of all of reality, which would be the case for the Christian tradition since it conceives of God as having an infinite Intellect, but that there must be something beyond Intellect because of the idea that unity precedes multiplicity and Intellect necessarily involves multiplicity. This "something" that is beyond intellect is the absolute undifferentiated unity that is the One, and the One is what is properly infinite because it is without boundaries. To be utterly undifferentiated is to be infinite, because differentiation involves the imposition of limits and boundaries, since it involves things standing over and against one another. These things could be either other corporeal beings or forms, and these cannot be attributed to the One.

Intellect, for Plotinus, is the first reality to emerge out of the One, bringing with it the totality of Being. "The intelligible is always coupled with intellect."[7] Intellect and Being are two sides of the same coin for him, because Intellect would not be Intellect without having something to think about, be it a concrete particular, an abstract idea or a form. Thinking always involves otherness, so, unlike Aristotle for example, thought cannot think itself. The reason for this is because thinking without content is impossible. In order for me to think, even if I am completely ignoring all input from the senses, I must have some content to think about: concepts, numbers, imaginary characters, past experiences, etc. Plotinus tells us that "one must include movement if there is thought, and rest that it may think the same; and otherness, that there must be thinker and thought; or else, if you take away otherness, it will become one and keep silent; and the objects of thought, also, must have otherness in relation to each other."[8] "Thought thinking itself" looks to be an empty phrase, since even thinking about thinking involves the otherness of the thinker stepping back and reflecting upon thinking and what it means to be thinking. Phenomenologically speaking, then, thought is always intentional. As Dominic O'Meara points out, through his critique of Aristotle in *Ennead* V.6.1-2, Plotinus argues that:

> All thought, including self-thought, is constituted through a duality of act and the object of thinking, and the object, as constitutive of thought, must exist prior to thought as well as in thought. In Plotinus's mind Aristotle's analysis of thinking leads to the conclusion that the Aristotelian god, as self-thought, cannot be what it claims to be, absolutely simple and ultimate.[9]

Therefore, when Intellect emerges out of the One, Being has to emerge along with it in order for Intellect to be able to think something. "The whole is universal Intellect and Being, Intellect making Being exist in thinking it, and Being giving Intellect thinking and existence by being thought."[10] Being cannot emerge prior to Intellect because it would then be unintelligible and therefore without organization or guidance (sheer multiplicity and chaos). Intellect cannot emerge prior to Being because if it did it would have nothing to think about, and, as we have seen, thinking for Plotinus must always be thinking of something. Being and Intellect/Thinking, then, must emerge simultaneously.

Given that all of reality is produced along with Intellect, since Intellect needs something to think about in order to be Intellect, and given that Plotinus believes unity must precede multiplicity, it must be the case that the rest of reality is radically different from the One and the One cannot be conceptualized through any reference with the rest of reality. Plotinus thus tells us that "all thing [together, the totality of being] are not an origin, and this is no more all things, or one of them."[11] The One, then, is neither Intellect (thinking) or Being, but rather radically beyond thinking and being. To say that the One is neither Intellect nor Being would mean that these two things cannot be predicated of it, so it cannot be the case that the One is like the Christian God who is infinite thinking and being. This notion takes Plotinus out of the usual Western ontological framework, where there is a distinction between the supreme infinite Being and all other finite beings, and places him in what can best be described as a "henological" framework.[12] That is, the One *is* the very generation of Intellect/Being, yet neither of these things. The One, then, is needed as a generative principle, but not in the sense of an efficient cause or an unmoved mover, but in the sense of a *purely* generative principle. A purely generative principle, unlike an efficient cause or an unmoved mover, is not a *Being* acting on other beings in order to or set them into motion or produce them, but rather simply *is* the very unfolding of beings. Furthermore, as Eric Perl points out in his article "The One as Pure Giving": "if the One were any thing at all, it would be included in the totality of that which is, distinguished from other beings, and hence determinate, complex, and therefore dependent."[13] If the One were "determinate, complex, and therefore dependent," like Being and Intellect, it would need *another* principle by which it is explained, so it would cease to be the One. Therefore, predicating anything whatsoever of the One undercuts the very function it is meant to serve at the center of Plotinus's system (that of an ultimate generative principle), and thus a contradiction is placed at the very heart of his metaphysics.

Further evidence for the notion that nothing can be predicated of the One is found in *Ennead* III.8 and 9, where Plotinus is explicit about the fact that the One is not Intellect and cannot be or have Intellect, which in turn means that the One cannot have being, since, as we have seen above, the two are necessarily connected. So, speaking of the One (also called "the Good"), Plotinus writes:

> Other things have their activity about the Good, but the Good needs nothing; therefore it has nothing but itself. Therefore, when you have said "the Good" do not add anything to it in your mind, for if you add anything, you will make it deficient by whatever you added. Therefore you must not even add thinking, in order that you may not add something and make it two, intellect and good. For Intellect needs to Good, but the Good does not need it.[14]

We see here that Plotinus believes that if we add thinking to the One, which some interpreters want to do as we shall see in the next section, we destroy its simplicity and perfection, which in turn undermines its ability to be the ultimate principle of reality. Intellect needs the Good, but the Good needs nothing. Furthermore, it is quite evident here that there cannot be *anything at all* predicated of the One if we are to call it "One" or "Good," which seems to radically undercut any of the positive pronouncements of the One that occur in *Ennead* VI.8.

Plotinus is also quite clear that you cannot add anything to the One, especially thinking, in *Ennead* III.9. He tells us that "the One does not have thought. So that which thinks is double, even if it thinks itself, and defective, because it has its good in its thinking, not in its being."[15] Furthermore, Plotinus argues:

> Thinking is not the primarily venerable; all thinking is certainly not venerable, only thinking about the Good, so the Good is beyond thinking. But the Good will not be conscious of itself. What, then, would its consciousness of itself be? A consciousness of itself as being good or not? Well, then, if it is of itself being good, the Good exists already before the consciousness; but if the consciousness makes it good, the Good would not exist before it, since it is of the Good. What then? Is it not alive either? No, it cannot be said to live…So, then, thinking must be excluded from the Good, for the addition causes diminution and defect.[16]

This paragraph provides a clear statement of Plotinus's apophatic understanding of the One. We see that it cannot be the case that the One is conscious even of itself because this would mean that consciousness somehow precedes Goodness, thus making consciousness the Good, which cannot be the case since consciousness is always directed *toward* the Good from which it emerged. We cannot even say that the One is alive because this too would be adding something to the One, and, as Plotinus writes, any addition "causes diminution and defect." With that in mind, we turn back to Schelling, whose Neoplatonism has a decidedly unique flavor.[17]

## Neoplatonic Emanation and Schelling's *Urgrund*

What we see through our excursion into Plotinus is that the One is *beyond* the category of Being by logical necessity. If it were Being itself it would have to be explained why it exists rather than not, thus ultimately leading to an infinite regress problem. Out of the One emanate thinking and Being, or, to rephrase it in categories that are more aligned with German Idealism, the Ideal and the Real. Precisely as is the case in German Idealism, the Ideal and Real are caught up in perpetual dialectical interplay. Thinking must be thinking *of something*, even if self-referential or pointed directly to the Ideal alone, thinking brings Being with it. Being cannot *be* without being articulated and structured. Pure Being without a rational structure, shaped by *Nous* in Neoplatonism, is unintelligible in principle—to make it intelligible one would have to think it, so springing the dialectical trap. Out of the One then, as we see in the section above, flow thinking and Being, thus making the One the *ground of reality*. Is this the picture that is best attributed to Schelling? Is Schelling a Plotinian kind of Neoplatonist? At least at this juncture of his authorship (his roughly "middle" period), I argue that is not the case for several reasons, which is why it is important for the purposes of elucidation to see the contrast.

First of all, Schelling's "One" is not the One at all, but rather God. This is important not for simple philosophical hair splitting regarding what very well could be an artificial distinction of name alone under which lies no difference whatsoever. Rather, as we will shortly see, God *is* Being itself rather than purely beyond Being like the One, *and* by serving as "his" own ground God has his feet simultaneously planted in Being and beyond

Being. Secondly, Schelling is running an argument for a Spinozistic kind of pantheism throughout the *Freedom Essay*. While a case can be made that Neoplatonism too has pantheistic tendencies, the notion of emanation from the One makes it difficult to see how exactly that would be the case. After all, for Spinoza God/universe/substance is Being itself, but that exhausts our ultimate metaphysical categories. There is nothing over and above or beyond this substance. Granted, Schelling is moving past substance metaphysics, but the neat Neoplatonic division between the One and everything else is not quite there in Schelling and he very much takes the Spinozistic picture of reality seriously at this point of his work. Thirdly and finally, Schelling is decidedly *not* working with an account of emanation. So, then, what kind of Neoplatonism are we talking about? One heavily influenced by the later Neoplatonists—the German mystics such as Böhme. However, Plotinus still serves as an indispensable point of reference, and, as Bruce Matthews convincingly argues all throughout his book, so does Plato of the *Parmenides* and *Timaeus*, the two chief inspirations of Neoplatonism and Plotinus himself. Furthermore, there is one striking similarity, a golden thread that connects Plotinus to Schelling: Parmenidean pure Being is unworkable without a principle *beyond* it to serve as the *ground* of Being—a dark ground that is beyond Being, Ideal, Real, reason, and so forth; itself perpetually and permanently unknowable in principle; his "indivisible remainder" which systematically undermines the possibility of a final, closed system of any sort.

The key conceptual metaphor, the one which will ultimately point to the limitations of philosophical conceptual thought itself, is the one of the *ground of Being*. We must first explore this before moving to Schelling's discussion of freedom proper and its implications for political philosophy. The most difficult hurdle to understanding the *Freedom Essay* in its entirety lies in unpacking what Schelling exactly means by this notion of ground. It is precisely why I began our excavation by a foray into Plotinus. Plotinus provides a (relatively) clear answer for the need of a grounding principle. As we have seen, Being cannot be explained without recourse to something that it is grounded in which itself cannot fall under the category of Being.[18] This, however, is still an oversimplification that doesn't do justice to Schelling's startlingly unique answer to this philosophical problem.

To contextualize the grounding metaphor I first want the reader to consider it through the lens of Nature itself and its relationship to a primal element—lightning. The ground of reality, if visualized as a literal ground in this instance, can tie up the philosophical imagination into a foundationalist stance such as the one of Descartes, which is precisely *not* where Schelling is headed. The ground grounds physical structures and these structures are built with means to safely dissipate electrical discharge. Lightning too is absorbed when it strikes the ground.[19] *However*, the *Urgrung* or "dark ground" cannot quite *ground* in this literal manner for it is, indeed *logically must "be,"* outside any and all categories of Being, including the ones that are obviously borrowed from Nature (whose Being is in a state of flux or becoming). Thus, the primordial grounding can be thought through the natural grounding metaphor only obliquely at best. To borrow from the *Daodejing*, a process worldview that is outside the bounds of Western ontology and its necessary fixation on Being, "nameless, it is the beginning of Heaven and Earth; named, it is the mother of the myriad creatures,"[20] and, furthermore, "there is a thing confused yet perfect, which arose before Heaven and Earth. Still and indistinct, it stands alone and unchanging. It goes everywhere and is never at a loss. One can regard it as the mother of Heaven and Earth. I do not know its proper name; I have styled it 'the Way.'"[21] What the mythical Laozi is showing here is that there is a principle or "thing" that occupies a paradoxical status of being changing yet unchanged, the wellspring of reality, rationally unknowable yet needing a name, that "he" will call "the Way" or Dao. It grounds the myriad creatures and makes them possible. Schelling too must name the principle, and while his comes from a vastly different conceptual schema than the one found in ancient Chinese thought, he too is making a very similar move to Laozi (at least on the relationship between Nature and that which makes it possible). What Laozi dubs "the Way" as a placeholder name, Schelling dubs the *Urgrund* or "dark ground." This name, however, can never capture in rational discursive thought what the dark ground "is," for to do so is to fold it back into the Western, largely static ontology of Being, and thus make it bereft of its explanatory power. What he has in mind is an ontology that very well might show the limits of ontology itself.

Taking us now to the text of the *Freedom Essay* itself, we see Schelling tipping his hat to the philosophy of Nature as a direct inspiration for the notion of grounding. He tells us that "the natural philosophy of our time has first advanced in science the distinction between being in so far as it exists and being in so far as it is merely the ground of existence."[22] That is, his philosophy of Nature, both in the Identity period roughly of 1801–1804 and in the more purely *Naturphilosophie* of 1797/1799, has already grappled with this fundamental distinction insofar as it makes the distinction between productivity and product that served as the guiding light for the argument developed in the last chapter. We had there a notion of Nature as first and foremost being a self-organizing *productivity*, making possible the transient *products* or entities/beings that we are and observe all around us. However, in writing the *Freedom Essay* and beginning anew with this distinction, Schelling is admitting implicitly and explicitly that there are leftover unanswered questions. The first unanswered question concerns the very possibility of a deduction of freedom from the confines of natural system. Even an organic system like the one developed by Schelling during the *Naturphilosophie* period has the danger of trapping freedom in the clash of positive and negative forces that make Nature possible. This loops us back to the beginning of this study where freedom was simply conceptualized as the unconditioned, tapping into Schelling's early Kantianism but now tacitly acknowledging a dissatisfaction with this approach. The second question interrogates how the dueling forces of polarity in Nature are themselves possible in the first place. That is, what conditions the conditions for the possibility of Nature? To answer this question from the confines of the *Naturphilosophie* is difficult because it requires further investigation into ontology and metaphysics.

The key paragraph which allows us to answer these questions is very much worth quoting at length. Schelling writes:

> Since nothing is prior to, or outside of, God, he must have the ground of his existence in himself. All philosophies say this; but they speak of this ground as of a mere concept without making it into something real and actual. This ground of his existence, which God has in himself, is not God considered absolutely, that is, in so far as he exists; for it is only the ground of his existence. It [the ground] is *nature*—in God, a being indeed inseparable, yet still distinct, from him. This relation can be explained analogically through

> that of gravity and light in nature. Gravity precedes light as its ever dark ground, which itself is not *actu* [actual], and flees into the night as light (that which exists) dawns. Even light does not fully remove the seal under which gravity lies contained. Precisely for this reason gravity is neither the pure essence nor the actual Being of absolute identity but rather follows only from its own nature or *is* absolute identity, namely considered as a particular potency. For, incidentally, that which is relative to gravity appears as existing also belongs in itself to the ground, and, hence, nature in general lies beyond the absolute Being of absolute identity. Incidentally, as far as this precedence is concerned, it is to be thought neither as precedence in time nor as priority of being. In the circle out of which everything becomes, it is no contradiction that that through which the One is generated may itself be in turn begotten by it. Here there is no first and last because all things mutually presuppose each other, no thing is another thing and yet no thing is not without another thing. God has in himself an inner ground of his existence that in this respect precedes him in existence; but, precisely in this way, God is again the *prius* [what is before] of the ground in so far as the ground, even as such, could not exist if God did not exist *actu*.[23]

This single paragraph contains enough philosophical insight to potentially fill an entire manuscript. It is simultaneously a summary and critique of over two millennia of Western metaphysics, and the basis for my read of the Schelling of 1809 as a kind of inverted Neoplatonism. First we begin with a pantheism of the Spinozistic variety, which itself has deep roots in Stoic discourse—God *is* the totality of reality, there is *only* God at the level of fundamental ontology, and nothing can be before, after, or outside of God. In this manner, the Neoplatonic categories of the One, thinking, Being, and matter (which is furthest from the One and gives rise to evil due to its distance), are condensed and consolidated into God, thus pointing to a kind of *identity* relationship. However, merely stating this in conceptual terms as the center point of this discourse is to barrel over all the complexity, nuance, and *actuality* of the discourse. It is merely an *empty abstraction*. Rather, the ground of God lies in God himself, the same yet in a sense different from him. The ground is the "same" because God is the grand totality of *all* existence, but simultaneously different because one "piece" of God grounds God. We must again deal with organic metaphors here to explain the process at hand. The neat mechanistic picture of classical thought, which makes God either the prime mover or creator *ex nihilo* makes too many assumptions and separates God from the rest of reality, thus creating a dualism that obfuscates just as much as it explains. Instead, what we see above is that there is no easy or neat way to differentiate *either* ontological or temporal priority in all the elements of the divine. God *simultaneously* needs the ground to ground himself, and yet serves as the condition for the possibility of God's own grounding. At first glance this seems either paradoxical or flat out contradictory, but that is only through the lens of mechanistic thinking. A mechanistic theory renders this notion nonsensical, for it needs a nice cascading effect with a clear first move, but an organic theory makes it workable. For example, a human heart can be thought of in the same theoretical parameters. The heart "grounds" one's existence insofar as it is needed for sustaining *all* other bodily functions, and yet it simultaneously depends on the rest of the organism for its own sustained survival and viability. It forms a feedback loop, albeit in a more mundane manner than the metaphysics being interrogated by Schelling above.

This brings us to the sticking point of the status of Nature in this picture. Very much *unlike* Neoplatonism, especially of the strictly Plotinian variety which sees Nature as the furthest away from the One or the Good, Schelling's Nature serves as the possibility for God's own ground *and* the movement of *difference* in the identity of identity and difference. God grounds himself in and through Nature insofar as the unfolding of creation through dynamic forces can *only* happen if there is a "place" in which it occurs, a potency of Nature. This is the realm of becoming or process: "we recognize rather that the concept of becoming is the only one appropriate to the nature of things."[24] Nature is the being that can only be understood as becoming, "a being indeed inseparable, yet still distinct, from him."[25] There is a certain sense of a *double* grounding here, found simultaneously in Nature but also in a "portion" of God that cannot be Nature as such. This is the space that makes possible the unfolding of freedom. As Schelling puts it,

> After the eternal act of self-revelation, everything in the world is, as we see it now, rule, order and form; but anarchy still lies in the ground, as

if it could break through once again, and nowhere does it appear as if order and form were what is original but rather as if initial anarchy has been brought into order. This is the incomprehensible base of reality in things, the indivisible remainder, that which with the greatest exertion cannot be resolved in the understanding but rather remains eternally in the ground.[26]

The above might very well be the single most referenced passage in Schelling's entire corpus, and that is for good reason. In it he has taken philosophy and rational understanding to its utmost limit without simply rehashing the Kantian noumeanon. We can know Nature, both philosophically/phenomenologically in its broad parameters and in excruciating detail scientifically; we can even know God as well, here both as a part of the pantheistic view by which God is to a certain extent coextensive with Nature and also philosophically/theologically; but *the ground itself* remains perpetually outside of reason. Echoing Kant but now working well past the confines of Transcendental Idealism, Schelling again borrows a piece of Neoplatonic (as well as theosophical and mystical) reasoning. Reason guides us through Nature, through the visible and invisible structures and processes of reality, but what Schelling is pointing out along with Neoplatonism is that reason has an upper limit—the assumption that what grounds reality is also rational itself is simply without evidence. After all, reason is a part of the order of reality, while that which grounds the order is a singularity point in which all the rules of reason dissolve back into chaos. Thinking of this from the standpoint of contemporary physics and cosmology, there comes a point in our scientific understanding where all the categories which we rely on are simply not operational. Time, space, even mathematical differentiation inevitably fall apart the closer one inches to the moment out which the universe unfolds during the Big Bang. As we have also seen, in the Neoplatonic framework if the One out of which reality emanates is predicated at all, it immediately ceases to be One, for any predication forces a doubling and splinters the One into two. This bit of philosophical reasoning dates back to Plato's *Parmenides*, and Schelling's debt to Plato is meticulously documented by Grant, Freydberg, and Matthews.[27] Furthermore, if the ground were rational it cannot in principle serve as ground. Its knowability and rationality would place it back into the confines of Being *qua* Being, thus depriving it of its capacity to ground Being.

Freedom emerges from the dark ground of Being and not Being itself, thus manifesting itself in an ordered world as a perpetual curveball, always bringing with it layers upon layers of contingency. It is the freedom for good *and* evil, as Schelling contends throughout the essay. In adding the "*and*" and avoiding the disjunctive, Schelling is following in the Kantian footsteps while simultaneously parting ways with them. Kant famously argues that humanity is a crooked piece of timber, carrying evil at our very core, but yet keeps freedom fundamentally *formal*—it is the condition for the possibility of experience, a fundamental posit or presupposition that cannot be touched theoretically for it falls squarely and solely in the realm of practical reason. That is, for Kant freedom is that without which we cannot even conceptualize ethical and political life, but we are incapable of having any direct proof of it because it transcends the limits of human reason. Instead of following Kant, as he did much more explicitly earlier in his career, Schelling here breaks substantively with him as he also breaks with purely idealistic outlook, telling us that "idealism is the soul of philosophy; realism is the body; only both together can constitute a living whole,"[28] and, furthermore, "idealism provides namely, on the one hand, only the most general concept of freedom, on the other hand, a merely formal one. But the real and vital concept is that freedom is the capacity for good and evil."[29] As such, he is no longer interested in formal or general proofs for anything, especially not freedom, instead seeking a philosophical outlook that is concretely grounded in our shared lived reality. Freedom means that evil can be, and very often is, chosen over good. Furthermore, God for Schelling is not the transcendent God of the Medieval and Modern periods, nor the purely pantheistic God of perfect order we find in Spinoza, but rather "a life."

Since all things emerge from God, including of course humanity, freedom too has its ultimate seat in God. How then does one preserve God's purity and goodness while making evil an explicit element of the Absolute? This is where we find the uniqueness of the Schellingian theodicy. Evil does not come from God as such, but rather from the chaotic ground that underpins all of reality (including God). As Werner Marx points out, this is the ground that's not really "ground" but rather "non-ground": "this concept characterizes that state within the process of God's becoming himself in which he is neither Being nor becoming, and thus in no sense a ground."[30] That is, here lies the very limitations of *all* reason, and especially of human reason, where any attempt to capture the lived reality of God or the underpinnings of the universe itself—any attempt to peer beyond the event horizon, to borrow from physics—defies any and all possible direct conceptualization. In God himself, the freedom that God maintains perpetually holds the possibility of evil at bay, but the same cannot be said for us humans. We are capable of evil in a multitude ways that are bewilderingly creative and shockingly mundane.

It should be pointed out here that while the prognosis for humans does not paint us in a particularly favorable light, it is still *not* the case that for Schelling we are somehow *inherently evil*. That is, this is not an account of a type of original sin that moves past the notion of evil as privation that dominates Western theodicies from Augustine to Leibniz and makes us into born villains, nor is there a sense of a Manichean conflict between two opposing factions with one essentially evil and the other good. Rather, humanity is *free*—nothing more or less. It is precisely this freedom that gives rise to both the *possibility* and *reality* of evil (as well as good). As Bernard Freydberg points out in *Schelling's Dialogical Freedom Essay*, "properly speaking freedom is neither good nor evil, although good and evil are each marks of a free act,"[31] and, furthermore, "the actuality of good demands the actuality of evil."[32] In order for good to shine through as good, it must stand in dialectical (or dialogical, in Freydberg's formulation) relationship with evil, and this dialectical relationship fundamentally necessitates that the two cannot be neatly untangled either in potentiality or in actuality—they simply do not make sense apart from each other in the same manner that tall and short, light and dark, infinite and finite, and so forth are incoherent except through comparison. If somehow all was "good" or all was "evil" in the world that would simply be the end of the analysis. It would be a brute fact of reality as such, and morality, political theory, and legality would not every have even occurred to us. This is why *humanity* must fight with these concepts and their implementation, for the rest of reality is beyond good and evil.

Given our capacity for good and evil, what exactly is it that tips the favor toward one or the other when a human being decides to act? Schelling's answer to this question is quite clear and highly suggestive for the nature of political life as it ultimately couched in *political* terms concerning the interplay between universal and particular will (concepts we have already investigated in the first chapter). Concerning the elevation of the particular will over the general will, with the general will here understood as the divine will yet to be separated from creaturely will, Schelling argues:

> The will steps out from its being beyond nature, in order as general will to make itself at once particular and creaturely, strives to reverse the relation of the principles, to elevate the ground over the cause, to use the spirit that it obtained only for the sake of the *centrum* outside the *centrum* and against creatures; from this results the collapse within the will itself and outside it. The human will is to be regarded as a bond of living forces; now, as long as it remains in unity with the universal will, these divine forces exist in divine measure and balance. But no sooner that the self-will moves to the *centrum* as its place, so does the bond of forces as well; in its stead rules a mere particular will that can no longer bring the forces to unity among themselves as the original will could...[33]

What we see here is Schelling's appropriation of Jacob Böhme's theosophical notion of the "*centrum*." The notion of the *centrum* in Böhme refers to the core in creatures that is inaccessible to reason, and which creatures share with the divinity: "God does not dwell in the external fleshly heart, but in the soul's *centrum*, in itself."[34] For Schelling as well as for Böhme,[35] evil is the direct result of individuality attempting to take the place of divine universality. Thus, what we see here is that the dark principle that is the core individuality of person, that which cannot be rationally accessed and remains perpetually unconscious, usurps the role of the general will which is in equilibrium in God/Nature and elevates the *individual* over the *universal*. The equilibrium in God/Nature—the principles of divine light and divine darkness, and the interplay of dueling polarities (respectively)—is usurped or set aside by individual humans when the individual self or ego becomes the totality of existence. This becomes the sole seat by which we proclaim judgment on all affairs, human or otherwise, and as Marx points out, "the elevation of the particular will over the universal will; precisely this is the realization of evil."[36] This elevation is the root, grounding cause of modernity's myriad failures. The elevation of the individual, that isolated atomic subject trapped within the confines of the Cartesian Theatre, wondering if it is alone among a sea of automatons, is made to be all that is really real. As such, reality becomes radically contracted to a single point. This single point then gets elevated in the work of Hobbes and Locke to a fundamental principle of political rule, never fully carried out given the various injustices perpetuated against countless individuals, yet, by consequence of overwhelming influence, into the very fabric of the Western psyche and made into the *ultimate and only* possible beginning for political organization. As Adorno and Horkheimer vividly show in *The Dialectic of Enlightenment*,[37] a totalizing notion of "progress" coming out of an extreme individualism ultimately result in a series of human tragedies and atrocities whose scale is difficult to grasp imaginatively and intellectually. Modernity has *simultaneously* elevated the standard of living of many in the West while at the same time perpetuating slavery, genocide, and an unparalleled and continuously accelerating destruction of the only environment suitable to support us. The Anthropocene is and has always been the logical conclusion of a system of thought and governance that sees only the individual human as the ultimate unit of value. Individualism becomes totalitarian.

The individual and communal, particular and universal, are of course always in dialectical interplay in Schelling and Hegel. It is nonsensical to speak of one without the other. However, Schelling's dialectical moves are not those that Hegel makes. There is no moment of *aufheben* in Schelling, no sublation to speak of. There is just the interplay between opposites, the tension, the strife of forces, the contingency of history, the tipping of the scales between one side to the other in perpetuity. What is clear nevertheless is that the pure elevation of the individual will over the universal will results in the lived reality of evil. The proverbial road to hell has been paved, brick by brick, by individuals perpetually favoring their own narrow interest ahead of the universal. While this insight has been articulated many times by many thinkers as to appear to be a truism at this point, it is one of very few that I am as sure of as I am of the reality of gravity, and, furthermore, the way that Schelling gets us here is unlike anything else in Western philosophy. What he teaches us here is that there is no final solution to this particular human all too human problem. It is the crux of real, concrete freedom manifesting itself in the world, not the merely formal analysis of freedom articulated from the philosopher's armchair. It is and will remain a perpetual reality that political organization and public policy has to deal with as long as there are any of us left on the planet. Freedom is the freedom for good *and* evil, and not even a perfect utopia will change that (which calls into question the very possibility of utopia in the first place). However, there are embedded in this insight hints of a possible remedy, an ability to treat this uniquely human disease. They are to be found in Schelling's discussion of the interplay between freedom and necessity. It is toward this interplay that we now turn.

## Freedom and Necessity in the Dark Ground (and their Political Implications)

Debates surrounding free will have a tendency to revolve around a fundamental problematic: how does one reconcile the seeming strong necessity of physical laws with what appears to be the brute reality of humans to make free decisions (often quite bad ones). One can move in several directions. Kant, who is easily the most towering influence on all that Schelling writes, will argue that freedom is practical posit, needed to explain the possibility of ethics and law but incapable of theoretical proof. He thus sidesteps or dissolves the problem. Hume, who strikes me as level-headed of a philosopher as possible, argues for what would now be described as a compatibilist position—yes, there are physical laws which obviously constrain our action, but human history and general behavior is impossible to explain without some recourse to freedom. Spinoza consistently follows through on his initial definitions and posits the earliest strong[38] formulation of the Principle of Sufficient Reason. This leads him to state that for *anything* that happens (or even *doesn't* happen) there must be a cause or reason, thus instantly eliminating the possibility of freedom. Finally, later thinkers such as Sartre, or at least Sartre of the early works (*Being and Nothingness* and *Existentialism is a Humanism*) will argue for what is now dubbed a "libertarian" conception of freedom. That is, we *are* our freedom. The status of intentional consciousness, which exists only insofar as it is actively consciousness *of* something, proves to Sartre that we are radically free because we can *always* redirect our intentionality in infinite directions. We are condemned to be free.

Schelling's solution is elegant and unique to him, and what it effectively does is to combine the various seemingly incompatible positions above. What allows him to make this move is the logical edifice he had constructed during the Identity period of his thought. Schelling writes:

> The intelligible being can, as certainly as it acts as such freely and absolutely, just as certainly act in accordance with its own nature; or action can follow from within only in accordance with the law of identity and absolute necessity which alone is also absolute freedom. For free is what acts only in accord with the laws of its own being and is determined by nothing else either in or outside itself.[39]

In the root of Absolute Identity, the category that emerges out of the *Urgrund*, all distinctions ultimately collapse, which means that in the most primal source of Being there cannot be a strict separation between necessity and freedom. Every free choice that humans make, if it is to be considered a truly free choice, dips into the unconscious *centrum*—that which is outside of temporality itself—and emerges back out *as free*. But, in the *centrum* itself, there can be no true distinction between freedom and necessity. While this has echoes of Kant and Fichte, who each argue that true freedom is the ability to self-legislate rather than have external impositions upon the self, we ought to again take seriously here Schelling's claim that he is not concerned with the *formal* concept of freedom which boils down to freedom as the condition for the possibility of self-legislation and nothing more, but rather the *real or actual* concept of freedom in all of its chaotic messiness. As such, it would be unfair to Schelling as well as Kant/Fichte to equate his position on freedom with their notion of self-legislation. After all, Kant and Fichte are *transcendental* thinkers *par excellence* while Schelling of the *Freedom Essay* has substantively broken with the transcendental approach by reintroducing the *real* into the heart of speculative philosophy. This foray back into Being itself would thus put Schelling back in the category of "dogmatist" for Kant and Fichte, but this is an unfair characterization given how radically distinct his thought is at this point of his authorship and forward, and how saturated it is with the critical approach that the two had inaugurated.

The element of the argument that we must consider here concerns Schelling's notion that freedom emerges *directly* from the dark ground, which goes even further down the proverbial rabbit hole than the notion of Identity. In the dark ground or *Urgrund*, the bond of forces that extend through and make Nature possible is still undifferentiated. It is the metaphysical equivalent of the physics of the Big Bang. This undifferentiating entails that every decision made by humans, guided by an pre-conscious or unconscious *will*, dips and folds back into an a-temporal realm only to re-emerge back into the mundane temporal world when humans act. Given that differences at this level of reality would be indistinguishable in principle, it logically follows that freedom and necessity in fact merge:

> Here lies the point at which necessity and freedom must be unified if they are at all capable of unification. Were this Being a dead sort of Being and a merely given one with respect to man, then, because all action resulting from it could do so only with necessity, responsibility and all freedom would be abolished. But precisely this inner necessity is itself freedom; the essence of man is fundamentally *his own act*; necessity and freedom are in one another as one being that appears as one or the other only when considered from different sides, in itself freedom, formally necessity.[40]

Other than demonstrating the connection of freedom and necessity, which has always been at the forefront of the German Idealist project, the above passage also anticipates key existential insights that will not be articulated until much later in the history of Western thought. "The essence of man is fundamentally *his own act*,"[41] is a sentence that very well could have been penned by Sartre in *Being and Nothingness, Existentialism is a Humanism*, and even *the Critique of Dialectical Reason*. It is the sentence that makes existentialism what it is, and it drives home the idea that humanity determines through each and every act its own essence. We *are* our freedom, for better or worse, which Schelling has shown is always the freedom for good and evil, and examples of both abound in history.

What Sartre of the *Being and Nothingness* period and the rest of his early output did not see however, and what the *later* Sartre and Schelling here clearly see, is that freedom and necessity are tangled together in a profound and somewhat strange way—a way that cannot be easily captured by the seemingly neat but ultimately false intuition that they need to be clearly distinguished and relegated to separate realms. We simply cannot have one without the other, and for Schelling that is true at the below-ground level of metaphysics. Where Schelling doesn't take the insight and the later Sartre does, is in the sphere of the body politic. In the political sphere, itself contingent upon Nature which is in turn contingent upon the dark ground, we cannot and ought not to address freedom without simultaneously addressing necessity. We will first do so here through the long-standing distinction between positive and negative freedom that has been the hallmark of political liberalism—a distinction that suffers from the excessive formalism that philosophy all too often suffers from—and we will subsequently turn to the later Sartre shortly thereafter.

In situating Schelling within a general nexus of political philosophy rather than pure metaphysics or the history of ideas, the distinction between positive and negative freedom not only shows how freedom and necessity are not disparate phenomena, but it also demonstrates the radical distinctness of his discussion of freedom. The 20th-century touchstone for the distinction between positive and negative freedom is found in Isaiah Berlin's "Two Concepts of Liberty."[42] Following the liberal tradition that spans from Locke to Mill, Berlin defends negative freedom or liberty in the following manner: "I am normally said to be free to the degree to which no man or body of men interferers with my activity. Political liberty in this sense is simply the area within which a man can act unobstructed by others."[43] That is, *negative* freedom is simply the *absence* of external coercion. For instance, in the present moment my negative freedom is in full display insofar as no one is preventing from writing what I wish to write, either literally through force and direct coercion (actual violence, threats of it, imprisonment, etc., all of which are not outside of the realm of possibility depending on one's political situation) or, perhaps even more insidiously, through censorship. Positive freedom on the other hand, "derives from the wish of the individual to be his own master. I wish my life and decisions to depend on myself, not on external forces of whatever kind. I wish to be the instrument of my own, not of other men's, acts of will. I wish to be a subject, not an object; to be moved by reasons, by conscious purposes, which are my own, not by causes which affect me, as it were, from the outside."[44] What this entails is that unlike negative freedom, which is the mere absence of external coercion, positive freedom demands much more—it demands internal self-legislation, the ability to direct one's actions through one's deliberative processes. As we will also see shortly, positive freedom is not simply the freedom *from* x, but also the freedom *to be or do* x. That is, positive freedom demands that conditions are set by society for the possibility of full human agency which do not merely leave people to their own devices.

In the original dictation of the "Two Concepts of Liberty," which was presented as an Inaugural Lecture at Oxford, Berlin observes that the positive conception of freedom has its direct roots in the Kantian notion of self-legislation: "Kant, who was perhaps the most profound secular defender of this point of view, built his concept of freedom upon it. I am free because I am autonomous: I obey laws which I have invented for myself."[45] The positive concepts of freedom or liberty, then, is not simply a lack of interference from external forces, such that I am left to my own devices, but rather a notion of directed self-determination. Like Rousseau would also have it, I obey rules and laws that are of my own making (or the making of the body politic I belong to). Thus, this notion opens up a space of not only freedom *from* x (negative freedom) but freedom *to do* x (positive freedom). Berlin argues all throughout the essay that the two concepts of positive and negative freedom are in dialectical/logical conflict with one another, and that we ought not to think of them in interplay. Indeed, they are diametrically opposed to each other such that the notion of positive freedom ultimately undermines *all* freedom, including and especially negative freedom.

Berlin's main worry when it comes to positive freedom, a worry that I share (albeit to a much lesser extent than he does), is that when we enact positive freedom or the ability to self-legislate/do x, we run the risk of having this freedom completely subverted by a state apparatus that will coercively force people to behave in certain ways because it is for their own good.[46] The argument here is that the notion of self-legislation is taken at the level of the general will such that it loses its original, individual self-directedness and becomes the purview of society writ large rather than the individual. In many ways this echoes Schelling's own worry in the *New Deduction of Natural Right*, such that Schelling argues that it is unwarranted for the general will to force the individual will to act in certain pre-approved ways. Hence the need of dissent, as we have seen in detail in Chapter 1 of this study. Berlin further claims that at the heart of the "distortion" that occurs when freedom is understood as positive is a claim concerning the metaphysics of what constitutes the essence of the human being or a self. Once we begin with a hidden unstated premise, there opens up a space for an external authoritarian regime to step in and claim that a person who is not "properly" self-determining is not *truly* human. That is, one is not adequately or truly realizing or enacting their positive freedom. Given the manner in which society has historically marginalized women, people of color (mainly following a black/white binary that is a direct by-product of the colonial project of modernity), and the LGBTQ+ community, as not "truly" or "fully" or "naturally" human, and thus in need of coercive control, Berlin's worry is not far-fetched at all. Furthermore, this debate concerning the nature of freedom is not a peripheral issue in the history of political thought, but in fact the dividing line between two competing tendencies—those of classical liberalism and communitarianism. While both are umbrella terms that hold a variety of disparate thinkers under their shade, one can roughly think of them as divides surrounding the basic unit of society. Liberalism sees the individual as the starting point while communitarianism sees the community as the starting point. On the liberal end sit thinkers such as Locke, Mill, Berlin, and Nozick, and on the communitarian end sit Aristotle, Plato, Confucius, Rousseau, Hegel, Marx, and so on.[47] While Schelling has his foot in *both* traditions depending on the time period of his authorship, I am not particularly interested in a precise taxonomy here. Instead, I want to explore how the *Freedom Essay* can branch into and provide insight into this general debate, and, furthermore, how the positions defended in the essay deconstruct the debate from within. In order to accomplish this aim we must recover and weave back together the disparate Schellingian threads concerning the political that have been the subject of this study.

I contend here that Schelling is fundamentally correct in coupling freedom and necessity together much more strongly than classical liberalism would permit, both for theoretical and practical reasons, and, furthermore, that this coupling shows the limitations of a neat division between negative and positive freedom. From the theoretical or more speculative perspective, the notion of negative freedom as lack of external coercive restraint is most decidedly *formal*. That is, the simple leaving of the Other to their own devices, which is indeed a necessary moment of freedom, says very little to nothing about what the *essence* of freedom actually is. It apophatically points to what freedom is *not*—the guidance or interference of an Other, but not what it *is*. What it *is* is obviously not a being or entity like the pen in my hand or the desk on which I write, but, as Schelling clearly articulates, a *capacity*, a *possibility for something* (for good and evil, as we have seen). By merely delineating freedom as simple non-interference the classical liberal picture has presented, at best, a single side of a coin, and, at worst, only a mere piece of that single side. This is because the notion of negative freedom, in strictly excluding necessity out of its analysis, has failed to account for the ways in which freedom *concretely* manifests itself in the world, regardless of the interference or lack of interference from external agents. "The positive is always the whole or unity; that which opposes unity is severing of the whole, disharmony, ataxia of forces,"[48] writes Schelling. In removing the positive from discussions of freedom, classical liberalism has done precisely what the above suggests—it has distorted and opposed the unity of the whole from the outset. It has done so by making each individual an ontologically radical microcosm, a monad that does *not* reflect the rest of reality but is rather the author and arbiter of its own good. Notions concerning the status of the whole or the general/public good have been perpetually sidelined in a quest for the individual good (whatever form that may take is of course up to the individual, with Mill's caveat that it doesn't harm others). This is not to say that a Schellingian incursion into this debate will magically tip the balance in politics and political theory toward some kind of communitarian utopia where humanity works collectively and organically toward shared goals. On the contrary, by making freedom the freedom for good *and* evil Schelling has simultaneously shown the limits of negative formal freedom and put utopian thinking to rest permanently. There is no possibility for a perfect human order, for to be human is to be a creature that can *always* choose evil, and, indeed, we often make this choice. The Schellingian incursion merely demonstrates the one-sidedness of theories of freedom that do not include in themselves discussion of necessity.

How, then, are we to interpret the interrelationship between freedom and necessity? Between positive and negative freedom? "For the free is what acts only in accord with the laws of its own being and is determined by nothing else either in our outside itself,"[49] writes Schelling. The initial answer certainly looks to be nearly indistinguishable from the Kantian notion of self-legislation that worries Berlin so much. We are free when we follow laws or rules of our own construction, determined only by ourselves and nothing else. This, however, is an incomplete picture of what Schelling has in mind, although it is certainly one element of the picture, as it was in the early work and its concern with the unconditioned. Despite his admitted heavy debt to Kant, Schelling never quite settles on purely Kantian solutions to philosophical problems. Furthermore, this Kantian position is also caught in an individualist account of the self[50] that is at odds with the recognitive framework articulated in the *System of Transcendental Idealism*, the organic-Spinozistic picture of Nature as a vast interconnected whole (and the organic state of the Identity period), as well as the final conclusions of the *Freedom Essay*. As he states there:

> The general possibility of evil consists, as shown, in the fact that man, instead of making his selfhood in the basis, the instrument, can strive to elevate it into the ruling and total will and, conversely, to make the spiritual into himself into a means.[51]

And, furthermore:

> Thus is the beginning of sin, that man transgresses from authentic Being into Non-Being, from truth into lies, from light into darkness, in order to become a self-creating ground and, with the power of the *centrum* which he has within himself, to rule over all things.[52]

In elevating the individual self, what Schelling dubs a mere "instrument" in the quote above, to the level of Absolute, each self with its own radically different *telos*, the classical liberal project has *systematically* elevated the possibility of evil into a governing principle. As we have already seen in the previous chapter regarding our primordial responsibility to Nature, the atomic self looks to rule over all, to dominate, to subsume *everything* within its gaze as an item for consumption and personal "enjoyment," ignoring the obvious fact that it is a mere part of a greater whole upon which it is radically dependent.

Necessity, then, *must* be accounted for in our theory of freedom for multiple reasons. First of all, as Schelling clearly points out above, the two form a dialectical copula—neither is reducible to the other (except in the dark ground itself where all distinctions get devoured), but they are conceptually bound up. If all was within the confines of strict causal necessity, and thus necessity was the only guiding principle of any and all experience, then freedom would not even occur to us as a possibility, conceptual or otherwise. All events, be they cultural, political, biological, or physical, would proceed as they always have and always would, guided by ironclad fate. We would simply have no way of thinking of freedom in the first place in the same manner as witnessing something so utterly alien to the human experience, so *radically different*, that we would have no means of processing it. The same thing would be the case if we were some kind of god-like creature who can do as they please with no consequence or no impediment. In a counterfactual world where our freedom had no limitation, it simply would not occur to us that anything could be otherwise for a creature such as us, unless of course we had recourse to other creatures who did not experience the world in the same manner, in which case we would be able to conceptually divide the problem but not apply it to ourselves. But we don't wrestle with this either/or phenomenologically and practically. Secondly, and directly following the above argument, the very lived reality of our day-to-day existence *constantly* enforces upon us that the interplay between freedom and necessity is not at all a mere conceptual puzzle to be solved permanently by the philosopher in a well-placed article or book, but rather a concretely tangible facet of all that we do. Layers upon layers of necessity build a bedrock on which free action is possible. We are dependent upon Nature itself, we need food, shelter, medicine, education, and so forth, in order to exercise our freedom. While the condition for the possibility of freedom (for good *and* evil) is contained in the dark ground, this too would end up being an empty formal abstraction if there wasn't a world, a Nature, in which this agency is instantiated.

It is precisely this realization that led Jean-Paul Sartre to break with his own methodological starting points as they are found in *Being and Nothingness*[53] by the later part of his career as he incorporates Marxist insights into his phenomenological approach. As such, what he develops in the two-volume *Critique of Dialectical Reason* is a nuanced take of how freedom and necessity intertwine in the very concrete level of political *praxis*. I'd like to focus here on Sartre's often ignored later work for the purposes of further elucidating what Schelling has in mind concerning the interplay between freedom and necessity. For Sartre of the *Critique of Dialectical Reason*, freedom is no longer to be understood only in the phenomenological manner of Being-for-itself, which, in its purely intentional character, can be characterized as nothingness for it is no one thing (we can also simply characterize it as freedom since one can always intend otherwise for Sartre). Freedom is rather to be understood in terms of *praxis* or work, which is always conditioned by structural-material *necessity* of some sort. To put it in Sartrean terms, it is conditioned by a milieu of *scarcity*. As he points out, "the whole of human development, at least up to now, has been a bitter struggle against *scarcity*."[54] That is, human beings manifest their freedom in a material realm (Nature) where necessity derives or structures our free actions. Simply put, there is much needed to survive; human desire is inherently endless, and yet there isn't an infinite amount of resources on the planet (although we certainly act in the West as if there is). Like in the Hobbesian war of all against all, our freedom clashes with others due to the very necessity that is conditioned in the world by the milieu of scarcity. To ignore necessity when discussing freedom, be it the necessity of the dark ground where the two concepts become *completely* entangled or the more mundane necessity that drives human action in the political realm, is to leave freedom severely under-theorized. This makes freedom an empty abstraction instead of a living force. It is either the empty abstraction of the pure determinist who sees necessity in all actions, even with ample evidence to the contrary, or the empty abstraction of the classical liberal who believes that freedom is simple non-interference.

For Sartre scarcity and necessity, terms that are bundled throughout the book,[55] have a strange double-relationship insofar as he is unwilling to state that they are an *a priori* brute fact of human existence, and yet we cannot possibly get away from necessity. It is simultaneously universal *and* contingent. He argues:

> In spite of its contingency, scarcity is a very basic human relation, both to Nature and to men. In this sense, scarcity must be seen as that which makes us into *these* particular individuals producing *this* particular History and define *ourselves* as men. It is perfectly possible to conceive of dialectical *praxis,* or even of labour, without scarcity. In fact, there is no reason why the products required by the organism should not be practically inexhaustible, while practical operation was still necessary in order to extract them from the earth. In that case, the inversion of the unity of human multiplicities through the counter-finalities of matter would still necessarily subsist. For this unity is linked to labour as to the original dialectic. But what would disappear is our quality as *men,* and since this quality is dialectical, the actual specificity of our History would disappear too. So today everyone must recognise this basic contingency as the necessity which, working both through thousands of years and also, quite directly, through the present, forces him to be exactly what he is.[56]

While this might sound somewhat contradictory since Sartre is stating that there is nothing absolutely necessary about the current arrangement and yet it simultaneously must be so due to the material conditions, it *directly* echoes Schelling's transformation of transcendental inquiry in the *Naturphilosophie,* his discussion of history at the end of the *System of Transcendental Idealism,* as well as his coupling of freedom and necessity in the *Freedom Essay.* When one naturalizes the transcendental both naturalism and transcendentalism are irrevocably changed—the *a priori* takes on new and different connotations. The conditions for the possibility of my existence, subjectivity, and survival are simultaneously necessary and universal, and yet underpinned by *contingency,* as Sartre astutely argues above. That is, in order to propagate the kind of creature that I am, Nature *had* to develop in a certain direction, but there is nothing in Nature itself which guarantees said development (for instance, if the planet had not had experienced the Cretaceous-Paleogene extinction event then it could very well be the case that the planet was still roamed by dinosaurs, making these words impossible to write). As Michael Monahan points out in "Sartre's *Critique of Dialectical Reason* and the Inevitability of Violence," freedom and necessity, *praxis* and scarcity intertwine and cross-influence one another. He writes:

> Scarcity exists as a milieu that explains human *praxis,* in that it inevitably… conditions that *praxis,* but does not strictly cause it… Scarcity thus exists both as a kind of *exis,* or passive mode of Being, in that the material world contains within it the possibility of universal destruction, and it is a *praxis,* or active manifestation of freedom, in that we interiorize that scarcity and act it out through others and ourselves…In other words, human *praxis* (freedom) is both the cause and consequence of scarcity. It is a cause insofar as our choices and actions make use of and even exacerbate scarcity, and it is a consequence insofar as choices and actions are always conditioned by and intelligible within a milieu of scarcity.[57]

This entails that what Sartre dubs "The First Encounter with Necessity" is always-already in an interplay with freedom in its concrete manifestation in materiality. We cannot theorize, or even truly think, human freedom without its entanglement with necessity (except in a purely abstract way that has no bearing on reality) for the two co-constitute each other. Necessity, if it is to be a living concept in the Schellingian manner, cannot be a purely logical construct, for all logical constructs are devoid of content and thus essentially inert, but rather a part and parcel of the lived material reality in which freedom finds its efficacy. Thus, one cannot theorize freedom without theorizing necessity, and one never manifests itself without the other in human affairs. Any theory that purports to speak of freedom *must* address the material conditions in which this freedom is made manifest, even if, as is the case in Schelling's *Freedom Essay*, this freedom is ultimately found in the *centrum* that is hidden in the dark ground which is outside of our Natural categories. When this freedom is made manifest in Nature these material conditions make our freedom a living possibility and, as is often the case, materiality itself *both* constrains and is constrained by our free actions. Even more simply put, and looping us back to our discussion of Berlin as well, without access to concrete resources—food, shelter, clothing, medicine, and education, for instance—talk of freedom is an empty abstraction at best and a vicious cruelty at worst.

## Arendt and Schelling on the Nature of Evil in the Body Politic

With this framework in place we move to the final portion of our study of Schelling's political thought—the reality of evil itself in the body politic, which is a direct consequence of freedom itself. The 20th century has historically played out around the twin lived realities of freedom as the possibility for good and evil. Vehement fights for greater and greater freedom and inclusion for marginalized and oppressed peoples—fights which continue, and, indeed, *must* continue well into the 21st century—have simultaneously been accompanied by the greatest atrocities the world has ever known. The wholesale slaughter of millions of human beings by totalitarian governments have amply demonstrated how the freedom of a few, the taking of selfhood and making it into a ruling principle,[58] can be so shockingly abused on a mass scale that would make the devil himself cringe. What is particularly striking about the myriad horrors of the 20th century is that they were not generally perpetrated just by mad emperors and tyrants, although variants of those are most certainly responsible, but rather by "ordinary" humans. In Hannah Arendt's now classic formulation, mentioned merely once in a text that gets more chilling with each re-read, evil is characterized by its shocking *banality*.[59] Eichmann in particular amply demonstrates Schelling's point that the taking of the abyss of forces and focusing them on a self allows a mid-level bureaucrat, one with almost no strong convictions other than personal advancement, can result in a thereto unimaginable human tragedy.

The portrait that Arendt paints of Eichmann is not a flattering one, and indeed it simply could never be that give the atrocities committed,[60] but it is nuanced and quite difficult to wrap one's mind around. The chief difficulty lies in the fact that her portrayal constantly subverts one's expectations—expectations that are a natural result of knowing even the roughest details surrounding World War II. What one expects going into the book (or perhaps what I expected on my first read as an undergraduate despite the subtitle) is a portrait of a diabolically evil genius, a mind warped by hate and blind adherence to ideology. After all, who but one such as that could organize the death of so many? One goes in expecting cosmic horror, because cosmic horror allows one to sleep a little more easily, to say "well, this is just an evil man through and through, no wonder he was capable of such actions." But we don't get *any* of those qualities. No cosmic evil is to be found. Instead of the chilling monstrosity of one such as Joseph Kallinger, a 20th-century serial killer who famously states that God told him to kill three million people after killing his own family in order to himself become God, we get a middle manager—a middle manager who orchestrated the worst atrocity in human history and was both directly and indirectly responsible for the death of millions (Kallinger by contrast took the lives of three people and had the kind of childhood that essentially guarantees psychopathic tendencies).

Arendt shows Eichmann through layers of complexity, or in many ways a *lack* of complexity since he is shown to be not particularly remarkable on a personal level. Eichmann, who came to position in the Nazi party after many years as a vacuum salesman, is shown to be at many instances remorseful for his actions, and according to his lawyer "feels guilty before God"[61]; he had never in fact "directly" killed anyone[62] (in the sense that he had literally pulled a trigger or operated the Nazi killing machinery), and Arendt herself believes that he was probably not capable of doing so; he was thought by himself and others around him to be a law-abiding citizen[63]; he was by all accounts kind to his wife, children, other family and friends[64]; a person who half a dozen psychiatrists and psychologists evaluated as "normal"[65]; by all measures and accounts one of mediocre intellectual ability[66]; and perhaps most shocking of all given his actions, a member of a vehemently anti-Semitic party who personally did not harbor any feelings of hatred for the Jews.[67] While structural racism and ethnocentrism can be used to explain the possibility of racist or anti-Semitic tendencies without a direct recourse toward personal dispositional beliefs, and the notion of the unconscious could explain hidden motives (as we have seen in Chapter 2 of this work), it is nevertheless difficult to fathom how one is capable of such monstrous evil without such strongly held beliefs regarding the Other. It is indeed the banality of such a person that makes Arendt's account all the more difficult. It forces us to admit along with Schelling that virtually *any* person can do evil on this scale, a truth that is difficult to process and admit.

It certainly cannot be said of Arendt's account that it is somehow sympathetic of Eichmann, and it most certainly is not the case that this is somehow a good person caught up in bad circumstances. Indeed, her account is quite damning, showing how human freedom can be *so easily* perverted or distorted, allowing itself to manifest as evil. Furthermore, the evil here is not only the banal evil born of Eichmann's own freedom, but also takes on a *structural* form. It becomes all the more evil because the free action of a relatively few orchestrators can subvert the freedom of an entire nation, guiding it toward horror. Eichmann and Himmler (as we will shortly see) are shown by Arendt to be examples *par excellence* of the Schellingian notion of selfhood retreating back into itself, denying all that is deemed Other in an absurdly systematic fashion. According to Arendt, Eichmann had an "almost total inability ever to look at anything from the other fellow's point of view."[68] Obsessed with personal promotion, be it the selling of vacuums or a career in the SS which he stumbled upon basically by chance, Eichmann becomes incapable of truly recognizing the horror that he himself has caused, and he explicitly denies himself the ability of recognizing anyone who is Other by avoiding at all cost the places where he shipped millions of human beings toward a gruesome death. Describing an instance of his own organizational efforts central to orchestrating the Holocaust, Arendt reports in a direct quote what Eichmann saw in a trip to Poland:

> The Jews were in a large room; they were told to strip; then a truck arrived, stopping directly before the entrance to the room, and the naked Jews were told to enter it. The doors were closed and the truck started off. "I cannot tell [how many Jews entered], I hardly looked. I could not; I could not; I had enough. The shrieking, and . . . I was much too upset, and so on, as I told Müller when I reported to him; he did not get much profit out of my report. I then drove along after the van, and then I saw the most horrible sight I had thus far seen in my life. The truck was making for an open ditch, the doors were opened, and the corpses were thrown out, as though they were still alive, so smooth were their limbs. They were hurdled into the ditch, and I can still see civilians extracting teeth with tooth pliers. And then I was off-jumped into my car and did not open my mouth any more. After that time,

I could sit for hours beside my driver without exchanging a word with him. I had enough. I was finished. I only remember a physician in white overalls told me to look through a hole into the truck while they were still in it. I refused to do that. I could not. I had to disappear."[69]

Faced with the possibility of recognition, of witnessing the Other and the Other recognizing him for what he is and revealing it back to him, Eichmann is instead frozen in horror. The momentary blink of recognition that he experiences one-sidedly, amplified by the visceral terror of the moment, forces Eichmann away from the Other and back into the self (so much so that he is rendered incapable of speaking to even his own driver). He becomes psychologically and philosophically incapable of witnessing how it is that his own free actions have destroyed the freedom and very being of the Other—indeed have done so for countless Others.

Arendt sees all of this with complete clarity. Asking herself and her reader how it is that the Nazi membership was even capable of such acts—acts of such abject dehumanization that they should have been rendered impossible by the very seeing of what is being done. She articulates the crux of this issue in this manner:

> The murderers were not sadist or killers by nature; on the contrary, a systematic effort was made to weed out all those who derived physical pleasure from what they did . . . Hence the problem was how to overcome not so much their conscience as the animal pity by which all men are affected in the presence of physical suffering. The trick used by Himmler—who apparently was rather strongly afflicted by these instinctive reactions himself—was very simple and probably very effective; it consisted in turning these instincts around, as it were, in directing them toward the self. So that instead of saying: What horrible things I did to people!, the murderers would be able to say: What horrible things I had to watch in the pursuance of my duties, how heavily the task weighed upon my shoulders![70]

While it is indisputably the case that evil has a banality to it, insofar as the people who are perpetrating it are quite often not the comic book villains that we desperately need them to be in order to set our mind at ease, I believe that the most significant insight that Arendt provides (among many insights) in *Eichmann in Jerusalem* is found in the quote above rather than in dubbing evil "banal." It is the complete retreat into the self, the disavowal and *a priori* refusal to recognize the Other that has at all times given rise to the reality of evil. The underlying mechanisms of freedom and recognition, which ground the formation of subjectivity itself and our very humanity, ought to guard against mass scale atrocities such as the Holocaust. After all, faced with the humanity of the Other in the moment of recognition the self has a natural revulsion toward violence. Recognition is always-already at play, given that it structures the very formation of the self, such that it guards against freedom's propensity for evil, more often than not falling on the side of good when it comes to interpersonal relations. This is why Schopenhauer in *On the Basis of Morality*, Rousseau in the *Discourses*, and Mengzi in the *Mengzi* are essentially correct in claiming that natural empathy (or the related virtue of benevolence in Mengzi) is aroused at the sight of suffering, human or otherwise, thus rendering humans generally incapable of the evil such as the Holocaust. And yet evil is found in all places and all times, sometimes in mass genocides and currently in the rapid destruction of countless species (on top of the myriad human sufferings we inflict on each other). How can this possibly be true simultaneously?

First of all, Arendt has already amply illustrated how it can be true in her quote above and her observations of Eichmann. One *must* retreat wholly into the self, to usurp the forces that are spread through the whole into the self in order to so completely dehumanize the Other. We see this clearly at play above, we have seen it historically in the institution of slavery, and we have seen it in all too many genocides. As Sartre succinctly puts it, "this is the contradiction of racism, colonialism and all forms of tyranny: in order to *treat man like a dog,* one must first recognize him as a man."[71] That is, in order to retreat back into the self and tell the myth of the wholly Other that must be subjugated and eliminated, you first recognize the Other as a human and in fact witness their suffering, and *only then* can you flip the script and completely dehumanize them. Secondly, this flip, which Himmler employed so horrifically during World War II, becomes at times a guiding principle at the *structural* level. Institutions, laws, organizations, etc., are put in place that can carry the process indefinitely. These form a calcified *praxis* (Sartre's "practico-inert") that can subsist in virtual perpetuity. Finally, the individual retreat in the self and the structural *praxis* intertwine to form a vicious feedback loop, each reinforcing the other and thus making evil endemic.

# Conclusion

When we finally take stock of the debates surrounding freedom in the political discourse, the Schellingian intervention, despite its initial relative inaccessibility and seeming abstractness, in fact becomes exceptionally useful and brutally concrete. It illuminates a host of issues that must be thought through in the political realm. The nature of positive and negative freedom, the interplay between freedom and necessity (at the ontological and practical level), and the reality of human evil each have *clear* and lasting repercussion on our political discourse. What Schelling has demonstrated is that a *living, actual* concept of freedom must break through various philosophical abstractions of modernity (and perhaps even postmodernity) in order to dynamically ground our thinking in what freedom is truly like. We have seen that *neither* negative nor positive freedom fully capture our lived political reality, and only a dynamic interplay of the two at the level of *praxis*, along with the ontological structure which makes this dynamic interplay possible in the first place, can tell anything resembling full story. Furthermore, no matter how well we tell the story, Schelling is correct in arguing that there is *always* an indivisible remainder that can never subsume the profound messiness of the world into neat philosophical categories. It is in fact the case that being free is to be left to do as you please, as defenders of negative freedom argue. However, this is a single one-sided element of a multifaceted reality, for freedom also entails the ability to *self-determine*, along the concrete need for policies that allow us to do as we please (such as the education required to understand that you really can't just do as you please all the time and still live among others). Furthermore, this cannot be a purely *individualistic* account as found in classical liberalism, for as we have seen in the chapters concerning recognition and Nature, our autonomy is not absolute but rather relative. We *are not nor have ever been* purely autonomous agents. Our subjectivity is made possible only through intersubjectivity, as the *System of Transcendental Idealism* demonstrates (along with insights that prefigure it, such as Fichte's account in *Foundations of Natural Right*, along with subsequent accounts in Hegel, Husserl, Taylor, Honneth, and so forth). The condition for the possibility of subjectivity and the enactment of freedom *must* in fact be intersubjective. Furthermore, the conditions for the possibility of *intersubjectivity* are to a large extent naturalized in the *Naturphilosophie*, such that our interdependence is demonstrated *both* from the standpoint of the Ideal and the Real (the subjective and the objective).

One also sees that freedom ultimately cannot be so easily decoupled from necessity. The two concepts have often been conceptualized as diametrical opposites, enemies of each other even (depending on the philosopher one asks), such that one falls into the traps of a strict necessetarian determinism or a purely unpredictable libertarianism. Yet one sees in Schelling that freedom and necessity are intertwined at a level beyond Being in the dark ground of creation, and then one sees how this plays out in a world of human *praxis*. Through the lens of Sartre's *Critique of Dialectical Reason*, we see his disavowal of his own highly libertarian position in *Being and Nothingness* and *Existentialism is a Humanism*, such that their interconnection becomes apparent in the more mundane plane of material reality made possible by the dark ground.[72] *Praxis is freedom*, and both of them are always-already shaped by necessity, by the scarcity that has always been an inescapable reality of all political life. As such, a theory of freedom such as the one of Robert Nozick or Isaiah Berlin, both of whom claim that one is free if and only if negative freedom alone is maintained, blindly ignore some harsh truths about human reality and the body politic. If we quit our theorizing at the point of negative freedom, enacting a society in which all we care about is that others stay out of our business, we fail at the level of both theory and policy. Without an examination of materiality, necessity, and need, all which condition the possibility of freedom/agency at a level that is essentially pre-theoretical, we can never even achieve negative freedom in the first place (at least in any meaningful sense for day-to-day existence). Furthermore, freedom and necessity are an inherent dialectical copula—they are *always in actuality* held in dynamic tension. As Sartre shows, the very heart of *praxis* is an interplay between the two.

Finally, we have seen through our comparison of Schelling and Arendt how evil is to be properly theorized. Acknowledging the brute fact of its perpetual possibility in the case of humans, a possibility that turns into a guarantee that evil will emerge given the very nature of our freedom, evil ought to be taken seriously as a *political* problem. Schelling's account explains how ordinary humans, such as Eichmann, can be capable of massive atrocities (and countless small transgressions). Barring some outliers of people who commit evil due to mental illness, who would be in an exceptionally small minority since the severely mentally ill are much, much more likely to have evil done to them rather than to do it themselves, evil is clearly shown as not being an aberration due to insanity. It is done *freely* by those who retreat deeply into the self, thus dehumanizing and demonizing the Other. As history has repeatedly demonstrated, quite literally anyone can occupy the category of Other, most often for reasons that are *completely* arbitrary. As Sartre once again astutely observes: "if the Jew did not exist, the anti-Semite would invent him."[73] It is for this reason that the self *must* be radically "expanded," so to speak. Humanity is at a literal tipping point—environmental degradation, a fracturing of the general will, a degradation of public discourse to a Manichean fever pitch where both sides claim the mantle of light, and wide-spread systemic issues in the form of racism/sexism, *must* be collectively and aggressively addressed in a world which often seeks to pretend that they don't exist despite all evidence to the contrary. We have seen throughout this study how a thinker who, according to Habermas, is not a political one, can help us think through and address these most pressing of issues, perhaps even let us chart a path through them. This path, however, is fraught with difficulty. I fervently hope that it will be the Hegelian dialectic that will have the final word; that the correct current problems and contradictions will be systematically resolved and we can begin to live in equilibrium with ourselves and Nature. I am less and less confident of this potential resolution at this juncture. I see before us nothing but obscenely difficult *practical* work and Schelling as an unlikely guide.

# Conclusion

## A Schellingian Political Philosophy: Merging the Negative with the Positive

We have now come to the end of our study of Schelling as a political thinker. Questions still loom: What kind of politics is Schelling concretely advocating for? What does the Schellingian body politic look like? No easy answer is possible here, and I would ultimately argue that no single approach is all that particularly desirable at this historical moment. Humanity has problems that need to be addressed—problems that were basically unthinkable even during my own childhood (which is not particularly far behind me). These include *global* political problems such as climate change and the Anthropocene; an ongoing crisis of racism, which, coupled with climate change, will only exacerbate already existent problems with immigration and borders; the specter of fascism rises again; we are automating work at an unprecedented rate, offloading human labor to machines who will quite soon autonomously reproduce; the rise of Artificial Intelligence, which as of now seems like a foregone conclusion while it was mere science fiction only a short time ago; and so forth. Add to that a seemingly endless pandemic and what can be succinctly described as the fracturing of the general will in American politics (along with what feels like the fraying of the social contract itself).[1] Yet humans are still not radically different than what we have been in the last few thousand years, and political systems are variations on ideas that were foreseen and articulated at the dawn of philosophy across multiple traditions. Even as modernity and postmodernity have broken with many of them, they are still playing a variation on the older themes. We thus must find ways in which to reconcile and live with the profound changes coming to the world in the next twenty to thirty years with politics that hits its limits due to the very constitution of the human—our biological, social, and phenomenological constitution. My own turn to Schelling in particular came directly out of my concerns for the environment and the endemic misrecognition that plagues humanity. He seemed to me to have gazed much further ahead than most, and gave answers to questions that we didn't even know we had.

Schelling himself has roughly *three* political outlooks, and none are neatly reconcilable with the others.[2] First we saw his almost classical liberal argument for the emergence of natural right. Then there is a strong anti-statist[3] stance that one finds as early as the *Oldest Systematic Program of German Idealism* (whose authorship we will likely never untangle but can point to the trio of Schelling, Hegel, and Hölderlin) and as late as the *Stuttgart Seminars* of 1810. Thirdly, and finally, there is a strong statist or "conservative" turn at the end of his life when he writes the positive philosophy. In the *Oldest Systematic Program* one finds a youthful statement that will be again reiterated by Schelling later in the *Stuttgart Seminars*:

> I want to show that there is no idea of the *state* because the state is something *mechanical*, just as little as there is an idea of a *machine*. Only that which is the object of *freedom* is called *idea*. We must therefore go beyond the state! – Because every state must treat free human beings like mechanical works; and it should not do that; therefore it should cease.[4]

While this document lacks a clear author and is too short to have rigorous argumentation, serving instead as a general outline for systematic Idealist philosophy, there are many Schellingian ideas running through it. The clearest and most striking idea is the notion that the state is a rigid mechanism that serves to thwart the freedom of people. Merging there the organicist worldview of the *Naturphilosophie*, with its explicit argumentation against mechanistic thinking, with the lifelong concern that freedom is the single most important factor of the human essence, and perhaps even the very essence of the human, one can see what the authors are worried about. The state imposes rigid laws that are enforced in a mechanical manner from the top-down on individual human beings. We have seen in the second chapter how such laws take on a life of their own because of the ways in which misrecognition can be legitimated through a state-sanctioned legal framework that makes this misrecognition official and structural (to give but one clear example). As long as the state is in place, it simply functions in this manner.

This is repeated *explicitly* by Schelling in the *Stuttgart Seminars*, which, ironically, are given to an audience primarily composed of government officials.[5] There Schelling provides a succinct systematic summary of his philosophical output, and again broaches political theory. Dovetailing from a theme one finds in many world scriptures, and philosophically in Rousseau (at least in the West), Schelling argues again as he did in his early works on *Naturphilosphie* that humanity has moved from an initial condition of a pre-philosophical immersion in Nature or Being itself toward a dissolution of this unity, which is a condition that is mirrored by Nature's own disunity with God.[6] In order to replace this natural unity humanity has turned to a different sort of unity: that of the *state*.[7] Schelling writes: "the natural unity, this second nature superimposed on the first, to which man must necessarily take recourse, is the [modern] *state*; and to put it bluntly, the [modern] state is thus a consequence of the curse that has been placed on humanity. Because man no longer has God for his unity, he must submit to material unity."[8] Keeping in mind Schelling's own ontological edifice—the edifice that has been the hermeneutic guiding principle of our entire study here—we see the political framework not as something *un*natural or a break with Nature's order, but rather as the final human "superimposed" natural potency on the lower level potencies. However, at this point of his authorship, Schelling is not even remotely convinced that this state is a means for concretely preserving freedom, which is the direction that he was initially headed in 1796 with the *New Deduction* and where he will ultimately end up in the 1840s in the positive philosophy. Instead he proposes the opposite conclusion:

> it is my opinion that the state *as* such can never find a true and absolute unity and that all states are merely attempts at finding such a unity; that is,

doomed attempts to become a whole and, as such, subject to the fate of all organic life, namely to bloom, to ripen, eventually to age, and finally to die.[9]

Given the historical record and various cracks that are emerging in the world order in the contemporary world,[10] this statement is in some ways difficult to dispute. The state never quite unifies people, it very often mistreats its own citizens in ways visible and invisible, and actual states emerge and die off.

Schelling's next move is even more radical than the one above, for the one above can be taken to be a merely descriptive point about human institutions. What he argues next is not simply that states have a tendency to not achieve their aim to a long-lost unity, but rather that they are the direct causal explanation for a state of war between states[11] and various human evils. As he puts it, "to put the finishing touches on the image of a humanity that has entirely succumbed to a material, and indeed, existential, struggle, we merely need to add all those evils that can only originate in the state, such as poverty and mass hysteria."[12] While no direct elaboration is forthcoming from Schelling as to why this tendency is indicative of all state apparatuses, it is not difficult to tease out from his general worldview. The state solidifies misrecognition in a systematic fashion; poverty emerges because of the notions of money and wealth, which are not a part of the Nature's order as such but only a relatively new development in the history of our species; and we are *always* engaged in some kind of struggle, be it against each other, other states, or Nature itself (ever-increasingly and to the detriment of quite literally *everything and everyone* on the planet). Finally, leaning into the framework of the *Freedom Essay* published just a short year before the *Stuttgart Seminars* were given, Schelling brings in the notion of evil as a positive reality to explain how this keeps on happening, telling us that "it could indeed be argued that evil itself... wages the most vehement war against all *Being*; indeed, it wishes to destroy the very ground of all creation."[13] In our move toward a new way of existing after our initial immersion in Nature and Being, we form a unity that can never be a true unity, a state, and this state exacerbates evil. What could save us from this process? According to Schelling, only God can do so.[14]

With this he lays the seeds of the positive philosophy as found in such works as the *Philosophy of Mythology*, *Philosophy of Revelation*, and *The Grounding of the Positive* philosophy. There he argues the need of a state as a mechanism to combat our propensity to evil,[15] in a seemingly reactionary move. Yet I am not at all certain that he is being all that reactionary. As Žižek astutely observes regarding the transition between the "middle" Schelling of the *Freedom Essay/ Stuttgart Seminars/Ages of the World* and the "late" Schelling of the 1840s,

> This Schelling,[16] of course, is very close to Marx: the state is an externally imposed false unity which cancels the antagonistic splitting of society; it functions as a substitute for the lack of true social unity. In contrast to Hegel, for Schelling (even for the late Schelling) the State is not an actualization of Reason but always a contingent, unauthentic substitute for the lost true unity . . . This means that the late "reactionary" Schelling is also not to be easily dismissed: he clearly perceived how, owing to man's original Fall—owing, that is, to his constitutive "out-of-jointedness," loss of the primordial organic unity—the State is a contingent substitute-formation, not a "natural," authentic form of social unity; and yet precisely as such, and for that very reason it is *unavoidable*. Schelling thereby undermined the false alternative of either glorifying the State as an ethical kingdom or endeavoring to abolish it as the instrument of oppression.[17]

While I do not always see eye-to-eye with Žižek's interpretation of Schelling,[18] we are in complete agreement on this issue. I advocate that we hold fast to Schelling's ambivalences and ambiguities, for they mirror the ambivalences and ambiguities of the world itself. That is, I am not particularly concerned that Schelling has serious changes in his thinking about philosophy in general and political philosophy in particular. Instead we should hold on to his insights without worrying about his precise location on the political spectrum. As often as not situating a thinker along the said spectrum obfuscates as much as it reveals.

The reasons for this are manifold. First and foremost, it allows us to mine for insight into concrete sociopolitical problems without adherence to preordained lines of interpretation that pigeonhole us into claiming that Schelling is this or that kind of thinker (a proto-anarchist or proto-Marxist, a liberal, a conservative or even reactionary, etc.). For instance, it is the case that the state has in very many instances been the tool of oppression, has created poverty and war, and has involved large groups of people in what are avoidable conflicts. It is thus in need of heavy criticism and reform. Likewise, as we have seen in the first chapter where a more classically "liberal" Schelling was at play, dissent in word and deed is necessary to keep a state honest—to keep it from coercively forcing its will on the people it is meant to directly serve. From the vantage point of the 21st century, it is also *simultaneously* the case that the state can and *must* serve as the coordinator for large-scale projects that isolated groups of people and/or individuals simply cannot undertake on their own. The manufacture and distribution of a COVID vaccine, for instance, is one simple example that is indicative of this phenomenon, and one that we are seeing unfold in real time. States threw unprecedented piles of money at speedy development of vaccines and treatments, they were able to impose coordinated lockdowns in order to save lives, and they have access to vast distribution channels that NGOs and private individuals simply do not and cannot ever really have. Also, despite their half-hearted attempts to address climate change, it is nonetheless the case that the problem is of such a staggeringly large nature that nothing other than a vast, international state effort is necessary (albeit perhaps insufficient, for we also need personal change) to even begin addressing the problem. It turns out that we must be both critical of the state and that we also need it with all of its deeply messy imperfections.

Secondly, for those of us working in political philosophy and critical theory, we must be mindful of how *new* problems emerge within one's framework that cannot be addressed with preestablished conceptual tools. The single biggest such phenomenon surrounds what I take to be the most important issue facing humanity: climate change. Until quite recently, political philosophy has not even broached the issue, instead focusing on the sociopolitical realm as if it is divorced from the Natural order. Indeed, many classical political theorists ranging from Aristotle to Hegel to Rawls, have *explicitly* thought that we are or even ought to be removed from Nature. That the social and political are different realms from the Natural. That is no longer tenable. In order to theory our responsibility to each other in the early 21st century we now have to theory our responsibility to Nature qua Nature. Nature itself is the condition for the possibility of any and all moral/political responsibility in the first place, and our pretense otherwise is what has led us to the mess we are in to begin with.

In order to rectify and correct this mess, if such a concerted large-scale action is even possible at this juncture,[19] we have to account for our responsibility to Nature. When we account for it, we have to understand not just scientifically, but *philosophically* what Nature is in the first place, and Schelling is one of a tiny handful of thinkers who has done this work. We must mine for insight wherever it is to be found if we to either make sense of the world or work toward bettering it (knowing with Schelling that the world will never resemble a utopia—the lived reality of evil we saw in Chapter 4 all but guarantees utopia's impossibility).

Finally, I want to make a renewed call here for something that Schelling advocates at the end of his life—the need for a philosophical, rational religion. A return to the messy contingency of positive philosophy, filtered here through the lens of political theory. Concerning the capacity of philosophy to achieve such an aim, Schelling writes: "if I see in philosophy the means for healing the fragmentation of our time, then I do not thereby mean a feeble philosophy that is mere artifact. I mean a robust philosophy of the type that can measure up to life."[20] This is the kind of philosophy that we need yet again when life is fragmented in ways that are unimaginable in Schelling's time, and religion increasingly falls by the wayside. It is also this kind of philosophy that is necessary to answer questions of *meaning*,[21] questions which the empirical sciences are woefully inadequate at answering. The question of meaning is not peripheral to the political project, but rather caught right in the middle of it. In our never-ending quest for supposed "progress," we have seemingly forgotten what we are progressing to and why we are progressing toward it, especially now that our technological progress has seemingly led us to the precipice of catastrophe. What is the purpose of our political and economic institutions? Are those institutions working for humans in a manner most consistent for fostering the well-being for individuals and the collective? Perhaps even more bluntly, why should we even get out of bed in the morning?

We are in dire need of a philosophy of life—a philosophy that will directly address the contingent search for meaning. Schelling thus proposes a new kind of metaphysics, and, as I have argued throughout the book, metaphysical questions are in many regards political questions. "Human affairs do not allow themselves to be governed by mathematics, physics, natural history (I revere these sciences highly), or even poetry and art. The true understanding of the world is provided by precisely the right metaphysics, which for this very reason has from time immemorial been called the royal science."[22] It is long past due that we restore metaphysics to its rightful throne and directly engage the public philosophically. No matter how much the sciences that Schelling rightfully reveres in the same manner that I do tell us about the world, they are simply incapable of answering the deeper questions of meaning, and some of those same sciences have now made possible the continued exploitation of the natural world. What does this metaphysics concretely look like? We have already seen the "negative," or critical, version from the inception of Schelling's thought until his middle period. It is an empirically informed, *a posteriori* inquiry which retroactively finds the necessity within the empirical contingency for an overarching cohesive worldview.[23] As Schelling further observes at the final stages of his authorship (in the *Grounding of Positive Philosophy*), "the science of reason, contrary to excluding experience, requires it."[24] It moves away from a static notion of substance to a dynamic notion of process, retaining transcendental elements as relatively stable channels of flow within a self-organizing system. Adding to this cohesive, but yet negative notion that is still operating at the conceptual level rather than the level of life itself is "positive" philosophy, which, due to its inherently contingent essence, can never be neatly summed up or tied up. It is an ongoing, meditative praxis on life itself, what Wirth dubs "the conspiracy of life," done from a life that cannot and will not ever stand still.

Despite the importance of the negative philosophical element, Schelling argues that negative philosophy captures life or Being itself only in thought.[25] Negative philosophy cleared the ground for positive philosophy to emerge, but positive philosophy is not merely parasitic on the negative. The negative "hands over its final concept to the positive as a demand."[26] A demand for what? For a new beginning—an "absolute beginning."[27] This new beginning does not look for Being itself, according to Schelling, but rather that which is "*above* Being,"[28] thus bringing him full circle back to Neoplatonism. While he was more critical of the Neoplatonic approach in earlier texts (presumably due to his lingering pantheism), while at the same time retaining a core Neoplatonic logic without which his work cannot be easily untangled, here he not only invokes the core concepts of the tradition but also praises it as inaugurating a positive philosophy in the ancient world.[29] Going further than mere praise, Schelling directly connects the Neoplatonic approach to positive philosophy itself due to the very structure of the distinction between positive and negative philosophy. While negative philosophy is a critical science of the conceptual, one that can be traced quite neatly from Leibniz to Kant to post-Kantian Idealism, positive philosophy must break free of purely conceptual thinking in order to theorize the mess that is life itself. But to theorize this mess it doesn't just start from the mess itself. Instead it begins with that which is beyond thought: "if positive philosophy starts out from that which is external to all thought, it cannot begin with a being that is external to thought in a merely relative sense, but only with a being that is *absolutely* external to thought."[30] What Schelling is referring to is of course God, or whatever one wishes to call the Being beyond all Being, and, as Kierkegaard will spend an entire pseudonymous authorship performatively demonstrating, the relation to this "Being" external to all thought is *existential* through and through. A positive philosophy, it seems to me, is not so much written, but rather lived. It entails a fundamental restructuring of what we are and ought to be, from the ground up, and we must continue to do it for the sake of life itself. Life itself must be channeled in different directions than our current trajectory if we are to avoid at least some of the evils that we are so prone to commit and recommit, and Schelling emerges again as an unlikely guide to this ongoing process. The positive philosophy he left us with is by no means a final word—it is yet another demand for a new beginning—one where philosophy is not merely theorized but rather *lived*.

# Notes

## Introduction

1. Jürgen Habermas, "Dialectical Idealism in Transition to Materialism: Schelling's Idea of a Contraction of God and its Consequences for a Philosophy of History," in *The New Schelling*, ed. Judith Norman and Alaistair Welchman (London: Continuum/Bloomsbury Academic, 2004), 43.

2. See Emiliano Acosta, "Recognition and Dissent: Schelling's Conception of Recognition and Its Contribution to Contemporary Political Philosophy," in *Recognition—German Idealism as an Ongoing Challenge*, ed. Christian Krijnen (Leiden: Brill Publishing, 2014), 143–64.

3. Theresa Fenichel, *Schelling, Freud, and the Philosophical Foundations of the Unconscious: Uncanny Belonging* (New York: Routledge, 2019).

4. Matt ffytche, *The Foundation of the Unconscious: Schelling, Freud and the Birth of the Modern Psyche* (Cambridge: Cambridge University Press, 2012).

5. S. J. McGrath, *The Dark Ground of Spirit: Schelling and the Unconscious* (New York: Routledge, 2012).

6. This approach is broadly inspired by Iain Hamilton Grant's *Philosophies of Nature after Schelling* and Jason Wirth's two studies of Schelling, *The Conspiracy of Life* and *Schelling's Practice in the Wild*. Rather than thinking of him as a historical curiosity of a bygone era, both thinkers show just how deeply relevant he is to contemporary issues, how truly *untimely* he is.

7. See Charlotte Alderwick, *Schelling's Ontology of Powers* (Edinburgh: Edinburgh University Press, 2021) for how the notion of "grounding" correlated to contemporary debates in the analytic tradition.

8. Dale E. Snow, *Schelling and the End of Idealism* (New York: SUNY Press, 1996).

9. Andrew Bowie, *Schelling and Modern European Philosophy: An Introduction* (New York: Routledge, 1993).

10. One of the most theoretically fruitful elements of Bowie's introduction is the engagement of Schelling with the 20th-century French turn toward *difference* (Derrida and Deleuze, in particular). Part of what this shows is simply how far ahead of his

time Schelling was on a variety of issues, which perhaps explains why commentators did not know quite what to do with his work for so long.

11  His body of work is what solidified my initial interest in German Idealism as an early graduate student, and he has continued to excavate neglected corners of what I take to be one of history's most productive and creative philosophical period.

12  Frederick C. Beiser, *German Idealism: The Struggle Against Subjectivism* (Cambridge, MA: Harvard University Press, 2002), 465–595.

13  Manfred Frank, *Eine Einführung in Schellings Philosophie* (Frankfort: Suhrkamp, 1985).

14  Xavier Tilliette, *Schelling une Philosophie en Devinir vol, 1 and 2* (Paris: Librairie Philosophique J. Vrin, 1970).

15  His biography of Schelling, simply titled *Schelling Biographie*, is also quite useful for situating Schelling in his historical milieu.

16  Bruce Matthews, *Schelling's Organic Form of Philosophy: Life as a Schema of Freedom* (New York: SUNY Press, 2011).

17  Bernard Freydberg, *Schelling's Dialogical Freedom Essay* (New York: SUNY Press, 2008).

18  See J. G. Fichte and F. W. J. Schelling, *The Philosophical Rupture Between Fichte and Schelling: Selected Texts and Correspondence (1800–1802)*, trans. and ed. Michael G. Vater and David W. Wood (New York: SUNY Press, 2012).

19  Immanuel Kant, *Critique of Pure Reason*, trans. and ed. Paul Guyer and Allen W. Wood (Cambridge: Cambridge University Press, 1998), A82/B108.

20  The more I study Leibniz in depth the more I am convinced that he does *not* in fact belong on this list for the simple reason that he more than perhaps any of the Idealists that follow him, be they critical or Absolute, has a metaphysical position deeply informed by his own studies into the natural world.

21  Immanuel Kant, *Theoretical Philosophy after 1781*, ed. Henry Allison and Peter Heath (Cambridge: Cambridge University Press, 2002), 183–270.

22  A statement that is later disputed by Schopenhauer in the *World as Will and Representation* due to Schopenhauer's insistence that we do in fact have a direct line to the noumenal insofar as we too are first and foremost will.

23  Immanuel Kant, *Critique of Judgement*, trans. Werner S. Pluhar (Indianapolis: Hackett Publishing, 1987), 15.

24  Ibid., 23.

25  J. G. Fichte, *The Science of Knowledge*, trans. and ed. Peter Heath and John Lachs (Cambridge: Cambridge University Press, 1982).

26  Ibid., 94.

27  Ibid.

28  Ibid., 96; footnote.

29  Ibid., 97–8.

30  Ibid., 104.

31  Ibid., 107.

32  G. W. F. Hegel, *The Difference Between Fichte's and Schelling's System of Philosophy*, trans. and ed. H. S. Harris and Walter Cerf (New York: SUNY Press, 1977).

33  Fichte, *Science of Knowledge*, 120.

34  Ibid., 127–8. I leave this final portion underdeveloped simply because Fichte himself is unsure where to go with it. He spends much of the 1794 *Wissenschaftslehre* trying to flesh this notion out, but he ultimately abandons it in favor of his practical philosophy because it does not produce the result he needs to make his system stable.

35  See Fichte and Schelling, *The Philosophical Rupture Between Fichte and Schelling*.

36  See Snow, *Schelling and the End of Idealism*, 14–24; Frederick Beiser, *The Fate of Reason: German Philosophy from Kant to Fichte* (Cambridge, MA: Harvard University Press, 1987), 44–127 (one of the most sustained discussions of the topic in English); and Dieter Henrich, *Between Kant and Hegel: Lectures on German Idealism* (Cambridge, MA: Harvard University Press, 2003), 82–96.

37  This is also now true for the reception of modern philosophers in the English-speaking world, especially among a newer set of analytic philosophers who have turned to the history of philosophy. See Michael Della Rocca, *Spinoza* (New York: Routledge, 2008).

38  Baruch Spinoza, *Ethics*, trans. Samuel Sherly and ed. Seymour Feldman (Indianapolis: Hackett Publishing, 1992).

39  See Della Rocca, *Spinoza*.

40  Spinoza, *Ethics*, 66; emphasis in original.

41  See Jason M. Wirth, *The Conspiracy of Life: Meditations on Schelling and His Time* (New York: SUNY Press, 2003). This is one of the primary works that rescues Schelling from the same dustbin of history to which Spinoza was once relegated, and is an indispensable read for anyone who wishes to study Schelling as a living thinker rather than a mere historical curiosity.

42  See Robert F. Brown, *The Later Philosophy of Schelling: The Influence of Boehme on the Works of 1809–1815* (Cranbury: Associated University Presses, 1977). Brown's study has both an excellent overview of Böhme's work as well as sustained engagement with the repercussion of his ideas for Schelling's overall intellectual trajectory between the publication of the *Freedom Essay* and the many drafts of the *Ages of the World*.

43  See McGrath, *The Dark Ground of Spirit*, 44–81.

44  Brown, *The Later Philosophy of Schelling*, 48.

45  This is seen all throughout Böhme's corpus, and one can see how it also influences thinkers such as Schopenhauer and the subsequent psychoanalytic tradition.

46  Jacob Boehme, *The Way to Christ*, trans. Peter Erb (New York: Paulist Press, 1978), 127.

47  See Jacob Boehme, *Mysterium Pansophicum: Or Thorough Report on the Earthly and Heavenly Mysterium*. This translation is found in F. W. J. Schelling, *Philosophical Investigations into the Essence of Human Freedom*, trans. Jeff Love and Johannes Schmidt (New York: SUNY Press, 2006), 85–98.

48  Boehme, *Mysterium Pansophicum*, 85.

49  Ibid.

50  Ibid., 86.

51  Ibid., 86–7.

52  For the sake of focus I have chosen to look at the two works that I take to be the most pertinent to our questions: *Ideas for a Philosophy of Nature* and *First Outline for a System of the Philosophy of Nature*. I find the second to be especially fruitful for the overall argument that I am making concerning the direct political responsibility we have to Nature.

53  F. W. J. Schelling, "New Deduction of Natural Right," in *The Unconditioned in Human Knowledge: Four Early Essays*, trans. Fritz Marti (Lewisburg: Bucknell University Press, 1980), 219–52.

54  Ibid., 221.

55  Ibid., 223.

56  Ibid.

57  Ibid., 224–5.

58  J. J. Rousseau, *Social Contract and Other Later Political Writings*, trans. and ed. Victor Gourevitch (Cambridge: Cambridge University Press, 1997).

59  Ibid., 59.

60  Ibid., 64.

61  See Isaiah Berlin, *Liberty*, ed. Henry Hardy (Oxford: Oxford University Press, 2017), 166–217.

62  See Laurence D. Cooper, *Rousseau, Nature, and the Problem of the Good Life* (University Park: Pennsylvanian University Press, 1999), ix.

63  Schelling, "New Deduction of Natural Right," 226; emphasis Schelling's.

64  Ibid., 223; footnote.

65  F. W. J. Schelling, *System of Transcendental Idealism*, trans. Peter Heath (Charlottesville: University Press of Virginia, 1978), 5.

66  See Grant's *Philosophies of Nature after Schelling* and Iain Hamilton Grant, "The Hypothesis of Nature's Logic in Schelling's *Naturphilosophie*," in *The Palgrave Handbook of German Idealism*, ed. Matthew C. Altman (London: Palgrave-Macmillan, 2014), 478–98.

67 See Schelling, *System of Transcendental Idealism*, 169 for a brief summary. That summary is developed into a full account in the next dozen or so pages.

68 See Robert R. Williams, *Hegel's Ethics of Recognition* (Berkeley: University of California Press, 1997). This book also has a very brief foray into Schelling's conception of recognition, but Williams argues that Schelling's notion is not as developed as either Fichte or Hegel's (see 39–45). While this is certainly true in one sense, given the relatively small amount of space that Schelling devotes to the idea in comparison to Fichte and Hegel, in another sense there emerges from a more holistic read of Schelling's overall work that recognition is an indispensable component of the potency of Nature that deals with the human social realm.

69 See Robert R. Williams, *Recognition: Fichte and Hegel on the Other* (New York: SUNY Press, 1992).

70 Schelling, *System of Transcendental Idealism*, 169.

71 Ibid.

72 Ibid., 170.

73 Hegel's ultimate position can also be described as coherentist, which means that he is simply not concerned with the idea of a single grounding principle. As a matter of fact, he would explicitly reject this project.

74 Schelling, *System of Transcendental Idealism*, 159.

75 McGrath, *The Dark Ground of Spirit*, 11.

76 Which itself in many ways breaks with this development given that the first edition has its foot in transcendental idealism and the other in the Identity Philosophy that is the hallmark of his early 1800s work.

77 The situation is different when one examines the primary Daoist works in China (*Daodejing*, *Zhuangzi*, and *Leizi*), where the concern for our treatment of Nature dates as far back as the 6th century BCE. It is also quite different in Native American thought where it is, and continues to be, of central importance. Likewise, one can find in elements of Chan and Zen Buddhism a concern for Nature qua Nature. Dogen's *Mountains and Waters Sutra* is one fantastic instance of an environmental philosophy.

78 I use the term "speculative" here in the German Idealist sense rather than its colloquial contemporary use.

79 Schelling, *Philosophical Investigations into the Essence of Human Freedom*, 29.

# Chapter 1

1 His later work can be characterized as a political *theology*, but this lies well outside the scope of the current project. For a look at this period of his thought, one should consult Saitya Brata Das, *The Political Theology of Schelling* (Edinburgh: Edinburgh

University Press, 2016) and Sean J. McGrath, *The Philosophical Foundations of the Late Schelling: A Turn to the Positive* (Edinburgh: Edinburgh University Press, 2021). Both of these works situate Schelling within a set of contemporary discourses concerning eschatology, and navigate through the canonical continental thinkers (Heidegger, Derrida, Benjamin, Levinas, etc.). While I have incorporated their insights throughout the work, my interest lies squarely at the intersection of metaphysics and classical/critical political thought (Locke, Hobbes, Rousseau, Hegel, Marx, Rawls, Adorno, Horkheimer, Habermas, Honneth, etc.). It is in this vein that I read Schelling's early work, and, as I point out in the Introduction, articulate a Schellingian Critical Theory that looks to address the myriad of political crises of the 21st century.

2 This phrase is found in a letter to Hegel written in 1795, shortly before the publication of the *New Deduction* while the two are on friendly terms.

3 I follow Emiliano Acosta in this conceptualization. In a rare piece on Schelling's political philosophy. Acosta argues that "dissent" plays a central role in the "New Deduction of Natural Right." I build on that work here. See Acosta, "Recognition and Dissent," 143–64.

4 F. W. J. Schelling, "New Deduction of Natural Right (1796)," in *The Unconditional in Human Knowledge*, trans. Fritz Marti (Lewisburg: Bucknell University Press, 1980), 221, 2.

5 Ibid., 221, 3.

6 Ibid., 222, 5.

7 Ibid., 222, 9.

8 Ibid., 223, 10.

9 Fichte's *Foundations of Natural Rights* and Schelling's "New Deduction of Natural Right" were written during roughly the same period of time (1795/6) and published roughly around the same time. Given that they were not explicitly collaborating on this project it is somewhat striking how closely they resemble and overlap one another in content if not in presentation. Perhaps this is due to an overlap in methodology and starting assumptions on both of their parts. The public falling out between the two does not occur until a few years later in the early 1800s, even though cracks were showing much earlier. Schelling wanted to have the *New Deduction* published before Fichte so that his work was not seen as derivative of Fichte's. For a discussion between the convergence and divergence of the two texts, see Michael Vater, "Schelling Aphorisms on Natural Right and (1976/7) and Fichte's *Grundlage des Naturrechts*," *Rights, Bodies and Recognition: New Essays on Fichte's Foundations of Natural Right*, ed. Tom Rockmore and Daniel Breazeale (New York: Routledge, 2019), 196–213.

10 J. G. Fichte, *Foundations of Natural Right*, trans. Michael Bauer and ed. Frederick Neuhauser (Cambridge: Cambridge University Press, 2000), 59.

11 Schelling, "New Deduction of Natural Right," 223, 12.

12 It might in fact be unique to Schelling alone in the West, at least during modernity.

13 As we will see in Chapter 3 of this study.

14 It is for reasons such as these that I find Schelling's work to be so deeply relevant to current political concerns. In light of the fact that Nature was seen as something to conquer and shape throughout the vast majority of modernity, Schelling stands as a lone outlier. He is very much untimely, which is why it is not at all surprising that the revaluation of his thought is only in full swing now, some two hundred years after his most productive period.

15 As I have already mention in the introduction, Iain Hamilton Grant decisively shows the prevalence of *Naturphilosophie* all throughout each phase of Schelling's philosophical output in his masterful reappraisal *Philosophies of Nature after Schelling*.

16 Schelling, "New Deduction of Natural Right," 223, 13.

17 Ibid., 223, 15 and accompanying footnote. The footnote is Schelling's own.

18 While Schelling remains at the forefront of this development from a historical lens, it would be irresponsible to claim that he is unique in his articulation of dissent as a primary mechanism for the assertion of freedom and agency. Hegel and Axel Honneth (who is following the early, unpublished Hegel) clearly have a similar notion in the form of a "struggle." For instance, see Axel Honneth's seminal *The Struggle for Recognition: The Moral Grammar of Social Conflicts*, Robert R. William's two studies on recognition (*Recognition: Fichte, Hegel and the Other* and *Hegel's Ethics of Recognition*), and my own reconstruction of recognition in Fichte, Hegel, and Honneth. Since this is a study on Schelling, I have set this work aside in order to allow Schelling to shine in his own light.

19 This is a central component of Axel Honneth's overall argument in the *Struggle for Recognition*. He argues throughout the book that freedom over the last two hundred years has emerged through a series of expanding struggles for inclusion of previously marginalized groups of human beings.

20 For example, the 2015 film *Suffragette* portrays women learning the Japanese martial art jiu-jitsu in order to defend themselves against policy violence. For an academic analysis, see Wendy Rouse and Beth Slutsky "Empowering the Physical and Political Self: Women and the Practice of Self-Defense, 1890–1920," *The Journal of the Gilded Age and Progressive Era* 13, no. 4 (2014): 470–99.

21 In *Hegel, Haiti and Universal History* Susan Buck-Morss argues that Hegel developed his account of recognition explicitly through his observations of what was happening in Haiti. While I am highly appreciative of the account of recognition in that work, I have some reservations that this was Hegel's primary inspiration. We simply lack the full historical evidence that would be necessary to corroborate this claim, and I think the German "*Knecht*" that has been translated as "slave" into English is much more

accurately construed as "bondsman" or "servant." As such, the more likely scenario that he had in mind is the division between the aristocracy and the commoners that would have been more indicative of life in Germany at the time. This, however, is a topic for an entirely different study. See Susan Buck-Morss, *Hegel, Haiti and Universal History* (Pittsburgh: Pittsburgh University Press, 2009).

22  Jeremy D. Popkin, *A Concise History of the Haitian Revolution* (Hoboken: Wiley-Blackwell Press, 2012), 5.

23  Laurent Dubois, *Avengers of the New World: The Story of the Haitian Revolution* (Cambridge, MA: Belknap/Harvard University Press, 2004).

24  David Geggus, *The Haitian Revolution: A Documentary History* (Indianapolis: Hackett Publishing, 2014).

25  C. L. R. James, *The Black Jacobins: Toussaint L'Overture and the San Domingo Revolution* (New York: Random House, 1963).

26  Popkin, *A Concise History of the Haitian Revolution*, 14.

27  Ibid., 2.

28  Dubois, *Avengers of the New World*, 30.

29  Popkin, *A Concise History of the Haitian Revolution*, 14.

30  Dubois, *Avengers of the New World*, 40.

31  Ibid., 45.

32  Ibid., 50.

33  See Dubois, *Avengers of the New World*, 58; Popkin, *A Concise History of the Haitian Revolution*, 18.

34  Dubois, *Avengers of the New World*, 52.

35  Ibid., 55.

36  Geggus, *The Haitian Revolution*, 25.

37  Ibid., 28.

38  Ibid., 29–32.

39  Ibid., 32.

40  Dubois, *Avengers of the New World*, 56.

41  C. L. R. James's *The Black Jacobins* is indispensable for analyzing the broader political picture.

42  Popkin, *A Concise History of the Haitian Revolution*, 126.

43  Ibid., 138.

44  Dubois, *Avengers of the New World*, 103–4.

45  Ibid., 126.

46  Ibid., 127.

47  Quoted in Popkin, *A Concise History of the Haitian Revolution*, 44. Also see Dubois, *Avengers of the New World*, 127; and Geggus, *The Haitian Revolution*, 88. Geggus has the full letter that was written to the General Assembly.

48  Schelling, "New Deduction of Natural Right," 224, 21.

49  Ibid., 224, 21.

50  Although Schelling does not conceptualize it in the stark Hobbesian terms of the "war of all against all," the net effect of unbridled freedom strikes me as being quite Hobbesian in nature.

51  Schelling, "New Deduction of Natural Right," 225.

52  This chaos is further exacerbated when we redefine freedom as the freedom for good and evil, as we will see in our exploration into Schelling's *Philosophical Investigations into the Essence of Human Freedom* at the final portion of the book.

53  Schelling, "New Deduction of Natural Right," 225, 30.

54  This is the difference between *Moralität*, primarily concerned with a notion of duty that is criticized by Hegel in the *Philosophy of Right* for its overt formalism and lack of concrete content, and *Sittlichkeit* or Ethical Life, which is realized only through actually existing institutions.

55  Schelling, "New Deduction of Natural Right," 226, 34.

56  For an overview of the general will as it unfolds in Rousseau and a dozen other thinkers, see *The General Will: An Evolution of Concept*, ed. James Farr and David Lay Williams (Cambridge: Cambridge University Press, 2015).

57  Judith N. Shklar, *Men and Citizens: A Study of Rousseau's Social Theory* (Cambridge: Cambridge University Press, 1969), 184.

58  J. J. Rousseau, *The Social Contract and Other Later Political Writings*, ed. and trans. Victor Gourevitch (Cambridge: Cambridge University Press, 2019), 52. Emphasis Rousseau's.

59  Ibid., 62.

60  Ibid.

61  See Patrick Riley, "The General Will Before Rousseau," in *The General Will: An Evolution of a Concept* (Cambridge: Cambridge University Press, 2015), 3–71. Riley unearths an amazing amount of literature in a relatively short space concerning how the concept was being used in theological circles to describe the will of God, which a long lineage that runs through much of the natural law traditions in Christianity and moves from the medieval period into modernity. Rousseau's version, however, is not a religious one, but a Platonic interpretation which remains viable (albeit unlikely given Rousseau's general disregard for metaphysical speculation).

62  See Shklar, *Men and Citizens*, 184–97; Tracy B. Strong, "The General Will in Rousseau and after Rousseau," *The General Will: The Evolution of a Concept,* 307–29.

63  David Lay Williams, "The Substantive Elements of Rousseau's General Will," in *The General Will: The Evolution of a Concept*, 219.

64  Immanuel Kant, *Practical Philosophy: The Metaphysics of Morals,* trans. and ed. Mary J. Gregor (Cambridge UK: Cambridge University Press, 1996), 409.

65  Ibid., 409.

66  Ibid., 411.

67  Ibid., 414–15.

68  Schelling, "New Deduction of Natural Right," 226, 36.

69  We will briefly turn to this text in the Conclusion of the book, as it remains one of tantalizingly brief glimpse into what overall political organization Schelling had in mind. I demonstrate there that there is no single answer possible to this question since he articulates at least *three* distinct possibilities for what political life ought to look like, and each of the three is substantially different. My ultimate contention is that there is no *a priori* way to know what political organization is suitable to the historical moment, so we may freely incorporate insight, tempered by empirical research from the social sciences, depending on what the current political climate has in store for us. As such, I ultimately reside in the non-ideal theory camp of political thought.

70  While I think that Rousseau has *definite* communitarian tendencies, insofar as he has a long-standing concern with the good of the community all throughout his writings, I tend to think that Tracy B. Strong is correct in pointing out that Rousseau's communitarianism is not found at the level of the general will (Strong, 312). Rousseau likewise has individualistic tendencies and is notorious for lacking particular care about his own inconsistencies.

71  On a personal note here, I was born and raised in a deeply communal culture, so the "intuitions" that were presented as obvious by folk in the analytic liberal tradition were often explicitly at odds with my own.

72  Schelling, "New Deduction of Natural Right," 227.

73  Ibid., 227, 42, 43, and 44; all emphasis Schelling's.

74  "Enter" here should not be taken to literally mean the coming in of an individual into society. We are always-already thrown into the social. It simply means that the actuality of freedom can only be theorized within a social context.

75  Schelling, "New Deduction of Natural Right," 228, 48.

76  The question of whether Schelling places primacy on the practical over the theoretical is much more complex than whether Fichte does so. While Fichte consistently prioritizes it in the *Foundations of Natural Right, System of Ethics,*

*Nova Methodo 1796/99*, and so on, Schelling is less explicitly concerned with it after his early more Fichtean period. Even in the early period Schelling is already concerned with theoretical issues in *Naturphilsophie*; issues which Fichte sees as illegitimate incursions into transcendental philosophy. Even a cursory read of their correspondence sees them clashing and eventually breaking their relationship over this issue (see *The Philosophical Rupture between Fichte and Schelling*).

77 Schelling, "New Deduction of Natural Right," 231, 64.

78 Ibid., 231, 66.

79 As such, Schelling turns out to be an important precursor to the communicative ethics of Critical Theory as developed by Habermas and Otto-Apel.

80 I tend to favor and argue for a virtue approach when it comes to morality. This, however, is neither the place nor time to establish such an argument. The simplest reason for my favoring a virtue approach lies in the fact of the inherent contextual nature of many if not most moral problems.

81 We often forget that the last great medieval thinkers (like Francisco Suarez, for instance) overlap the beginning of modernity, and untangling those two neatly from the renaissance is really a matter of argumentative convention and methodology rather than strict chronology, and even then the division is somewhat dubious.

82 Schelling, "New Deduction of Natural Right," 231, 66.

83 Ibid., 231, 68.

84 Ibid., 232, 70.

85 This essay too is a work of pantheism. However, in making the distinction between the ground of God and God himself Schelling inches ever closer to an apophantic conception of God as is found in much of German mysticism, Neoplatonism, and the Eastern Orthodox Church (his influence on Orthodox theology makes itself especially felt in the work of Sergey Bulgakov, Vladimir Soloviev, and Pavel Florensky, all of whom are essentially ignored in Western scholarship).

86 Schelling, "New Deduction of Natural Right," 232, 72.

87 Ibid., 232.

88 It is yet again striking here how much Hegel seems to borrow from Schelling (who has never been thought of as a political thinker) when he later discusses the exact same issue in the *Philosophy of Right*. Both the language invoked and the substantive concepts discussed have unmistakable parallels. That is not to claim that the Hegelian account is not highly original and, admittedly, more robustly developed than Schelling's sketch here—it is simply worth pointing out that the two are circling around the same cluster of ideas, each bringing forth groundbreaking work from these ideas.

89 Schelling, "New Deduction of Natural Right," 233, 76.

90  We can interchangeably say either moral or political ("ethical," in Schelling's phrasing) because at this point Schelling has blurred the distinction between morality and politics, making political a public display of our moral responsibility.

91  Schelling, "New Deduction of Natural Right," 233.

92  Perhaps counterintuitively, this position does not bind me to any strong sense of, or connection to, liberalism as such. My lifelong contention with liberalism is that it takes what is a necessary corrective of individual oppression and turns it into a sole governing principle, thus depriving both theory and policy of the tools necessary to address structural and systemic issues that affect the body politic as a whole.

93  This is true methodologically rather than stylistically. A re-examination of the original German text leads me to the same conclusion—he rushes the final portion of the deduction and leaves the end of this understudied text rather incomplete. However, I hope that other scholars will prove me wrong on this particular point.

94  Schelling, "New Deduction of Natural Right," 235.

95  Ibid., 233, 77.

96  Schelling is a few years away from developing the notion of the identity of identity and difference that is the hallmark of texts such as *Bruno*, *Von der Weltseele*, and the late *Naturphilosophie*. I flag this because with this distinction we might be better equipped to solve the conceptual puzzle above, but the fragmentary nature of the final portion of the *New Deduction* makes this difficult even with that apparatus in place.

97  Schelling, "New Deduction of Natural Right," 234, 85.

98  Ibid., 234, 86.

99  The other text being *System of Transcendental Idealism*. While obviously not a full-blown work of political theory like the "New Deduction of Natural Right" (or something like Hegel's *Philosophy of Right* or Fichte's *Foundations of Natural Right*), the *System of Transcendental Idealism* occupies a similar space as Hegel's *Phenomenology*. That is, it is a systematic attempt of unifying two disparate branches of human learning—mainly, philosophy of Nature and transcendental idealism—into a unified whole (whether it succeeds is an entirely open question). In doing so, like Hegel of the *Phenomenology*, Schelling articulates a set of arguments and principles that are *clearly* and *explicitly* political.

100 Having lived through politically motivated violence (albeit thankfully from some distance) during the Balkan wars, I am almost entirely in favor of peaceful and nonviolent means of dissent, especially in current circumstances. It is really only in extraordinarily horrific circumstances, such as the Haitian case, where no further options are open to the populace that I think such actions are justified.

101 With the exception of a short exposition by Robert William in *Hegel's Ethics of Recognition*, Francesco Forlin's piece "To Decide or Not to Decide: Recognition,

Intersubjectivity, and the (Un)expected Role of Unexpectedness" (whose aim is to discuss the role of recognition in decision theory, and thus outside the scope of the current study), and Acosta's article on dissent discussed above, the literature on Schelling's account of recognition is virtually nonexistent. Ludwig Siep alludes to it in his study on Hegel's Jena period in *Anerkennung als Prinzip der praktischen Philosophie: Untersuchungen zu Hegels Jenaer Philosophie des Geistes*, but it plays a relatively minor role there.

102  It would be foolish to argue that Schelling is a recognition theorist on the same scope and level as Fichte and Hegel. Fichte develops his entire political project around recognition and its centrality throughout the Hegelian corpus is unquestionable. By comparison, Schelling devotes only a dozen or so pages on the idea in the *System of Transcendental Idealism*.

# Chapter 2

1  See Bert van den Brink and David Owen, *Recognition and Power: Axel Honneth and the Tradition of Critical Social Theory* (Cambridge: Cambridge University Press, 2007); Tony Burns and Simon Thomson, *Global Justice and the Politics of Recognition* (New York: Palgrave-Macmillan, 2013); Shane O'Neill and Nicholas H. Smith, *Recognition Theory as Social Research: Investigating the Dynamics of Social Conflict* (New York: Palgrave-Macmillan, 2012); Danielle Petherbridge, *The Critical Theory of Axel Honneth* (Lanham: Lexington Books, 2013); Hans-Christoph Schmidt am Busch and Christopher Zurn, *The Philosophy of Recognition: Historical and Contemporary Perspectives* (Lanham: Lexington Books, 2010); and Volker Schmitz, *Axel Honneth and the Critical Theory of Recognition* (New York: Palgrave-Macmillan, 2019).

2  Williams, *Recognition*, 73.

3  To be fair to Fichte, who is in many relevant ways as profound of a thinker as Schelling and Hegel, his is the first *published* account that deals explicitly with the notion of recognition as a centerpiece of transcendental idealism. There are echoes of recognition in Rousseau and Spinoza, but nothing quite like what is argued for and rigorously developed in German Idealism.

4  Fichte, *Foundations of Natural Right*, 18.

5  Ibid., 24.

6  Ibid., 29.

7  Ibid., 39.

8  For a translation of the original formulation of the *Wissenscaftslehre*, the English reader should see Fichte, *The Science of Knowledge*. A new translation is forthcoming from Daniel Breazeale, whose work on Fichte is indispensable. I have not had a chance to consult the new translation, however.

9 Fichte, *Foundations of Natural Right*, 31–5.

10 I think there is a price to be paid for the infamy of the Master/Slave dialectic—it inaugurated a potent misread of recognition as a purely antagonistic process, especially as it was received in French philosophy after Alexandre Kojève's *Introduction to the Reading of Hegel*. Kojève ends his account in a very Marxist fashion with the slave realizing their subjectivity in and through labor, regardless of the fact that Hegel himself doesn't end the recognitive account well into the *end* of the *Phenomenology* with forgiveness and reconciliation in the spiritual life of a people. See G. W. F. Hegel, *The Phenomenology of Spirit*, trans. Terry Pinkard (Cambridge: Cambridge University Press), 388, 670.

11 Hegel, *Phenomenology of Spirit*, 103, 167.

12 Ibid., 107, 175; emphasis Hegel's.

13 Ibid., 110, 184–5.

14 Ibid., 111–12, 187.

15 Ibid., 112–13, 189.

16 Ibid., 115, 195.

17 Ibid., 388, 670.

18 Schelling, *System of Transcendental Idealism*, 155.

19 Ibid., 161.

20 As we will see in the chapter that immediately follows this one, this particular insight is one that recurs throughout Schelling's *Naturphilosophie*, which is evidence that Schelling's transcendental idealism is conditioned and contingent upon his philosophy of nature. This is one of the central reasons with his break from Fichte, both philosophical, and, as evidenced by their letters, ultimately personal. See *The Philosophical Rupture between Fichte and Schelling* and *Statement on the True Relationship of the Philosophy of Nature and the Revised Fichtean Doctrine*.

21 Consciousness exists as an activity, but our language has certain limitations of expression which is why it is often easier to think of it as a thing.

22 For an in-depth discussion of the radical break with solipsistic subjectivism, see Frederic Beiser's magisterial *German Idealism: The Struggle against Subjectivism 1781-1801*.

23 "It is the act whereby the intelligence raises itself absolutely above the objective. Since this act is an absolute one, it cannot be conditioned by any of the preceding acts . . ." (Schelling, *System of Transcendental Idealism*, 155.)

24 Schelling, *System of Transcendental Idealism*, 161.

25 Ibid.

26 The mapping of the distinction between theoretical as ideal and practical as real occurs throughout the whole of the *System of Transcendental Idealism*. It is Schelling's distinction, not my own.

27 Schelling, *System of Transcendental Idealism*, 162.

28 Ibid., 163.

29 Ibid.

30 Ibid., 155.

31 Working merely through the Kantian categories and their schematization, the *a priori* intuitions and the transcendental deduction would easily span a volume. Seeing how Fichte and Schelling appropriate and transform the Kantian project would add another volume on top of that.

32 Schelling, *System of Transcendental Idealism*, 174.

33 He does so doubly, both in the notion of "mirroring" which Leibniz uses many times to explain how the complexity of the world can be reducible to monads which do not directly interact with one another, and in invoking the idea of a "harmony" between the intelligences, which has notes of Leibniz's idea of a preestablished harmony.

34 G. W. Leibniz, *Philosophical Essays*, trans. Roger Ariew and Daniel Garber (Indianapolis: Hackett Publishing, 1989), 42.

35 Schelling too has this in mind insofar as subject and object will coincide at the level of fundamental ontology, especially shortly thereafter in his work in the Identity Philosophy.

36 Ibid., 169.

37 I do not mean to imply here that Schelling is a virtue theorist. Despite my own proclivity for virtue ethics, there is not much evidence to corroborate such a claim. This is simply an analogy that works along a similar logical trajectory.

38 It is not the case that Schelling ignores the messy contingency of history. He explicitly addresses that at the end of the *System of Transcendental Idealism*. It is simply that, unlike Hegel for instance, he doesn't theorize misrecognition as misrecognition when he introduced this historical contingency.

39 Unfortunately, it is impossible to trace every line of influence in a volume such as this one.

40 See Schelling, *Freedom Essay*, 25.

41 McGrath, *The Dark Ground of Spirit*, 125.

42 Ibid., 150.

43 I am speaking in generalities here, of course. It is undoubtedly the case that there are still many *explicitly* and *unapologetically* racist people and organizations on the planet.

44 I say portion here because I don't fundamentally believe that any one thinker can ever completely cover any particular issue, especially one as historically complex as race and racism.

45 Shannon Sullivan, *Revealing Whiteness: The Unconscious Habits of Racial Privilege* (Bloomington: Indiana University Press, 2006), 23. Emphasis mine.

46 Ibid., 24.

47 I am admittedly theoretically less comfortable with this pragmatist idea since I am still of the mindset that *something* such as a transcendental ego or individual monad is necessary to hold the bundled ego together, but this is a debate for another time and place. As I argue in the subsequent chapter on Nature, I take the transcendental conditions to be relatively stable avenues or channels of flow along which the processes of Nature take place, and this would include the recognitive processes which make subjectivity possible in the first place.

48 Sullivan, *Revealing Whiteness*, 46.

49 Ibid.

50 Ibid., 47–8.

51 Ibid., 48–9.

52 Ibid., 49.

53 Sigmund Freud, *The Freud Reader*, ed. Peter Gay (New York: Norton Press, 1989), 627.

54 Ibid., 573, 579–80.

55 We see education being explicitly attacked now for simply teaching elements of Critical Race Theory, a term that until the last two years or so has been largely confined to academia. Here one can see conscious and unconscious racism directly at play, often in the same instant, as seemingly well-meaning people cannot accept *basic facts* about our collective mistreatment of the Other. It is both terrifying and fascinating to observe.

56 F. W. J. Schelling, "Stuttgart Seminars," in *Idealism and the Endgame of Theory*, trans. and ed. Thomas Pfau (New York: SUNY Press, 1994), 206–7.

# Chapter 3

1 F. W. J. Schelling, *Ideas for a Philosophy of Nature*, trans. Errol E. Harris and Peter Heath (Cambridge: Cambridge University Press, 1988), 57. Schelling somehow saw the logic of capitalist production before it got into full swing.

2 See Beiser, *German Idealism*, 506–9.

3   Ibid., 506; emphasis his own.

4   Iain Hamilton Grant's *Philosophies of Nature after Schelling* emphatically drives this point home all throughout. This work serves as *the* key touchstone in the secondary literature for what I aim to accomplish here.

5   Both are Schelling's own metaphors that I have appropriated here.

6   That he would get some of his science wrong is trivially true—he is working at what is basically the infancy of the fields of biology and chemistry. That other philosophers will disagree with some, or perhaps all, of his philosophical positions is also not even remotely surprising, given the nature of our field.

7   Confucius, *Analects*, trans. Edward Slingerland (Indianapolis: Hackett Publishing, 2003), 4.15.

8   See Beiser, *German Idealism*; Iain Hamilton Grant, *Philosophies of Nature after Schelling* (London: Bloomsbury Academic/Continuum Press, 2006) and "'Philosophy Becomes Genetic': The Physics of the World Soul," in *The New Schelling*, ed. Judith Norman and Alistair Welchman (London: Bloomsbury Academic/Continuum Press, 2004), 128–51; Ben Woodard, *Schelling's Naturalism: Motion, Space and the Volition of Thought* (Edinburgh: Edinburgh University Press, 2020).

9   Schelling, *Ideas for a Philosophy of Nature*, 5.

10  My read of the notion of recognition that runs throughout the German Idealist tradition and the work of contemporary theorists such as Charles Taylor and Axel Honneth (among others) is that the contemporary focus on naturalizing the notion of recognition comes at a cost of missing key structural features that make it prone to a myriad of objections. Thus, while I am sympathetic to a naturalist worldview, I don't think that it paints a full picture. See "Recognition and Political Ontology: Fichte, Hegel, and Honneth" (PhD diss., Marquette University, 2015).

11  F. W. J. Schelling, *First Outline of a System of the Philosophy of Nature*, trans. Keith R. Peterson (New York: SUNY Press, 2004), 212; emphasis Schelling's.

12  Schelling, *Ideas for a Philosophy of Nature*, 11.

13  See John Sallis, *The Return of Nature: On the Return of Sense* (Bloomington: Indiana University Press, 2016). The book is a beautiful meditation on Nature itself, heavily incorporating Schellingian themes for a contemporary examination of Nature as Nature.

14  Schelling, *Ideas for a Philosophy of Nature*, 30.

15  I suspect that this might be one of the key reasons why Schelling was neglected for such a long period of time. He is untimely in the Nietzschean sense.

16  Snow, *Schelling and the End of Idealism*, 186.

17  Schelling, *Ideas for a Philosophy of Nature*, 9.

18  Think here of Marx's key distinction between use and exchange value. It should also be added that I am in no way implying that one can be *reductive* in one's explanations.

That is, one ought not to explain economics in terms of Nature alone, for it is a different emergent property. In the Schellingian parlance, it lies at different order potency.

19  See Edward Beach, *The Potencies of God(s): Schelling's Philosophy of Mythology* (New York: SUNY Press, 1994) for how the notion plays out in the later Philosophy of Mythology.

20  Schelling, *Ideas for a Philosophy of Nature*, 51.

21  Ibid.

22  Grant, *Philosophies of Nature after Schelling*, 11.

23  See Chapters 2, 5, and 6 of Grant's *Philosophies of Nature after Schelling*.

24  Schelling, *Ideas for a Philosophy of Nature*, 51.

25  Ibid., 65.

26  Schelling, *System of Transcendental Idealism*, 199–214.

27  I believe that Deleuze often overplays his hand when accusing the German Idealists of being philosophers of pure identity in *Difference and Repetition*, but that is a discussion best left for another project.

28  Bowie, *Schelling and Modern European Philosophy*, 74.

29  See Axel Honneth, *The I in We: Studies in the Theory of Recognition*, trans. Joseph Ganahl (Cambridge: Polity Press, 2012) for an extended discussion of the recognitive element of this general idea.

30  Aldo Leopold, *A Sand County Almanac* (Oxford: Oxford University Press, 1949), 202.

31  Schelling, *Ideas for a Philosophy of Nature*, 87.

32  This is an admitted philosophical fiction even in Hobbes and Locke, but I might just be old-fashioned enough to think that one ought not to build society upon a fiction, and a pernicious one at that.

33  This would require a conception of logic that is indebted to Schelling/Hegel rather than a purely formal logic.

34  See Confucius, *Analects*, 1.11, 4.20, 15.21.

35  I argue here, as well in my previous work on Fichte and Hegel, that the ultimate damage of misrecognition is at the level of ontology. That is, it results in distorted or stunted intersubjectivity.

36  See the Fraser/Honneth debate in *Redistribution or Recognition?*

37  As I revise this post-lockdown, I should note that the US economy is struggling to fill vacant positions due to a lack of appropriate pay and, frankly, often terrible working conditions, so perhaps not all is forgotten.

38  The tendency to portray Schelling and Hegel into philosophical opposites in the newly emerging contemporary scholarship on Schelling is, for a lack of a better adjective, rather strange. While I do not for a second think they are somehow aligned on all issues, their commitment to Absolute Idealism in the early years of the 1800s makes them complimentary thinkers. I also find philosophy to be working at its best and most interesting when it is engaged in the project of addressing our most pressing problems, so I admittedly have almost no interest in picking one thinker as the sole fountain of insight.

39  Grant, *Philosophies of Nature after Schelling*, 62.

40  For a discussion of the influence of Plato in general, and Plato's *Timaeus* particular, see Matthews, *Schelling's Organic form of Philosophy*, 103–35. Matthew's discussion of the Platonic influence on the very young Schelling is especially illuminating.

41  Schelling, *Ideas for a Philosophy of Nature*, 44.

42  Ibid., 47.

43  One gets a different picture of Plato when reading dialogues such as the *Timaeus* and *Parmenides*, though. Plato's greatest critic is still Plato.

44  The exceptions to this claim are found in his later positive philosophy works where he examines religious institutions. See McGrath and Brata Das. Also, he argues in 1810 that the state is inherently oppressive, which is a radical claim to say the least, and one that I examine in the conclusion of our study.

45  See Louis Althusser, *Reading Capital* (New York: Verso Books, 2016).

46  We will delve into further detail on this ontology in the second portion of this chapter dedicated to the *First Outline of a System of the Philosophy of Nature*.

47  See Michael Monahan's *The Creolizing Subject* (New York: Fordham University Press, 2011) for a fuller engagement in the interplay between the biological reality of race and its phenomenological lived experience.

48  Charles Mills' *The Racial Contract* remains the best place to begin interrogating the social-constructivist account of race. As it ought to be clear from my blurring of distinctions that I am not committed to any single view on the issue as a definitive answer. The phenomenon of race is at once too complex, and too interwoven with a wide range of social, economic, medical, biological, and other factors to truly have either a single definitive origin point (or a single answer to the problem of racism, which I hope in some distant future will be decoupled from race itself).

49  Here we can turn to Schelling's articulation of *history* as a concrete human praxis at the end of the *System of Transcendental Idealism* and his own rethinking of it in terms of temporality in the three surviving versions of the *Ages of the World*.

50  While coming close to the notion of "identity," the *System* never completely makes this move, leaving the transcendental and natural investigations in relatively sequestered domains, with the sociohistorical adding a strong layer of contingency

into the mix—a layer that already hints at Schelling's subsequent break with a notion of "system" altogether.

51  See Grant, "The Hypothesis of Nature's Logic in Schelling's *Naturphilosophie*," 478.

52  *Die Weltseele* is a very close second, but I have a tendency to characterize that work as being an expression of the Identity Philosophy first and foremost.

53  Keith R. Peterson; Translator's Introduction to *First Outline for a System of the Philosophy of Nature* (New York: SUNY Press, 2004), xi.

54  Ibid., 13. (All emphasis is Schelling's own.)

55  It might not be entirely fair to lump Laozi and even Zhuangzi in the same framework since the concern with Being comes from the Western tradition. However, the Daoists are process thinkers—the Dao designates the underlying processes of the world that make individual things possible. This definition cannot of course do justice to their multifaceted insights. One of my scholarly aims is to bring German Idealism in general, and Schelling in particular, into dialogue with thinkers outside the Western framework since I believe that they have very many overlapping insights.

56  Schelling, *First Outline*, 14–15.

57  Ibid., 15.

58  Ibid.

59  Spinoza, *Ethics*, Book I, def. 3.

60  We can think here of Aristotle's insistence that substance is "this man" or "this horse" in his *Categories*, which would be precisely the view of substance that is antithetical to Schelling's since those simply designate finite *products* rather than *productivity*.

61  Schelling, *First Outline*, 16.

62  Ibid.

63  Aristotle, *Categories*, 2a15.

64  Schelling, *First Outline*, 18; footnote.

65  It is here that ontology and empirical data coincide. While all science operates on what is basically probabilistic evidence, never claiming that x *must* be the case, ontology takes over and asks the next question—what are the universal necessary structures that make x possible in the first place? This is precisely what Schelling is trying to uncover, and it points to a significant overlap between the task of ontology/metaphysics and empirical investigation.

66  Schelling, *First Outline*, 32.

67  Ibid., 53.

68  Ibid; emphasis his.

69  Ibid., 57; emphasis his.

70  I do not mean to imply here that children playing is equivalent to chaos. Their play serves many different purposes. The point that needed to be driven home is that activity alone exhausts itself into nothing.

71  The finer points and details of precisely how this works at the atomic, subatomic, chemical, biological, and ecological level are never going to be discovered by philosophy as such. The empirical sciences are obviously the most well-suited methodologically to show the *how* in its amazing precision. As philosophers, we simply look for logical necessity and to the overall conceptual picture, along with the normative implications of this picture. Science itself is not suited to normative details.

72  Schelling, *First Outline*, 105.

73  It must be noted here that what I am proposing here is precisely the kind of project that would be vehemently opposed by postmodernism, some contemporary forms of critical theory (I have Habermas in mind in particular), and various sub-factions of analytic philosophy. We can think here of Foucault's and Lyotard's insistence on the death of grand theory, Habermas' various takes on the notion that we are in a "post-metaphysical" epoch, or the general analytic dictum that nature ought to be left to the natural scientist (despite the supposed disappearance of logical positivism, it seems to me that the analytic framework still operates with some positivist presupposition. It is however as difficult to generalize across all of analytic philosophy as it is across continental). While a step-by-step engagement with these various viewpoints would take us very far afield indeed, I would like to note here that this book, and this chapter in particular, serves as a small counter-narrative to this 20th- and 21st-century trend. The forgetting of the whole seems to have brought with it the death of the parts. Our forgetting of Nature and its ontological, interconnected structure, might prove to be the costliest mistake that humanity has ever made. Philosophy can ill afford to continue to neglect Nature and leave it either to Environmental Ethics alone or to the natural sciences.

74  Schelling, *First Outline*, 105.

75  Symeon the New Theologian, *The Discourses* (New York: Paulist Press, 1980), 152–3.

76  Anestis G. Keselopoulos, *Man and the Environment: A Study of St. Symeon the New Theologian* (Crestwood: St. Vladimir Seminary Press, 2001), 8; emphasis mine.

77  Hopefully this will change, and there are some movements toward this change even in public discourse, especially among younger populations who are terrified of what's coming ahead.

78  Francis Bacon, *Select Philosophical Works* (Indianapolis: Hackett Publishing, 1999), 75.

79  It is not as though policy makers are still reading Bacon, but simply that within our forgetting of Nature there are many details that are further forgotten.

80 Bacon, *Select Philosophical Works*, 147.

81 I do not wish here to appear as though Bacon and Descartes are the villains in some nefarious plot. Many of the theoretical moves they made are perfectly rational from within their historical context and their implications are made manifest only *centuries* later when philosophy has already left the central position it occupied in human inquiry. Nevertheless, ideas have consequences, and one cannot ignore the fact that the world would not look the way it does if it wasn't for the Western European enlightenment tradition.

82 Descartes, *The Philosophical Writings of Descartes: Volume I* (Cambridge: Cambridge University Press, 1985), 142–3; emphasis mine.

83 I am painting with fairly broad strokes when it comes to Kant here. To be fairer to his views of Nature one must take into account the *Metaphysical Foundations of Natural Science* and the *Critique of Judgement*, both of which play a direct influence on many aspects of Schelling's project. Nevertheless, the *noumenal* remains the sticking point between Kant and post-Kantian Idealism.

84 J. G. Fichte, *Gesamtausgabe der Bayerischen Akademie der Wissenschaften* (Stuttgart-Bad Cannstaat: Frommann Verlag, 1991), I–8, 78.

85 J. G. Fichte, *System of Ethics* (Cambridge: Cambridge University Press, 2005), 342.

86 F. W. J. Schelling, *Statement on the True Relationship of the Philosophy of Nature to the Revised Fichtean Doctrine* (New York: SUNY Press, 2018), 13.

87 G. W. F. Hegel, *Elements of the Philosophy of Right* (Cambridge: Cambridge University Press, 1991), 194, 231.

88 This is understandable both for Fichte and Hegel, and perhaps even more so going back to Bacon, given the harshness of life for the average individual in their historical epoch. It is unfortunately often the case that hindsight exposes faults where none were apparent. The Owl of Minerva does indeed only fly at dusk.

89 See Tom Regan, *The Case for Animal Rights* (Oakland: University of California Press, 2004).

90 See Christopher D. Stone, *Should Trees Have a Standing? Law, Morality and the Environment* (Oxford: 2010).

91 Honneth, *The Struggle for Recognition*, 115.

92 Although it can certainly purge us from the planet with more extreme weather events, albeit with no intentionality behind it.

93 While it could be argued that it is *policy* and *activism* that will achieve this aim rather than metaphysics, a claim which I would be the last to argue against, it must also be pointed out that our metaphysical positions, often in the form of unexamined or calcified presuppositions, are *precisely* how we got the change in policy in the first place. Modernity radically rethought what the political world and world in general

ought to look like, and this was first and foremost a philosophical position made manifest in the form of the American, French, and Russian revolutions.

94  Schelling, *Statement on True Relationship*, 13–14.

95  When I use "whole" here I am referring our particular tiny portion of the Universe. The creative forces of the Universe as a whole are thankfully far outside our scope of influence.

96  For instance, as I revise this particular portion of the book, there has been a heat dome developing in the Pacific Northwest that was not accounted for even by our best statistical models and would have been essentially impossible without climate change. Records were broken by as much as *five to six* degrees, which is a staggering number when we are talking about warm weather for the region. A town in Canada, which is not exactly known for its warm climate, reached 121 degrees and was tragically destroyed by a fast moving fire. I am afraid that this is just the beginning, but hopefully we learn from this in the long run.

97  We very well might fail, but try we must. It is imperative.

# Chapter 4

1  The order between the *Naturphilosophie* and *System of Transcendental Idealism* is a little difficult to pin down decisively since some of the work was revised *after* the completion of the *System*, as is the case for the *Ideas for a Philosophy of Nature*, while other work was done shortly beforehand or even in tandem with it. The *System* itself clearly straddles both the insights found in the philosophy of Nature and those that are more purely transcendental in the classical Kantian sense, which adds a little further complexity for a strict chronological account.

2  Schelling, *Freedom Essay*, 25.

3  See Freydberg, *Schelling's Dialogical Freedom Essay*.

4  I think that a cogent argument can be made that German Theosophy is an offshoot of Neoplatonism, especially if one traces the development through the work of Meister Eckhart. Also see ffytche, *The Foundation of the Unconscious*, 33.

5  Werner Marx, *The Philosophy of F.W.J. Schelling*, trans. Thomas Nenon (Bloomington: Indiana University Press, 1984), 60.

6  Plotinus, *Enneads*, trans. A. H. Armstrong (Cambridge: Loeb Classic Library, 1967), III.8.9–3.

7  Ibid., III.8.9–13.

8  Ibid., V.1.4–37.

9   Dominic O'Meara, *Plotinus: An Introduction to the Enneads* (Oxford: Oxford University Press, 1993), 50.

10  Plotinus, *Enneads*, V.I.4–27.

11  Ibid., III.8.9–44.

12  More work would need to be done to determine whether Schelling too can fit under this framework. My initial sense is that he can't quite be saying the same thing, but he is certainly close to it.

13  Eric Pearl, "'The Power of All Things': The One as Pure Giving in Plotinus." *American Catholic Philosophical Quarterly* 71, no. 3 (1997): 305.

14  Plotinus, *Enneads*, III.8.11–11.

15  Ibid., III.9.7–5.

16  Ibid., III.9.9–10.

17  It should be added that his position on the heavily Plotinian variety of Neoplatonism changes quite a bit between 1809 and the later positive period. In the positive period he *explicitly* defends a more classical Plotinus inspired version. We will see this in our conclusion to the study, which ends with reflections on his late authorship.

18  After years of working on this issue, I too see no other answer. For instance, I do not think that the answer given by thinkers such as Scotus, Spinoza, and even Leibniz, is ultimately workable. All three predicate Being largely univocally to any existing substance including God, arguing that God's existence is necessary by virtue of God's essence. While this is an oversimplification of a vast amount of argumentation that dominates the Medieval and Modern period for different reasons, I think the Schellingian, Neoplatonic, and Heideggerian concern that Being cannot be explained by recourse to itself is very much warranted. Although this is a work on political philosophy, this question remains my core metaphysical concern.

19  In the purely natural process, there is polarity feedback loop between cloud and ground, which drives a different but related Schellingian point across. I am speaking here of the process of protecting a human-built structure.

20  Laozi, *The Daodejing of Laozi*, trans. Philip J. Ivanhoe (Indianapolis: Hackett, 2003), chapter 1.

21  Ibid., chapter 25.

22  Schelling, *Freedom Essay*, 27.

23  Ibid., 27–8.

24  Ibid., 28.

25  Ibid., 27.

26  Ibid., 29.

27  See Grant's *Philosophies of Nature after Schelling*; Freydberg's *Schelling's Dialogical Freedom Essay,* and Matthew's *Schelling's Organic Form of Philosophy*. All three demonstrate how various dimensions of Schelling's thought go back to Plato again and again.

28  Schelling, *Freedom Essay*, 26.

29  Ibid., 23.

30  Marx, *The Philosophy of F.W.J. Schelling*, 67.

31  Freydberg, *Schelling's Dialogical Freedom Essay*, 52.

32  Ibid., 67.

33  Schelling, *Freedom Essay*, 34.

34  Boehme, *The Way to Christ*, 264.

35  Ibid., 117, 127.

36  Marx, *The Philosophy of F.W.J. Schelling*, 70.

37  Theodore Adorno and Max Horkheimer, *Dialectic of Enlightenment*, trans. Endmund Jephcott, ed. Gunzelin Schmid Noerr (Stanford: Stanford University Press, 2002).

38  Perhaps even the *strongest* use of the PSR since he thinks that *both* the existence and non-existence of an object or event must be explained.

39  Schelling, *Freedom Essay*, 50.

40  Ibid.

41  Ibid.

42  Isaiah Berlin, "Two Concepts of Liberty," in *Liberty*, ed. Henry Hardy (London: Oxford University Press, 2002), 166–218.

43  Berlin, *Liberty*, 169.

44  Ibid., 178.

45  Isaiah Berlin, "Two Concepts of Liberty: Original Dictation (A)" https://berlin.wolf.ox.ac.uk/published_works/tcl/tcl-a.pdf

46  Berlin, *Liberty*, 179–80.

47  This is a fairly rough divide since Hegel adopt elements of *both* traditions, Locke provides caveats to individual rights (such as the Lockean proviso), and Marx calls into question nearly all of the classical takes. However, there is enough overlap to give us a grounding in an overall debate.

48  Schelling, *Freedom Essay*, 38.

49  Ibid., 50.

50 Matt ffytche reads the Schelling unconscious through the lens of individualistic liberalism in *The Foundations of the Unconscious: Schelling, Freud and the Birth of the Modern Psyche*. (See Chapters 3 and 7 for a sustained discussion). While I agree that Schelling was indeed concerned with individual freedom as it is conceptualized by modern liberalism, I think that much of his ontological edifice, as well as large swaths of his work that bear upon political philosophy, do not point to a broadly liberal read of his work. His emphasis on dialectical interplay between self and Other, his organic conception of Nature, and his heavy critique of individualism in the *Freedom Essay*, all point in a different direction—one that cannot separate individual from community as neatly as classical liberalism would like. Nevertheless, Schelling *always* aims to preserve the uniqueness of human individuality, albeit without a recourse to *individualism*.

51 Schelling, *Freedom Essay*, 54.

52 Ibid., 55.

53 For an engagement between Schelling and Sartre's early work as found in *Being and Nothingness* see Manfred Frank's "Schelling and Sartre on Being and Nothingness," in *The New Schelling*, ed. Judith Norman and Alistair Welchman (London: Bloomsbury/Continuum, 2004), 151–67.

54 Jean-Paul Sartre, *Critique of Dialectical Reason: Volume One,* trans. Alan Sheridan-Smith (London: Verso, 1991), 123. (Emphasis Sartre's own).

55 For instance, see "Necessity as a New Structure of Dialectical Investigation," Sartre, *Critique of Dialectical Reason*, 220–8.

56 Sartre, *Critique of Dialectical Reason*, 123–4.

57 Michael Monahan, "Sartre's *Critique of Dialectical Reason* and the Inevitability of Violence: Human Freedom in the Milieu of Scarcity," *Sartre Studies International* 14, no. 2 (2008): 51.

58 Schelling, *Freedom Essay*, 54.

59 Hannah Arendt, *Eichmann in Jerusalem: A Report on the Banality of Evil* (New York: Penguin Books, 1963).

60 Controversy around his portrayal in the book has followed Arendt since the publication of the work, with the initial impression being that it somehow downplays his evil. I find the book all the more chilling because I fear that Arendt is precisely correct: evil is not a characteristic of monsters and supervillains, but of boring humans.

61 Arendt, *Eichmann in Jerusalem*, 21.

62 Ibid., 22.

63 Ibid., 24.

64 Ibid., 26.

65  Ibid., 25.

66  Ibid., 28–9.

67  Ibid., 30.

68  Ibid., 47–8.

69  Ibid., 87–8.

70  Ibid., 105–6.

71  Sartre, *Critique of Dialectical Reason*, 111.

72  While Sartre would most certainly avoid the Schellingian ontological edifice, which is clearly theistic to an extent that Sartre would be uncomfortable with, it is nonetheless the case that their conclusions concerning how freedom plays out in Nature and materiality line up perfectly.

73  Jean-Paul Sartre, *The Anti-Semite and Jew: An Exploration of the Etiology of Hate*, trans. George J. Becker (New York: Schocken Books, 1948), 13.

# Conclusion

1  It's difficult to generalize outward from this claim and I do not wish to. The American political context which I spend much of my time reflecting on does not describe or neatly map on to what is going on elsewhere. But we are all creatures of our place and time, and one must begin theorizing from somewhere.

2  Žižek echoes this claim in his *Indivisible Remainder: Schelling and Related Matters* (New York: Verso, 1996), 39–41.

3  In many ways at this juncture Schelling is anticipating Marxist and Anarchist ideas that won't emerge and come to full fruition in those thinkers until about a half-century later. This explains Marx's and Bakunin's disappointment with the later lectures in Berlin, which clearly go in the opposite direction.

4  See "The Oldest Systematic Program of German Idealism," in *Philosophy of German Idealism*, ed. Ernest Behler (New York: Continuum, 1987), 161.

5  See editor's note in F. W. J. Schelling, *Idealism and the Endgame of Theory*, ed. and trans. Thomas Pfau (New York: SUNY Press, 1994), 195.

6  Ibid., 226–7.

7  Ibid., 227.

8  Ibid.

9  Ibid.

10. To be fair, there are *always* cracks and struggle in the realm of politics.
11. Schelling, *Idealism and the Endgame of Theory—Stuttgart Seminars*, 228.
12. Ibid.
13. Ibid., 232.
14. Ibid., 228.
15. For a full discussion of the role of the state in the late Schelling, see McGrath, *The Philosophical Foundations of the Late Schelling*, 226–40. McGrath reconstructs and excavates the various published and unpublished lectures on the *Philosophy of Revelation* in order to *precisely* show how Schelling's very infrequent remarks about the state, remarks which are strewn here and there in the late work, fit in with his political theology and, especially, *eschatology*. On page 226 of the text, McGrath writes: "any effort to reconstruct Schelling's late political thinking on the basis of his slim but profound treatments on the subject of the relation of the State to the Church, on the one hand, and the relation of the State to the person, on the other, must keep in mind the essential distinction between utopian eschatological politics and political eschatology." Given that my knowledge of eschatology begins and ends with what Brata Das and McGrath have written in their respective books, I leave this discussion in their very capable hands.
16. The middle Schelling of the *Freedom Essay* through the *Ages of the World*, that is.
17. Žižek, *The Indivisible Remainder*, 41–2.
18. I have misgivings about psychoanalytically reading whole texts. Nevertheless, his political philosophy is both important and insightful for understanding much that is at stake in the 21st century.
19. I believe that it is, but cannot discount the fact that we are most certainly not doing our full share (either collectively or individually).
20. F. W. J. Schelling, *The Grounding of Positive Philosophy*, trans. Bruce Matthews (New York: SUNY Press, 2007), 96.
21. See Schelling, *Positive Philosophy*, 92. There he argues that while *Naturphilosophie* and science in general can answer questions of *how* humans and other natural entities emerge, they can never, in principle, answer the oldest of all metaphysical questions: why is there something in the first place?
22. Schelling, *Positive Philosophy*, 107.
23. From my admittedly limited understanding of Kripke, it seems to me that Schelling beat him to some of his core insights by about a century. Perhaps some of the gap between analytic and continental thought, a largely arbitrary distinction, can be bridged through German Idealism.
24. Schelling, *Positive Philosophy*, 131.

25  Ibid., 144.

26  Ibid., 154.

27  Ibid. This notion of an "absolute beginning" connects back up to themes that are found again a century later in the work of Derrida, who untangles and deconstructs binaries in a manner suggestive of Schelling, but spends lots of time problematizing notions such as absolute beginnings in fascinating ways.

28  Ibid., 154.

29  Ibid., 164.

30  Ibid., 179.

# Bibliography

Acosta, Emiliano. "Recognition and Dissent: Schelling's Conception of Recognition and its Contributions to Contemporary Political Philosophy." In *Recognition—German Idealism as an Ongoing Challenge*, edited by Christian Krinjen. Leiden: Brill, 2014.

Adorno, Theodore and Max Horkheimer. *Dialectic of Enlightenment: Philosophical Fragments*. Translated by Edmund Jephcott and Edited by Gunzelin Schmid Noerr. Stanford: Stanford University Press, 2002.

Alderwick, Charlotte. *Schelling's Ontology of Powers*. Edinburgh: Edinburgh University Press, 2021.

Althusser, Louis. *Reading Capital*. New York: Verso Books, 2016.

Altman, Matthew C., ed. *The Palgrave Handbook of German Idealism*. London: Pallgrave-Macmillan, 2014.

Arendt, Hannah. *Eichmann in Jerusalem: A Report on the Banality of Evil*. New York: Penguin Books, 1963,

Aristotle. *The Complete Works of Aristotle: Two Volumes*. Edited by Jonathan Barnes. Oxford: Oxford University Press, 1984.

Bacon, Francis. *Selected Philosophical Works*. Edited by Rose-Mary Sargent. Indianapolis: Hackett Publishing, 1999.

Beach, Edward Allen. *The Potencies of God(s): Schelling's Philosophy of Mythology*. New York: SUNY Press, 1994.

Behler, Ernst, ed. *Philosophy of German Idealism*. London: Continuum, 1987.

Beiser, Frederick C. *The Fate of Reason: German Philosophy from Kant to Fichte*. Cambridge, MA: Harvard University Press, 1987.

Beiser, Frederick C. *German Idealism: The Struggle against Subjectivism 1781–1801*. Cambridge, MA: Harvard University Press, 2002.

Berger, Benjamin and Daniel Whistler. *The Schelling-Eschenmeyer Controversy, 1801: Nature and Identity*. Edinburgh: Edinburgh University Press, 2020.

Berlin, Isaiah. *Liberty*. Edited by Henry Hardy. Oxford: Oxford University Press, 2017.

Berlin, Isaiah. "Two Concepts of Liberty: Original Dictation (A)." https://berlin.wolf.ox.ac.uk/published_works/tcl/tcl-a.pdf

Boehme, Jacob. *The Way to Christ*. Translated by Peter Erb. New York: Paulist Press, 1978.

Boehme, Jacob. "Mysterium Pansophicum: Or Thorough Report on the Earthly and Heavenly Mysterium." In *Philosophical Investigations into the Essence of Human*

*Freedom*, edited and translated by Jeff Love and Johannes Schmidt, 85–98. New York: SUNY Press, 2006.

Bowie, Andrew. *Schelling and Contemporary European Philosophy: An Introduction*. London: Routledge, 1993.

Brata Das, Saitya. *The Political Theology of Schelling*. Edinburgh: Edinburgh University Press, 2016.

Brown, Robert F. *The Later Philosophy of Schelling: The Influence of Boehme on the Works of 1809–1815*. Lewisburg: Bucknell University Press, 1977.

Bruno, G. Anthony, ed. *Schelling's Philosophy: Freedom, Nature, and Sytematicity*. Oxford: Oxford University Press, 2020.

Buck-Morss, Susan. *Hegel, Haiti and Universal History*. Pittsburgh: University of Pittsburgh Press, 2009.

Burns, Tony and Simon Thomson. *Global Justice and the Politics of Recognition*. New York: Palgrave-Macmillan, 2013.

Confucius. *Analects*. Translated by Edward Slingerland. Indianapolis: Hackett Publishing, 2003.

Cooper, Laurence D. *Rousseau, Nature, and the Problem of the Good Life*. University Park: Pennsylvanian University Press, 1999.

Deleuze, Gilles. *Difference and Repetition*. Translated by Paul Patton. New York: Columbia University Press, 1994.

Della Rocca, Michael. *Spinoza*. New York: Routledge, 2008.

Descartes. *The Philosophical Writings of Descartes: Volume I*. Cambridge: Cambridge University Press, 1985.

Dubois, Laurent. *Avengers of the New World*. Cambridge, MA: Harvard University Press, 2004.

Esposito, Joseph L. *Schelling's Idealism and Philosophy of Nature*. Lewisburg: Bucknell University Press, 1977.

Fenichel, Theresa. *Schelling, Freud, and the Philosophical Foundations of the Unconscious: Uncanny Belonging*. New York: Routledge, 2019.

ffytche, Matt. *The Foundation of the Unconscious: Schelling, Freud and the Birth of the Modern Psyche*. Cambridge: Cambridge University Press, 2012.

Fichte, J. G. *Foundations of Natural Right*. Edited by Frederick Neuhauser and Translated by Michael Bauer. Cambridge: Cambridge University Press, 2000.

Fichte, J. G. *Gesamtausgabe der Bayerischen Akademie der Wissenschaften*. Stuttgart-Bad Cannstaat: Frommann Verlag, 1991, I–8.

Fichte, J. G. *The Science of Knowledge*. Edited and Translated by Peter Heath and John Lachs. Cambridge: Cambridge University Press, 1982.

Fichte, J. G. *The System of Ethics*. Edited and Translated by Daniel Breazeale and Günter Zöller. Cambridge: Cambridge University Press, 2005.

Fichte, J. G. and F. W. J. Schelling. *The Philosophical Rupture between Fichte and Schelling: Selected Texts and Correspondence (1800–1802)*. Translated and Edited by Michael G. Vater and David W. Wood. New York: SUNY Press, 2012.

Forlin, Francesco. "To Decide or Not to Decide: Recognition, Intersubjectivity, and the (Un)expected Role of Unexpectedness." *Philosophy Study* 7, no. 9 (2017): 493–9.

Frank, Manfred. *Eine Einführung in Schellings Philosophie*. Frankfort: Suhrkamp, 1985.

Frank, Manfred. "Schelling and Sartre on Being and Nothingness." In *The New Schelling*, edited by Judith Norman and Alistair Welchman, 151–67. London: Bloomsbury/Continuum, 2004.

Fraser, Nancy and Axel Honneth. *Redistribution or Recognition? A Political-Philosophical Exchchange*. Translated by Joel Golb, James Ingram, and Christiane Wilke. London: Verso Press, 2003.

Freud, Sigmund. *Civilization and its Discontents*. Translated and Edited by James Strachey. New York: W.W. Norton and Company, 1961.

Freud, Sigmund. *The Freud Reader*. Edited by Peter Gay. New York: Norton and Norton Company, 1989.

Freydberg, Bernard. *Schelling's Dialogical Freedom Essay*. New York: SUNY Press, 2008.

Gabriel, Markus. *Transcendental Ontology: Essays in German Idealism*. London: Bloomsbury Academic, 2011.

Geggus, David. *The Haitian Revolution: A Documentary History*. Indianapolis: Hackett Publishing, 2014.

Grant, Iain Hamilton. *Philosophies of Nature after Schelling*. London: Bloomsbury/Continuum, 2006.

Grant, Iain Hamilton. "'Philosophy Becomes Genetic': The Physics of the World Soul." In *The New Schelling*, edited by Judith Norman and Alistair Welchman, 128–51. London: Bloomsbury Academic/Continuum Press, 2004.

Grant, Iain Hamilton. "The Hypothesis of Nature's Logic in Schelling's *Naturphilosophie*." In *The Palgrave Handbook of German Idealism*, edited by Matthew C. Altman, 478–98. New York: Palgrave-Macmillan, 2014.

Habermas, Jürgen. "Dialectical Idealism in Transition to Materialism: Schelling's Idea of a Contraction of God and the Consequences for a Philosophy of History." In *The New Schelling*, translated by Nick Midgley and Judith Norman, edited by Judith Norman and Alistair Wlchman, 43–89. London: Bloomsbury/Continuum, 2004.

Habermas, Jürgen. *Moral Consciousness and Communicative Action*. Translated by Christian Lenhardt and Shierry Weber Nicholsen. Cambridge, MA: MIT Press, 2001.

Habermas, Jürgen. *Postmetaphysical Thinking: Philosophical Essays*. Translated by William Mark Hohenegarten. Cambridge, MA: MIT Press, 1992.

Habermas, Jürgen. *Truth and Justification*. Translated by Barbara Fultner. Cambridge, MA: MIT Press, 2005.

Hegel, G. W. F. *The Difference between Fichte's and Schelling's System of Philosophy*. Translated and Edited by H. S. Harris and Walter Cerf. New York: SUNY Press, 1977.

Hegel, G. W. F. *Elements of the Philosophy of Right*. Edited by Allen W. Wood and Translated by H. B. Nisbett. Cambridge: Cambridge University Press, 1991.

Hegel, G. W. F. *Encyclopedia Logic*. Translated by T. F. Geraets, W. A. Suchting, and H. S. Harris. Indianapolis: Hackett Publishing, 1991.

Hegel, G. W. F. *Phenomenology of Spirit*. Translated and Edited by Terry Pinkard. Cambridge: Cambridge University Press, 2018.

Hegel, G. W. F. *Philosophy of Mind*. Translated by W. Wallece and A. V. Miller. Revised by M. J. Inwood. Oxford: Oxford University Press, 2007.

Hegel, G. W. F. *Philosophy of Nature*. Translated by A. V. Miller. Oxford: Oxford University Press, 1970.

Hegel, G. W. F. *The Science of Logic*. Translated and Edited by George Di Giovanni. Cambridge: Cambridge University Press, 2010.

Henrich, Dieter. *Between Kant and Hegel: Lectures on German Idealism*. Edited by David S. Pacini. Cambridge, MA: Harvard University Press, 2003.

Hobbes, Thomas. *Leviathan*. Edited by C. B. Macpherson. New York: Penguin Books, 1985.

Honneth, Axel. *The Struggle for Recognition: The Moral Grammar of Political Conflicts*. Translated by Joel Anderson. Cambridge: Polity Press, 1995.

Honneth, Axel. *The I in We: Studies in the Theory of Recognition*. Translated by Joseph Ganahl. Camridege: Polity Press, 2012.

James, C. L. R. *The Black Jacobins: Toussaint L'Ouverture and the San Domingo Revolution*. New York: Vintage Books, 1963.

James, David. *Rousseau and German Idealism: Freedom, Dependence, and Necessity*. Cambridge: Cambridge University Press, 2013.

Kant, Immanuel. *Critique of Pure Reason*. Translated and Edited by Paul Guyer and Allen Wood. Cambridge: Cambridge University Press, 1998.

Kant, Immanuel. *Critique of Judgement*. Translated by Werner S. Pluhar. Indianapolis: Hackett Publishing, 1987.

Kant, Immanuel. *Practical Philosophy*. Translated and Edited by Mary J. Gregor. Cambridge: Cambridge University Press, 1996

Kant, Immanuel. *Theoretical Philosophy after 1781*. Edited by Henry Allison and Peter Heath. Cambridge: Cambridge University Press, 2002.

Keselopoulos, Anestis G. *Man and the Environment: A Study of St. Symeon the New Theologian*. Crestwood: St. Vladimir Seminary Press, 2001.

Laozi. *The Daodejing of Laozi*. Translated by Philip J. Ivanhoe. Indianapolis: Hackett Publishing, 2003.

Leibniz, G. W. *Philosophical Essays*. Translated by Roger Ariew and Daniel Garber. Indianapolis: Hackett Publishing, 1989.

Leopold, Aldo. *A Sand County Almanac*. Oxford: Oxford University Press, 1949.

Locke, John. *Two Treatises of Government*. Edited by Peter Laslett. Cambridge: Cambridge University Press, 1960.

Markell, Patchen. *Bound by Recognition*. Princeton: Princeton University Press, 2003.

Marx, Werner. *The Philosophy of F.W.J. Schelling*. Translated by Thomas Nenon. Bloomington: Indiana University Press, 1984.

Matthews, Bruce. *Schelling's Organic Form of Philosophy: Life as the Schema of Freedom*. New York: SUNY Press, 2011.

McGrath, Sean J. *The Dark Ground of Spirit: Schelling and the Unconscious*. New York: Routledge, 2012.

McGrath, Sean J. *The Philosophical Foundation of the Late Schelling*. Edinburgh: Edinburgh University Press, 2021.

McNay, Lois. *Against Recognition*. Cambridge: Polity Press, 2008.

Mengzi. *Mengzi: With Selections from Traditional Commentaries*. Translated by Bryan W. Van Norden. Indianapolis: Hackett Publishing, 2008.

Mills, Charles. *The Racial Contract*. Ithaca: Cornell University Press, 1999.

Monahan, Michael. *The Creolizing Subject*. New York: Fordham University Press, 2011.
Monahan, Michael. "Sartre's *Critique of Dialectical Reason* and the Inevitability of Violence: Human Freedom in the Milieu of Scarcity." *Sartre Studies International* 14, no. 2 (2008): 51.
Oliver, Kelly. *Witnessing: Beyond Recognition*. Minneapolis: Minnesota University Press, 2001.
O'Meara, Dominic. *Plotinus: An Introduction to the Enneads*. Oxford: Oxford University Press, 1993.
O'Neill, Shane and Nicholas H. Smith. *Recognition Theory as Social Research: Investigating the Dynamics of Social Conflict*. New York: Palgrave-Macmillan, 2012.
Osteric, Lara, ed. *Interpreting Schelling: Critical Essays*. Cambridge: Cambridge University Press, 2014.
Pearl, Eric. "'The Power of All Things:' The One as Pure Giving in Plotinus." *American Catholic Philosophical Quarterly* 71, no. 3 (1997): 305.
Petherbridge, Danielle. *The Critical Theory of Axel Honneth*. Lanham: Lexington Books, 2013.
Plato. *Complete Works*. Edited by John M. Cooper. Indianapolis: Hackett Publishing, 1997.
Plotinus. *Enneads*. Translated by A. H. Armstrong. Cambridge: Loeb Classic Library, 1967.
Popkin, Jeremy. *A Concise History of the Haitian Revolution*. Hoboken: Wiley-Blackwell, 2012.
Regan, Tom. *The Case for Animal Rights*. Oakland: University of California Press, 2004.
Riley, Patrick. "The General Will Before Rousseau." In *The General Will: An Evolution of a Concept*, edited by James Farr and David Lay Williams, 3–71. Cambridge: Cambridge University Press, 2015.
Rouse, Wendy and Beth Slutsky. "Empowering the Physical and Political Self: Women and the Practice of Self-Defense, 1890–1920." *The Journal of the Gilded Age and Progressive Era* 13, no. 4 (2014): 470–99. Doi: 10.1017/S1537781414000383
Rousseau, J. J. *The Discourses and Other Early Political Writings*. Edited and Translated by Victor Gourevitch. Cambridge: Cambridge University Press, 1997.
Rousseau, J. J. *The Social Contract and Other Later Political Writings*. Edited and Translated by Victor Gourevitch. Cambridge: Cambridge University Press, 1997.
Sallis, John. *Delimitations: Phenomenology and the End of Metaphysics*. Bloomington: Indiana University Press, 1995.
Sallis, John. *The Return of Nature: On the Beyond of Sense*. Bloomington: Indiana University Press, 2016.
Sartre, Jean-Paul. *The Anti-Semite and the Jew: An Exploration on the Etiology of Hate*. Translated by George J. Becker. New York: Schoken Books, 1948.
Sartre, Jean-Paul. *Critique of Dialectical Reason: Volume 1*. Translated by Alan Sheridan-Smith and Edited by Jonathan Rée. London: Verso Books, 1976.
Schelling, F. W. J. *The Ages of the World (1811)*. Translated by Joseph P. Lawrence. New York: SUNY Press, 2019.
Schelling, F. W. J. *The Ages of the World (1813)*. Translated by Judith Norman. Ann Arbor: The University of Michigan Press, 1997.

Schelling, F. W. J. *The Ages of the World (1815)*. Translated by Jason M. Wirth. New York: SUNY Press, 2000.
Schelling, F. W. J. *Bruno: On the Natural and Divine Principe of Things*. Translated and Edited by Michael G. Vater. New York: SUNY Press, 1984.
Schelling, F. W. J. *Clara: or, ON Nature's Connection to the Spirit World*. Translated by Fiona Stienkamp. New York: SUNY Press, 2002.
Schelling, F. W. J. *First Outline of a System of the Philosophy of Nature*. Translated by Keith R. Peterson. New York: SUNY Press, 2004.
Schelling, F. W. J. *Frederich Wllhelm von Schelling's sämmtliche Werke; 14 vols*. Edited by K. F. A. Schelling. Stuttgart and Augsburg: J.G. Cotta, 1856-61.
Schelling, F. W. J. *The Grounding of the Positive Philosophy: The Berlin Lectures*. Translated by Bruce Matthews. New York: SUNY Press, 2007.
Schelling, F. W. J. *Historical-Critical Introduction to the Philosophy of Mythology*. Translated by Mason Richey and Markus Zisselsberger. New York: SUNY Press, 2007.
Schelling, F. W. J. *Idealism and the Endgame of Theory: Three Essays by F.W.J. Schelling*. Edited and Translated by Thomas Pfau. New York: SUNY Press, 1994.
Schelling, F. W. J. *Ideas for a Philosophy of Nature*. Translated by Errol E. Harris and Peter Heath. Cambridge: Cambridge University Press, 1988.
Schelling, F. W. J. "New Deduction of Natural Right." In *The Unconditional in Human Knowledge: Four Early Essays (1794-1796)*, translated by Fritz Marti, 219-52. Lewisburg: Bucknell University Press, 1980.
Schelling, F. W. J. *On the History of Modern Philosophy*. Translated by Andrew Bowie. Cambridge: Cambridge University Press, 1994.
Schelling, F. W. J. *Philosophical Investigations into the Essence of Human Freedom*. Translated by Jeff Love and Johannes Schmidt. New York: SUNY Press, 2006.
Schelling, F. W. J. *Philosophy of Revelation (1841-42): and Related Texts*. Translated by Klaus Ottmann. Putnam: Spring Publications, 2020.
Schelling, F. W. J. *The Philosophy of Art*. Translated and Edited by Douglass W. Scott. Minneapolis: University of Minnesota Press, 1989.
Schelling, F. W. J. *Statement on the True Relationship of the Philosophy of Nature and the Revised Fichtean Docrine*. Translated by Dale E. Snow. New York: SUNY Press, 2018.
Schelling, F. W. J. *System of Transcendental Idealism*. Translated by Peter Heath. Charlottesville: University Press of Virginia, 1978.
Schmidt am Busch, Hans-Christoph and Christopher Zurn. *The Philosophy of Recognition: Historical and Contemporary Perspectives*. Lanham: Lexington Books, 2010.
Schmitz, Volker. *Axel Honneth and the Critical Theory of Recognition*. New York: Palgrave-Macmillan, 2019.
Schopenhauer, Arthur. *On the Basis of Morality*. Translated by E. F. J. Payne. Indianapolis: Hackett Publishing, 1995.
Schopenhauer, Arthur. *Prize Essay on the Freedom of the Will*. Edited by Günter Zöller and Translated by E. F. J. Payne. Cambridge: Cambridge University Press, 1999.
Schopenhauer, Arthur. *The World as Will and Representation: In Two Volumes*. Translated by E. F. J. Payne. New York: Dover Publications, 1958.
Shklar, Judith N. *Men and Citizens: A Study of Rousseau's Social Theory*. Cambridge: Cambridge University Press, 1969.

Siep, Ludwig. *Anerkennung als Prinzip der praktischen Philosophie: Untersuchungen zu Hegels Jenaer Philosophie des Geistes*. Hamburg: Meiner, 2014.
Snow, Dale E. *Schelling and the End of Idealism*. New York: SUNY Press, 1996.
Spinoza, Baruch. *Ethics*. Translated by Samuel Sherly and Edited by Seymour Feldman. Indianapolis: Hackett Publishing, 1992.
Stojkovski, Velimir. "Recognition and Political Ontology: Fichte, Hegel, and Honneth." PhD diss. Marquette University, 2015.
Stone, Christopher D. *Should Trees Have a Standing? Law, Morality and the Environment*. Oxford: Oxford University Press, 2010.
Strong, Tracy B. "The General Will in Rousseau and After Rousseau." In *The General Will: The Evolution of a Concept*, edited by James Farr and David Lay Williams, 307–29. Cambridge: Cambridge University Press, 2015.
Sullivan, Shannon. *Revealing Whiteness: The Unconscious Habits of Racial Privilege*. Bloomington: Indiana University Press, 2006.
Symeon the New Theologian. *The Discourses*. New York: Paulist Press, 1980.
Taylor, Charles. "The Politics of Recognition." In *Multiculturalism: Examining the Politics of Recognition*, edited by Amy Gutmann, 25–75. Princeton: Princeton University Press, 1994.
Tilliette, Xavier. *Schelling une Philosophie en Devinir Vol, 1 and 2*. Paris: Librairie Philosophique J. Vrin, 1970.
Tilliette, Xavier. *Schelling: Biographie*. Paris: Calmann-Lévy, 1999.
Van den Brink, Bert and David Owen. *Recognition and Power: Axel Honneth and the Tradition of Critical Social Theory*. Cambridge: Cambridge University Press, 2007.
Vater, Michael. "Schelling Aphorisms on Natural Right and (1976/7) and Fichte's *Grundlage des Naturrechts*." In *Rights, Bodies and Recognition: New Essays on Fichte's Foundations of Natural Right*, edited by Tom Rockmore and Daniel Breazeale, 195–211. New York: Routledge, 2019.
Williams, David Lay. "The Substantive Elements of Rousseau's General Will." In *The General Will: The Evolution of a Concept*, edited by James Farr and David Lay Williams, 307–29. Cambridge: Cambridge University Press, 2015.
Williams, Robert R. *Hegel's Ethics of Recognition*. Oakland: University of California Press, 1997.
Williams, Robert R. *Recognition: Fichte and Hegel on the Other*. New York: SUNY Press, 1992.
Wirth, Jason. *The Conspiracy of Life: Meditations on Schelling and His Time*. New York: SUNY Press, 2003.
Wirth, Jason. *Schelling's Practice in the Wild: Time, Art, Imagination*. New York: SUNY Press, 2015.
Wirth, Jason, ed. *Schelling Now: Contemporary Readings*. Bloomington: Indiana University Press, 2005.
Woodard, Ben. *Schelling's Naturalism: Motion, Space and the Volition of Thought*. Edinburgh: Edinburgh University Press, 2019.
Zhuangzi. *The Essential Writings: With Selections from Traditional Commentaries*. Translated by Brook Ziporyn. Indianapolis: Hackett Publishing, 2009.
Žižek, Slavoj. *The Abyss of Freedom*. Ann Arbor: University of Michigan Press, 1997.
Žižek, Slavoj. *The Indivisible Remainder: On Schelling and Related Matters*. London: Verso, 1996.

# Index

Absolute  12, 19
   Ideal and Real  104
   as organism  93
Absolute Idealism  12, 19, 51
   human institutions  105–7
   Ideas and Reality  102–4
Acosta, Emiliano  30, 196 n.3
Arendt, Hannah  172–6, 179

Bacon, Francis  122–3
Being
   Identity  143–4
   negative and positive
      philosophy  188–9
   *vs.* Neoplatonic generative
      principle  147
   Neoplatonism  145–9
   *New Deduction of Natural Right*  27
   ontological naturalism  111
   opposition to freedom  144, 156
   as product  152
   as productivity (*see* nature)
   with thinking (in
      Neoplatonism)  146–7, 149
Beiser, Frederick  5, 86
Berlin, Isaiah, *see* freedom
Böhme, Jakob
   *centrum*  13–14, 158
   non-ground  15
   the will  14–15
Bowie, Andrew  5, 96

communitarianism  45, 46

dark ground (of being)

   ground of God  154, 156–7
   non-ground  151
   "outside" rationality  155–7, 177, 189
   relation to Daoism  151
   relation to freedom  156, 161–2, 178
dissent  30, 31, 56, 57
   civil rights movement  32
   dissent of nature  128, 138
   with freedom  39
   Haiti  35–6
   relation to the political  48
   suffrage movement  32
Fichte, Johann Gottlieb
   break with Schelling  11
   influence on Schelling  8
   nature  125
   practical philosophy  49, 69
   recognition  28, 30, 63–65, 70
   *Wissenschaftslehre*  9, 27, 49
      difference  10
      subject positing  9
      synthesis  10, 11
Frank, Manfred  5
freedom
   conditions for possibility  152
   with dissent  39
   emergence from Dark
      Ground  156, 161
   evil in the political  173–6, 179
   as form of right  54–5
   *Freedom Essay*  23
   good and evil  156–7, 160
      relation to will  158–9
   Kant  7
   with necessity  161–3, 168, 171

*New Deduction of Natural Right* 16,
  26–7, 48
positive and negative
  Berlin 163–5
  Schellingian critique 165–8
practical philosophy 16–17, 40, 55
praxis/education 20, 47, 162,
  169–71, 177–8
with recognition 20, 30, 48
relation to general will 39–40, 45–7
Spinoza 12
the state 182–4
the state and evil 184–5
as unconditioned 27–8, 39, 141
Freud, Sigmund 81–82

general will
  check to freedom 39–40
  Haiti 37–8
  relation to absolute will 51–2
  relation to good and evil 158–9
  relation to individual will 39, 41, 43,
    46–7, 61
  with rights 51, 53
Grant, Iain Hamilton 88, 94, 102,
  197 n.15
ground of Being
  *Freedom Essay* 150
  as God 149, 153
  grounding metaphor 151
  *Naturphilosophie* 92
  as productivity 152

Habermas, Jürgen 1, 211 n.73
Hegel, G. W. F. 28, 30, 48, 197 n.21
  *aufgehoben* 93
  nature 126
  recognition 65–6
Hobbes, Thomas 16, 22, 28, 127
Honneth, Axel 2, 18, 60, 100, 128

Ideal
  human institutions 105–7
  ontology 102
  race and social construction 107–8

relation to real/reality 103–4, 108–9,
  149, 156

Kant, Immanuel
  categorical imperative 49–50
  concepts and intuitions 6
  freedom 7, 27, 49, 156
  general will 43, 44
  judgment 8
  practical philosophy 49
  supersensible 8
  system 6, 8

Laozi/Daoism 151, 210 n.55, *see also*
  Dark Ground
Leibniz, G. W. 72–3
Locke, John 16, 22, 28, 127

McGrath, Sean, J. 21, 77, 195–6 n.1,
  218 n.15
morality/ethics 40, 48
  relation to the absolute will 52
  responsibility to nature 135
  theoretical/practical philosophy 49

nature 12, 13
  Böhme 15
  conditions of possibility of nature/
    life 77, 92, 112, 118, 131,
    136, 152
  consciousness 77, 107
  grounding principle 21
  human institutions 105–7, 133–4, 185
  identity philosophy 19
  interconnectedness 96–9, 101, 129
  *New Deduction of Natural
    Right* 16, 27–8
  the organic 118–19
  as organizing principles 113, 114
  our relation/responsibility 22, 28,
    90–1, 99, 130–1, 139
  polarities 22, 92, 100, 107, 114–15
  as possibility for God 154
  primordial responsibility 128–
    32, 134–5

as productivity/productive forces   21, 22, 114–15
recognition and dissent   137–8
self-organization   13
*System of Transcendental Idealism*   18
unconscious   21, 77
*Naturphilosophie*
  dueling polarities   114–18
  dynamic process ontology   89, 100, 112–13, 115, 118–19, 130
  Ideal and Real (*see* Ideal)
  naturalism   88, 136, 170
  nature as product   22, 128
  nature as productivity   22, 112–15, 130, 133
  philosophy and nature   91, 114, 136
  potencies   93, 94–5
  transcendentalism   88, 136, 170
  unconditioned   111
  wholism   100
Neoplatonism
  good and consciousness   149
  as guide   188–9
  intellect   145–7
  the one   145
  one as generative principle   147–8
*New Deduction of Natural Right*   16–17, 27

ontology, *see also* Being
  process   87, 89, 107

*Philosophical Investigations into the Essence of Human Freedom* (*Freedom Essay*)   23, 76, 142
  capacity for evil   156–9
  freedom's correction   144
  God and nature   154
  identity philosophy   143
  pantheism   153
  "progress"   159

rational religion   187–8
recognition
  Fichte   63–5, 70
  forming the subject   48
  general overview   59–61
  with the general will   45
  mirroring/reflection   71–2
  misrecognition   74, 77, 81–3, 108, 176
  nature and misrecognition   100–1
  necessity of the other   74
  recognition and evil   174–6
  recognition and nature   137–8
  relation to freedom   20, 69, 74
  relation to natural potencies   95–6
  Schelling's notion   20, 67
  subjectivity and preconditions   67–8, 70, 73
  theoretical and practical reason   69–71
  unconscious (*see* unconscious)
right
  connection to dissent   29, 32
  as duties   49–51
  the general will   43–4
  Haiti   34
  history   50, 51
  Kant   44
  in liberalism   28, 31
  original right   54
  rights of nature:130–3
  subject agency   53
Rousseau, Jean Jacques   17, 41–3, 49–50

Sallis, John   207 n.13
Sarte, Jean-Paul   40, 162–3, 169–71
Snow, Dale   4–5, 91
Spinoza, Baruch
  monism and the absolute   12, 113, 124
  pantheism controversy   11, 12
subject/object
  consciousness   76
  Fichte   9–11
  habit   79–80
  interconnectedness   129, 131
  Kant   6–8
  *New Deduction of Natural Right*   16

reflection and the world   71–3, 91
self as primordial will   69–70, 73
social subject   48
*System of Transcendental Idealism*   19
union with nature   90–91
Sullivan, Shannon   78–81
*System of Transcendental Idealism*   18, 61, 62

theology (political), *see also* McGrath, Sean, J.

Brata Das, Saitya   195–6 n.1, 209 n.44, 218 n.15
Tilliete, Xavier   5

unconscious
    ground of recognition   137
    in nature   21, 77
    with racism   78–82

Wirth, Jason   12, 188, 193 n.41

www.ingramcontent.com/pod-product-compliance
Lightning Source LLC
Chambersburg PA
CBHW062216300426
44115CB00012BA/2085